D1605864

THE FLICKER BETWEEN THE FRAMES

When Rudolph Valentino was projected onto the silver screen, audiences rarely wondered what took place in between frames. They were too enamored with the action in front of their eyes. Now comes *Valentino Speaks* and a new image of the "Great Lover" that takes us into the spaces between life-times where what you will find is a brilliant display of thought.

This is a book that challenges its readers to examine their views on any number of issues. And, with the spirit of Rudolph Valentino as your guide, you do so with elegance and grace, with neither confrontation nor conceit. Indeed, Valentino's observations on life propel you on a uniquely beautiful mind, heart, and soul expanding experience!

Valentino Speaks addresses 180 topics in a series of gem-like vignettes organized alphabetically by subject matter. They are all brief and very much to the point, ranging from the mundane to the esoteric to the spiritual and are presented with sparkling clarity. Each essay or rumination, however, is not intended to be the last word on the subject. Instead, see it as a jumping-off point for further consideration or discussion.

A veritable treasure trove of useful information, this project was penned by Wayne Hatford, acting as scribe. Also the author of *Letters from Janice: Correspondence from the Astral Plane*, Hatford is no stranger to the art of channeling, and the cadence, language, and style of speaking in this tome, so clearly reminiscent of Valentino's voice in other writings, attest to his ability in that arena.

As to the purpose of this work, Valentino, himself, says..."we are always in need of a little fine-tuning. That is what this book promotes, if one wishes to avail oneself of it. A sharpening of the senses, an uptick in awareness, an even better understanding of the beauty of soul, those are the attributes of *Valentino Speaks*."

This book provides both a fascinating read and an enjoyable journey in consciousness. Start at A and proceed through to Z, or use it as a meditation, picking a page or topic at random each day. Whatever your method, you are about to embark on a remarkable voyage, exploring this world...and the next...in stellar company.

Welcome aboard and **buon viaggio**!

Valentino on....

Love: "Love works however it's offered – as a sumptuous feast in the mansion of a rich man or as crumbs on a pauper's table. Love is, in and of itself, all that we truly ever need."

Romance: "Becoming right with romance involves really learning how to give and receive. Both must be well-practiced in order for us to become fully engaged. Think of these two verbs as a matched set, each one providing the other with an incentive. It does take two to tango. Natacha and I took that lesson to heart. Hopefully, too, so shall you."

Relationships: "It is said that two ought to be greater than one. Indeed, so it seems. But the paradox is that it often takes two to be able to see the ONE. When we choose to partner with another person, we're much more likely to feel our inter-connectedness with the Universe. Intimacy always reminds us that we're part of the WHOLE."

Beauty: "Beauty, like honey, tastes better unfiltered ~ no wardrobe or special make-up required!"

Forgiveness: "A sigh of relief is heard each time someone in the world forgives. Forgiving opens up space for new developments to occur. Indeed, it's in the act of forgiving that whatever's been clogging our emotional entrails suddenly gets released."

Poetry: "What is every poet's dream? To shed light on thoughts so that they may truly be seen."

Soul: "What is soul? God individuated, that which is immortal. As opposed to personality, the real deal. The personality is but a costume to be changed upon occasion, capable of morphing to suit our needs, whereas the soul represents our core self, the essence of who we are, a multi-faceted subset of the ONE. It is a conglomeration in a single package, expressing the distillation of innumerable life-times."

Sex: "Sex enhances vibration. Each time we're sexual, we increase our vibratory rate, defying time by temporarily losing all sense of it. Two people having sex with each other are like a pair of locomotives simultaneously speeding down adjacent tracks, sexual climax being the final station on the main line."

Money: "When beholding prosperity, be it yours or someone else's, acknowledge it. In so doing, we are confirming the lack of scarcity in the Universe. In other words, abundance reigns, in all planes. Rejoice, therefore, in each other's good fortune! In being resentful of another person's prosperity the only thing we're likely to accomplish is to short circuit our own. My friends, the laws of abundance are extraordinarily simple. To the extent that we're able to see ourselves as having the resources we need, so shall it be."

Hope: "Hope fuels our progress. Like Love, it's always working on our behalf. By hoping, we define our preferences, the first step in bringing about a desired result."

Happiness: "Laughter is connected to happiness at the point at which it meets itself, coming and going. Health is also entwined therein, at the very same juncture. That we often pair health and happiness in the same breath is not accidental. They are birds of a feather. That said, laughter's role in this pairing is one of facilitator. Quantifiably potent, its healing properties are perhaps even more effective than other therapeutic agents. It IS to laugh. The more we laugh, the happier and healthier we are all the more likely to become."

Beliefs: "How you see things depends on how you choose to see them. The bottom line is that nothing really means anything unless you believe that it does."

VALENTINO SPEAKS

THE WISDOM OF RUDOLPH VALENTINO

CUES AND VIEWS FROM THE OTHER SIDE

WAYNE VINCENT HATFORD

Con la collaborazione dello spirito di
RODOLFO VALENTINO GUGLIELMI

"Always strive to remember who you are."

Ex libris_____

Publisher's Cataloging-In-Publication Data
(Prepared by The Donohue Group, Inc.)

Hatford, Wayne Vincent. ☐

Valentino speaks : the wisdom of Rudolph Valentino, cues and views from the other side / by Wayne Vincent Hatford.

p. : ill. ; cm.

"Con la collaborazione dello spirito di Rodolfo Valentino Guglielmi."
Includes bibliographical references.
ISBN: 978-0-9833436-0-8

1. Valentino, Rudolph, 1895-1926--(Spirit)--Philosophy. 2. Spirit writings. 3. Spiritualism. 3. Valentino, Rudolph, 1895-1926. I. Valentino, Rudolph, 1895-1926 (Spirit) II. Title.

BF1311.V3 H38 2011
133.9/3   2011922925

Whitley Heights Publishing
Palm Springs, CA
www.valentinospeaks.com

ISBN: 978-0-9833436-0-8
LCCN: 2011922925

Design & Layout by Mark E. Anderson, aquazebra.com

AQUA ZEBRA™

This book is manufactured in the United States of America.

Acknowledgments

Grazie Mille to all those who helped make this book possible.

In Spirit
Rudolph Valentino Guglielmi
Black Feather
Meselope
Helen Hatford Good
Alice Vincent Hatford
Gus and Tillie Henke
Janice Horn
William Mumford Jr.
Charles and Margaret Vincent
Eva Walker

My Parents:
Bernice Henke Hatford
Robert W. Hatford

In The Flesh
Daniel Alvear
Lynn Bell
Steven Benjamin
Frank and Liza Bizzarro
G. Robert Cash
Darcy Sean Clarke
Tamara Diaghilev
Erik Engel
Alice Garabedian
Tom Hayes
Walter Kreuckl
Kenneth M. Leavitt

Donna Good Mereno
June Hatford Nugent
C. Jack Schwarz
Julie Soquet
Kurt Wagner

**For their work and dedication
to the memory of Rudolph Valentino**

Edoardo Ballerini
Kevin Brownlow
Allan Ellenberger
Donna Hill
Sylvia Valentino Huber
Emily Leider
Tracy Terhune
Jeanette Valentino Villalobos
Jeanine Villalobos
And so many more!

Also
Silvio Alovisio
Giulia Carluccio
Antonio Miredi
Paolo Orlandelli
Fabio Salvatore

Fondazione Rodolfo Valentino
Museo Valentino & The Town of Castellaneta, Italy

A Special Thanks to
Robert G. Prescod for having been instrumental
in bringing this book to fruition.

Offered in the Spirit of Love and Service

FOREWORD

"You ask about poetry and why I am partial to it. The answer is simple. Poems may be thought of as paintings on a page. The words are shadings and colorings whose purpose is to give shape to thought."

R. Valentino Guglielmi

In 1923, Valentino wrote and published a metaphysically-oriented book of poetry entitled *Day Dreams*. The poems contained herein, written more than eighty years later, follow in that tradition. They have been included to underscore certain key points and principles and are inscribed with a personal wish of love to all those who read them.

As you begin *Valentino Speaks*, I invite you to suspend your disbelief. Yes, it is so, those on the other side can and do communicate with us all the time. Rudolph Valentino is just another in a long line of helpful souls who, from their particular vantage point, have chosen to share their wisdom. You may, of course, react to what he has to say any way you want. The only thing I ask is that you keep an open mind.

Wayne Vincent Hatford
Palm Springs, 2011

TABLE OF CONTENTS

INTRODUCTION 1

TOPICS

ACTORS & ACTING 9

ADVENTURE 11

ANCIENT EGYPT 13

ANGER 15

ANIMALS & PETS 16

ANOTHER GOLDEN RULE 17

APPEARANCES 17

ARTISTS 18

ART OF BEING 19

ASTRAL BODY 20

ASTRAL PLANE 22

AT-ONE-MENT 23

ATTRIBUTES OF LOVE 24

AUGURIES 25

AURAS 27

AUTOMATIC WRITING 28

AUTOMOBILES 29

AWARENESS 34

BAD VIBES (MALPRACTICE) 36

BE-ATTITUDE 39

BEAUTY 40

BEING YOURSELF. 41

BELIEFS 43

BIRTH. 43

BIRTH NAMES. 45

BLISS 46

BOOKS 47

BULLFIGHTING (MAN VERSUS NATURE). 48

CASTELLANETA (VALENTINO BIRTHPLACE). 50

CAUTION 51

CELEBRITY. 51

CHANCE (FORTUNA). 52

CHANGE. 54

CHILDREN 54

CHOICE 55

CITIES 57

CLOCKWISE 59

COLOR 61

COMITY 61

COMMUNICATION. 63

COMPASSION. 65

CONFIDENCE. 66

CONSCIOUSNESS 68

CORPORATION. 70

COSTUMES 71

CREATING PERSONAL REALITY 73

CREATIVITY 80

CREMATION. 82

CURIOSITY. 83

DANCE 83

"DA RICORDARE" (THINGS TO KEEP IN MIND) 87

DEATH 89

DESIRE. 95

DESTINY. 98

DIET. 98

DOUBT 99

DREAMS. 101

DRUGS 106

ECOLOGY 107

EDUCATION 108

EGO 110

E-THEREAL MAIL 111

EVOLUTION 111

EYES 113

FAMILY. 115

FEAR. 119

FEELINGS 119

FEET. 120

FIRE 124

FLOW 125

FORGIVENESS. 127

FREEDOM 130

FREE WILL 131

FRESH START 132

FRIENDSHIP 134

FUN 135

GEMSTONES. 137

GOD 140

GOLD 143

GOSSIP 145

GREED 146

HABITS. 147

HANDS. 148

HAPPINESS 151

HEALING 155

HEALTH & DIS-EASE 156

HELP MATES 159

HOME. 160

HOPE 165

HUBRIS 166

HUGS 167

INSPIRATIONAL THOUGHTS (APHORISMS) 168

INTERNAL DIALOGUING. 169

JANUS (BEGINNINGS & ENDINGS) 171

JUSTICE 172

KARMA 175

KEY (CATALYSTS) 178

KINSHIP 181

KNOWLEDGE 183

LABYRINTHS 186

LANGUAGE 187

LIBERTY 190

LIFE 191

LIFE AS A MOVIE 192

LIFE GOALS 194

LOVE 195

MAGIC 199

MARRIAGE 203

MEDIA 204

MONEY 206

MOON 208

MOTION (MOVEMENT) 210

MUSIC 212

NAMASTE 215

NATURE 216

NEIGHBORS 219

OBJECT MEMORY 220

OPERA 221

ORBS OF LIGHT 223

PARADOXES 223

PASSION 224

PEACE 226

PERMUTATIONS 226

PERSONALITY 227

PHOTOS 230

PHYSICAL BODY 231

PHYSICAL MOVEMENT (EXERCISE) 232

PHYSICAL SPACE 233

POETRY 233

PORTALS 234

POTENTIAL 235

PRAYER & MEDITATION 237

PRIDE 238

QUALITY 239

QUATREFOIL 240

REINCARNATION 241

RELATIONSHIPS (INTIMACY) 244

RELIGION 247

ROMANCE 248

SACRIFICE 250

SATISFACTION 250

SCENT 251

SERVICE 252

SEX 253

SHARING 256

SILVER 257

SILVER CORD 257

SINGING 258

SMILE 259

SOUL 260

SOUL GROUPS 263

SOUL MATES 265

SPHERES & PLANETS 266

SPIRIT GUIDES (PERSONAL ANGELS) 268

SPIRITUAL WISDOM 273

SUFFERING 274

SUICIDE 275

SUN 277

SUPPORT 278

SURPRISE 280

SURRENDER 281

THREE DIMENSIONAL WORLD 281

THOUGHT 282

TIME 283

TRAVEL 287

UNIVERSE 288

VALENTINO ON VALENTINO 289

VANITY 290

VEIL 291

VIBRATION 294

Vogue (Personal Style) 295

Voice.. 298

War... 299

Who We Are 301

Words.. 301

Writers 302

X (A Rumination) 303

XXX (Kisses) 303

Yes 306

You 308

Zebra (Integration)................................. 309

Afterword 311

Coda: The Life and Times of Rudolph Valentino 312

Epitaph... 316

Reflections.. 316

Partial Bibliography................................. 318

Other books by Wayne Hatford 318

Valentino-related books in progress................... 319

Internet Resources 319

Museum 320

Memorial Service.................................... 320

About the Author 321

"Love binds us to each other as well as to the dimensions we inhabit. In essence, it's our reason for being, **the** reason why every-thing IS."

R. Valentino Guglielmi

Photo courtesy of the Academy of Motion Picture Arts & Sciences.

INTRODUCTION

> Men should be judged not by the tint of their skin
> The gods they serve, the vintage that they drink
> Nor by the way they fight or love or sin
> But rather by the quality of thought they think.

(Intertitle card from *The Young Rajah*
starring Rudolph Valentino, Paramount, 1922.)

How to describe Rudolph Valentino in the language of his time? "He was respectful of himself and others. He was reverent in how he dealt with spiritual matters yet jaunty in the manner in which he moved throughout the world. He was himself, at heart the southern Italian gentleman, the young man whose tendency it was to be simpatico towards everyone." He was also very much a lightning rod. If ever there was a person of interest, it was he. The tabloids loved him! And so did his many legions of fans.

Primarily known as an actor, Rudolph Valentino was really a man for all seasons. In addition to being a movie star, he wore a number of other hats during that life-time, for example, auto mechanic, physical fitness buff, exhibition dancer, writer, equestrian and photographer, just to name a few. In short, he was like all of us, a complex and multi-faceted individual full of hope and contradictions. But what of his inner being, the eternal self? That is the Valentino you will come to know here, the part of him that most of you have not had the pleasure of meeting before ~ on screen or off.

How was this book born? Of course, I already knew a little about Valentino's career before beginning this project. And, I had also seen what was arguably one of his best films, *The Four Horsemen of the Apocalypse*, at a San Francisco silent film festival. Even so, as of early 2004 my knowledge of him was rather limited.

In June of that year, however, things changed. Within the space of three weeks, I experienced a number of coincidences that were all Valentino-related. Photos, books, videos and unexpected connections all suddenly came my way, showing up in my life with way too much synchronicity for me not to pay attention. The biggest surprise though was yet to come. By the end of the month I instinctively felt that I wanted to try connecting with him through automatic writing, a technique that I had not practiced since I channeled my previous book, (*Letters from Janice*, Uni-Sun, 1987) about a friend's experiences with the transition known as death.

Desirous of establishing contact, I was delighted to discover that I had! A message came through and based on its content as well as how it was signed, it immediately became clear that I was in touch with Valentino's essence. Our first writing session was brief but informative. However, starting with session two and going forward we have been able to effectively align our energies for the purpose of writing this book. The whole process has been facilitated by our respective spirit guides and the soul essences of my grandmother, Alice Vincent Hatford, and other members of the Vincent clan. Working together as a group they provided the technical assistance required to make it happen. Others, too, sometimes joined the ranks, offering their help on an ad-hoc basis.

As a result, communication between us has flourished. Of course, I initially had to work on suspending my disbelief just as I had to do when I first channeled my friend Janice. But the evidence that I was in contact with Valentino's essence was undeniable. So I settled in, during the next few years producing the sixty automatic writing sessions that form the basis of this book. Doing this work has been a wonderful experience, something I've been thankful for since day one. Not only has it helped me transform my own thinking, it also provided both of us with an opportunity to re-boot, to start over again with each other karmically. Have Valentino and I had any previous entanglements? Yes, rather intense ones too, which is the answer to the rhetorical question why me? Once I began to recall some of the visuals, he was able to share details about three in particular. We knew each other in medieval Italy, during the 9th century on the Arabian peninsula and several thousand years ago in the land of the Pharaohs. "Three on a match, one that has illuminated all of our interactions thus far." A play on words, courtesy of Valentino. What he means is that all of our interactions have been due to our original vibrational match, the same one that continues to light our path today. In other words, we go way back.

That said, I am not the first person to have channeled Rudolph Valentino nor am I likely to be the last. Indeed, it has been well-documented that since his death in 1926 Valentino has had a history of speaking through others, most notably in the role of metaphysical teacher. Why is he so keen on communicating in this manner? Because to share is to love. That is the reason Valentino speaks to us from beyond, to share what he has learned, an expression of love. And now he sends his love one more time, presenting us with all new material!

Never having read any of his writings prior to starting this project, I did not have a sense of how Valentino might have expressed himself during that life-time. However, after our third session together I decided to locate and read copies of *Day Dreams*, the book of poetry he wrote in 1923, and *My Private Diary*, a journal of his European travels originally published in a magazine. In so doing, I discovered that the material in the three channeled sessions we had already completed closely resembled his other writings in terms of style and tone ~ even though the content was quite different. To me that was the ultimate confirmation that we were indeed in contact.

In educating myself about Valentino's personal and professional life I found it rather fascinating that he had also been open to channeling. June Mathis, the screenwriter friend who helped shape his career, was perhaps the first person in Hollywood to broach the subject with him. Embracing what he soon found to be a natural inclination, over time he participated in a number of automatic writing sessions and séances, especially with Natacha

Rambova, his second wife. He was also known to have channeled on his own, using the information he received to write poetry and in general provide guidance.

According to biographers Valentino was interested in spiritualism, gave credence to the concept of past lives and subscribed to the idea that the soul survives the death of the physical body. He also firmly believed in God. Although he was never particularly religious in the traditional sense, he was born and raised a Catholic. Natacha, on the other hand, was strongly attracted to ancient religions, an interest she pursued for the rest of her life, at one point even becoming a respected Egyptologist. During their marriage she actively supported her husband's interests in all things metaphysical.

To quote Natacha, writing shortly after his death: "Rudy was really psychic. We used to do mechanical writing quite a bit. A spirit would take command of the hand and pen and move the entranced medium to write on paper what was being dictated." Although Valentino may have been in contact with a number of spirit entities in this manner, he apparently communicated more with two in particular, Meselope, an Egyptian of the Hermetic brotherhood primarily associated with his wife, and Black Feather, a native American and his own personal spirit guide.

Since the inception of this project I've been communicating with the entirety of Rudolph Valentino rather than with just some portion of him. Indeed, I conceive of Valentino's essence as being inclusive of all his experience and knowledge to date ~ in all times and places. I'd like to propose, therefore, that he be conceptualized as something far greater than his former self, keeping in mind that names are nothing more than a frame of reference.

What I say here about Rudolph Valentino can easily be applied to everyone. Without exception, our respective life experiences are vast in comparison to what can be understood and utilized in the context of any one incarnation. In making this point, I am reminded of another that is perhaps even more salient: That all the information in this book was sourced from Universal Mind. However, in order for it to be expressed it first needed to be focused. Valentino's essence was able to do just that, distilling larger themes into more manageable ideas and then funneling them across the dimensional divide in such as way so as they might be shared. In order for any of this to occur, however, I first had to be a willing participant ~ something I was from beginning to end.

Although all information that ever was or shall be is theoretically available to us, it is not always so easy to access it on our own. Rudolph Valentino's gift here is to offer us pearls of wisdom, or as some might put it, an invitation to tango with a master dancer. Each essay or rumination, however, is not intended to be the last word on the subject. Instead, see it as a jumping-off point for further consideration or discussion. Valentino, like each of us, is still evolving. Though he speaks to us from the totality of what he knows, he does not yet know it all. Neither does anyone else for that matter, in the body or out. As he states unequivocally "that honor is reserved for the Creator." Therefore, take the information offered here as one soul entity's point of view, keeping in mind that you are the final arbiter of what is true for you.

I contend that spiritual awareness rather than his work as an actor is the true legacy of Rudolph Valentino. That said, this book is not intended to enshrine him or put any laurels on his head. Such would be the opposite of what he seeks to accomplish and at odds with the intent. Valentino is on a journey, just as we all are. He is not looking for any special recognition. His only hope is that you will find the ideas expressed in these pages to be helpful in deciding how you want to live your lives.

Valentino Speaks contains 180 thought-provoking vignettes on a wide variety of subjects, many of which have never been explored before through this type of lens. They are all brief and very much to the point, prescriptive suggestions for dealing with the challenges we all have to face. To quote Valentino: "our book is about helping people thrive in the midst of momentous change by focusing on the most creative aspects of ordinary dilemmas." As stated in the foreword, there are also a number of poems that have been included in order to underscore certain key points and principles. They tend to be playful, thought-provoking and hopefully, as Valentino himself put it "sometimes even a little like paintings on a page." That at least was the intent.

Because it's relevant, I'd like to point out that Rudolph Valentino was multi-lingual, speaking Italian, French, English and Spanish, all with great aplomb. He also knew a bit of German. Indeed, he was quite the communicator, even attempting to sing at one point. In 1923, he made a vanity record as a present for his wife, today the only remaining evidence of his voice.

Now, more than eighty years later, he has once again been given an opportunity to speak!

Valentino often inserted Italian, Spanish or French words into our channeled communication which, as it turned out, were always perfect for the occasion. To be true to his intent, I have left all non-English words intact, followed by their translations. That I am a former French and Spanish teacher who also speaks Italian has been most helpful and is perhaps yet another reason why, on the deepest of levels, Valentino and I have chosen to collaborate: we both know the same languages.

Now a bit more about the process. So that an automatic writing session may be accomplished, it is first necessary to establish an etheric link. The actual mechanics are fairly straightforward, mostly involving creating the time and space for it to occur. To that end, I have designed a ritual whose purpose is to clear the air vibrationally, anchor myself in the moment and call forth the necessary guides and technicians, those on the other side who help us to effect our communication. As soon as everything is in place Valentino's essence signs in and we begin.

During each session the power resides at the point of my pen as there is a force present, separate from my own, that is moving it. Of course, I am also involved but have set aside some of my own energy in order to allow Valentino to come through. At certain times the writing is very fast-paced. At others it's slow and deliberate. I may hear the words in my head as I write or I may not. However, all that does not matter.

What is important is that I'm able to get out of the way to a certain extent so that communication can take place. In fact, I am in a partial trance, my "NOW" focused solely on what is before me. Time seems to disappear, folding into itself. I do not consciously know what I have written until later when I transcribe it. Very little editing was required. What you read in these pages, therefore, is exactly what Valentino's essence wanted to say about each topic.

Explaining abstract ideas is always challenging. Nevertheless, with Valentino as the source and myself as the scribe, we have done our best to accurately convey all intended meanings. In these pages, Valentino shares his thoughts in a crisp, charming and again slightly playful manner, using alliteration as a teaching device. Truth is universal yet it must constantly be told and re-told in order to be fully grasped. *Valentino Speaks* aims to do just that. We hope to jog your memories so that you remember even more of what you already know.

Valentino's goal in writing this book is to help each of us achieve greater degrees of awareness, inner alignment and personal growth. To that end, he offers many examples of 'ways to be.' Keep in mind, however, that there is no one right path. How you 'are' at any given moment simply reflects the sum of your choices to date. Valentino's way of being, though not necessarily yours or mine, serves to remind us all of our own gifts, abilities and unlimited potentials.

Valentino Speaks is arranged alphabetically so that any topic of interest will be easy to find. Each is self-contained and does not have to be read in sequence. This book then is a compendium of the wisdom of Rudolph Valentino, a practical guide to the movie called "Life." You are invited to accept or reject any part of it as you see fit, according to its resonance with your inner self.

The final sentence of an article Valentino once wrote for *Movie Weekly* magazine now seems rather prophetic. **May the memory of my shortcomings fade when the thread of my days has run**

through the loom of life and only the best art that I had it in me to give remains. The tapestry of the life that was Rudolph Valentino's has long since been completed. However, the best in him continues to inform. **Le stelle non smettono mai di brillare** ~ *stars never stop shining.* Valentino shines in this book like he never has before. Again, I feel very fortunate for having been able to work on this project. It's been a constant joy!

Note: on the following pages, all italic questions and comments are mine; everything else is Rudy.

--- ❖ ---

Actors & Acting

An actor without a part is no one, or so it has been said. It's a good thing we always have some part to play. Actually, there's never a time when we don't!

What is the secret of a good actor then, especially if the medium is moving pictures? An actor's true brilliance lies in his or her ability to be still while in motion. Those who can most successfully project the stillness of their characters within the context of movement are those who are the most gifted.

The converse is equally true. In Hollywood parlance, the isolated frames of a film are known as stills. When each still, in and of itself, conveys some inner facet of the character being depicted, it is proof of an inspired performance. Taken collectively and placed within a framework of motion, they come together to form each actor's body of work.

You have indeed gotten to the bottom of what I was all about on the screen and in my daily life. I was blessed, especially in front of the camera. I had the ability to inhabit my characters, that is to say, to imbue them with the essence of soul. That is why they seemed so real. Nevertheless, this was not an exclusive gift granted to Rudolph Valentino, not at all! Everyone can do what I used to do. We all inhabit our roles, whatever they may be. It is always preferable, however, to do so without taking ourselves too seriously. A light touch will bring you much you see.

My formula for playing any part in life is simply to feel it. Ask yourself what is really there? What essentials must your character express? Furthermore, be aware of the 'realities' that are to be projected on the rhetorical screen of life and how they might affect or be affected by your character.

We all are actors, yes we be, for Actors Guild members are we, always playing our respective parts. How is this so? We all have stories to tell and tell them we must ~ through the use of any and all available modalities, on screen or off. Truth be told though, we are never off-screen, even when we are supposedly alone.

'Dancing through life' was my strategy. However, if the idea of dancing is not to your liking, choose a different metaphor, your own carefully crafted 'how to be.' Then, let things flow. You'll definitely put on a good show. There's nothing very complicated here, dear readers.

In essence, adopt a frame of mind or an attitude towards life that works best for you. Mine was the dance, as epitomized by the tango. But there are also any number of other readily available metaphorical constructs that can be equally as effective. Use my model, if you will, peruse those of your peers or choose one that you yourself devise. Remember, there is no one size fits all.

Which then shall be your preferred method? Which pitch to best effect your affect? Once these questions have been answered to your satisfaction, stick with it. Hang your hat on the stance you have chosen, subject, of course, to change.

As far as acting is concerned, some get paid, most do not! Structure your scenes. Light yourself well. Block your moves too, even if it's hard to tell if you're doing it right. Usually you are!

An actor is he or she who acts, i.e. WE. Actors literally take action and run with it. As actors, we function as catalysts and catalysts are, by their very nature, enthusiastically disposed to the task of bouncing thoughts around a set, literally our 'field of play.'

Acting is an essential part of the art of being. In fact, they are inexorably entwined. The preferable way 'to be' in life is natural. Be who you truly are and you will indeed go far.

As actors we are eternally on set, cameras rolling, ever on our marks. It's funny but we do always seem know our lines even if we never rehearsed them before. We also seem to be perpetual students, always striving to improve our skills.

Consider this: we are first and foremost actors, no matter what else we may choose to do. To act, in fact, is to support the vital substratum of Universal Energy that nurtures us all, the 'that which lies beneath' of our existence. It is interesting to note also that life requires that we all become well-schooled in the fine art of expressing ourselves.

Personalities come and go bump in the night, or during the day, as the case may be. The point is that they often conflict. What is the constant in this observation? That we lob our thoughts back and forth, again as though we were tossing a ball around on a playing field. That's what we're here to do. It's just part of the game of life, always in progress. There is never a time-out either. Seems like it's always our turn.

I play, you play, we play, they play – all parts and roles. Although these are literally just forms of the same verb, practically speaking they describe what we all do: act. And as we act, characters come to be, fleshed out, as they say. But in fact all characters already are. This you shall come to see more clearly as you evolve and grow into whoever it is that you are seeking to become.

Acting ~ I love it! Always have. As your consciousness joins forces with the spirit of acting, allow yourself to become part of that spirit. To do so is like eating a piece of the world's most delicious pie. You, too, will love the experience. It's called 'being in the flow.'

You must first define your character. Only then can you decide how best to play your part. Next, just do it. But in order to do, as always, you must first BE.

This is the actor's creed, simplified: BE, then do what comes naturally!

ADVENTURE

Adventures are opportunities for us to become more conscious. I submit, for example, that you are on an adventure right now. It started the moment you opened this book.

The spirit of adventure requires us to go where we have never been before, to wherever the four winds take us.

Indeed, the concept of adventure implies that in order to be able to experience one we must first put ourselves out there. In other words, we must be willing to try something new. However, in so doing we most likely will not be able to foresee the results of our endeavors.

Being in integrity with adventure demands that our physical bodies get involved. They must in order for personal epiphanies and breakthroughs in consciousness to take place. Although adventure is frequently linked with travel, that is a conceptual limitation. Adventures can be initiated in myriad ways and within endless numbers of frameworks. And, as long as the physical body is in some way part of the experience, they can happen at any time and place, including in our home environments.

Sometimes just one word can trigger an idea that will lead to some sort of an adventure. Then subsequent choices will turn that idea into a series of unexpected events and consequences. Indeed, that is always the delicious part.

What constitutes adventure? There are no constraints. Anything can be an adventure if you deem it so. The question to ask is have I done this before? If the answer is no and you want to do it now, you're at the beginning of an adventure.

Whatever falls into the category of 'seeming to be new' inspires adventure. It's not so much the adventure itself, however, that's important. It's what we learn from it. Changed perspectives are usually the result, an integral part of the evolutionary process. If we can't change our points of view, we can't evolve. It's as simple as that. Therefore, be open to adventures of any size, shape or flavor. At the very least, they will always reward us with greater understanding. Indeed, our task in life is to continually move from the realm of the known into the unknown, be it in direct or crab-like fashion.

Physical risk, though often associated with adventure, need not be one of its essential components. Actually, risking our bodies in thoughtless ways is counterproductive to personal growth. Calculated risk, on the other hand, is another thing. When doing anything that involves the safety of the physical body, be sure to check in with both gut and logic. Although our spirit guides may, upon occasion, intervene to save the day, the responsibility for our safety and well-being ultimately rests in our own hands.

In order to have an adventure all we need is the intention. Indeed, we have only to focus our consciousness in that direction and then choose our prescription. It may be one that's easy to take, like a sugar-coated pill, or it could be a little more difficult to swallow. In all cases, however, the soul inherently knows the parameters of what is being required, gently reminding us at the outset to make appropriate choices.

In truth, most people need very little encouragement to be adventuresome. And, when we allow our life circumstances to move from the ordinary to the extraordinary, whatever we are doing automatically becomes an adventure.

Ancient Egypt

Pharaonic Egypt was truly the land of the Golden Mean. Symmetry, proportion and balance ruled the day. There, all was math and spatial relationships. The ancient Egyptians used geometrical shapes and placements in order to create energy grids that worked in conjunction with the magnetic forces of the Earth. Each of these shapes had their own particular power and use. When juxtaposed according to pre-determined mathematical calculations, they acted in concert, as energy generators and modulators.

People in ancient Egypt had only to place themselves within these prescribed grids in order to be able to harness certain energies. The overall purpose of this was to dedicate power to specific tasks, especially those that had to do with governing the entity that was then the nation of Egypt. These grid lines were extremely important. They were usually constructed in temple complexes or at burial sites and were the exclusive province of the Pharaoh, the

High Priests and a few other learned people.

Those who harnessed the energies I speak of here were able to accomplish great things on behalf of the Egyptian state, working with the Earth's magnetic field in order to realize common goals.

The rulers of Egypt used these same concepts to protect their land and thwart potential enemies. They were also employed to accomplish any number of other things, for example, constructing buildings and monuments in what we might think of as record time, ensuring the yearly ebbs and flows of the river Nile and anchoring the identity of the Egyptian people. All this was quite the balancing act! Nevertheless, Egypt had thousands of years of peace and prosperity as a result.

What was known in ancient Egypt is retrievable and so shall it be. The story of this great land is encoded in all of our hearts.

Egypt was a paradise then as well as being a feast for the eyes and all of the other senses. Metaphysics were the rule rather than the exception. And, we strove to find balance in whatever we could or would do.

Again, everything in ancient Egyptian life was based on the science of shapes, spatial relationships and mathematical computations. This was the main precept and that society's guiding principle. At the same time, however, the ancient Egyptians knew how to honor and work with their environment. Egypt was an arid land. How else could they have made it bloom?

A parallel notion is to be found in the game of chess. First of all, mathematical principles have a role in how the game is played. Secondly, all of the pieces create different dynamics depending on their placements. And finally, the field of play, the board, if you will, is suspiciously analogous to your dimension. Remember it was the Egyptians who were among the first to capture the idea that living in the Earth Plane is a flat screen experience, not at all the three dimensional thing we perceive it to be.

The common denominator in all of Egypt's accomplishments and renown was again its reliance on mathematics. In particular, the numbers 3, 5 and 7 were of great importance. Why? Because they were quite efficacious in the computation of certain formulas.

Though often seen today as having been a rather mystical and amorphous land, the reality is that pharaonic Egypt was a highly organized and precise society. Everything had its purpose and place. For centuries, the Egyptian nation was supported and maintained by intense concentrations of thought, primarily generated by its priestly contingents, their minions and various and sundry supporters. It was a prime example of what mankind can accomplish.

In ancient Egypt, Light was everywhere. Its inhabitants had only to avail themselves of it.

ANGER

When seized by anger, we may sometimes choose to act impetuously or even irrationally.

On an emotional level, anger often provokes blinding or bewildering sorts of feelings. If unrestrained, it can overwhelm our faculties, preventing us from making sound and reasonable judgments. Nevertheless, anger must be experienced and dealt with by every human being.

When anger is overly indulged, it tends to intensify, begetting itself and possibly spinning out of control. Therefore, allowing anger to rule your life is at best counter-productive and at worst may lead to self-undoing.

When angry, the best thing we can do is just to acknowledge it and then let it go.

ANIMALS AND PETS

Our consciousness is not above the consciousness of animals. It is simply of different stuff, serving other purposes and goals. Animals, too, have souls. Therefore, things work much the same for them as they do for us. A major difference, however, is that when animals are disincarnate they continue life on their own levels in the Astral.

In death, you and your pets may choose to be in close proximity with each other but that is not a given. There needs to be some mutually beneficial reason for that to occur. In the meantime, you may visit former pets if you wish but they are limited in coming to you unless you and they have exceptionally strong bonds.

If you recall, I was once very close to a number of dogs. However, I can't manifest them as a group. Neither can I see them all at one time. Any attempt on my part to do so would cause consternation ~ primarily because they would not be able to handle it energetically. Therefore, I have to focus my thoughts on one pet at a time in order for us to be able to relate to each other in the Astral.

Pets are often among our closest companions, never tiring of our presence. However, there is one caveat: if we choose to have a pet, we have a responsibility to it. Adopting a pet is like adopting a child. It means making a life-time commitment.

Pets are our natural friends, loving and faithful. Once they are in our lives, we become their world. That said, not everyone should have a pet. There's a certain disposition that's required, a kind heart being the main prerequisite. Again, you must be willing to see pets as children and care for them as such. It is a responsibility that you must clearly accept should you decide to adopt one.

If you want to know what pure love looks like, picture your dog looking into your eyes or think of your cat purring in your lap ~ being there for you as you are for them. There's partnership practice at play in the way that you and your pet relate to each other.

Yes, we get to practice relating with our pets ~ hopefully transferable to our own species, in partnership and marriage.

ANOTHER GOLDEN RULE

I would like to say a few words about the idea of loving what you are not doing. Sounds strange, I know, but being envious of work or a project that is being done by someone else is akin to beating yourself up.

So love what you are not doing and what others therefore are doing. Why? Because they do it for you as you do whatever you are doing for them. There is no individuality on the action axis of the Earth Plane. We all work for and with each other all of the time.

Loving each other's work, therefore, whether or not we are personally involved with it, is key to having a more conscious, peaceful and tranquil existence. Jealousy and envy are feelings that should be monitored and neutralized whenever they are detected.

Love your neighbor's work and value his or her skills. Our gifts find their source in the Creator and we all need to express them. As soon as we realize that each of us has something unique to offer petty differences start to fade, becoming irrelevant.

APPEARANCES

Fashion is naught for what's being sought. It's not worth the trouble to obsess about. Glamour, seductive as it may be, also counts for naught. It's like a shadow flickering on a wall, perceptible though never very substantial.

Presenting yourself well has far less to do with fashion than one might suspect. In the final analysis, it's always the inner self that leaves the strongest impression anyway. How you ultimately appear to others, therefore, is based far more on who you really are than on any external factor. Character is indeed higher than intellect. Though gold and glitter may sometimes attempt to influence our hearts and minds, their effects are temporal at best.

If you want to make a good impression, the tried and true advice still applies. Be neat and clean. And, dress as well as you can given your economic status. But beyond that it's in the soul where our true power of presentation lies.

What counts most as far as appearance is concerned is smiling, exuding good will and having a sparkle in your eyes. All other considerations pale in comparison. A smile is the best accessory one could ever hope to have, and it's free! So, smile. By smiling you are inviting others to share in your joy.

Good will, my friends, opens many a door. Whenever you express it, others usually respond in kind. Working in tandem, smiles and good will are quite an effective pair. Indeed, they are the secret of a glowing appearance.

Our eyes, even more than our smiles, tell the whole story. They reveal our true i-dentity, letting others know exactly who we really are. Keep this in mind then as you are afoot in the world: the eyes are the mirrors of eternity in whose reflection we come to be known.

ARTISTS

The best in art always remains unresolved, open for discussion. In general, being able to access the child within is an important part of the creative process. It is especially imperative, however, for artists to be able to view life through the eyes of youth, no matter what their chronological age. It is then and only then that they can truly be fruitful in their endeavors.

For artists to be at the top of their game, they must be 'in the flow.' Obviously they can't produce very much if they are feeling out of sorts. Inspiration counts too, whether it results from seeing a fly land on a piece of fruit, enjoying a walk on the beach or observing a camel being silhouetted by the afternoon light. Inspirations may come from any quarter, especially given that they are not all that likely to be used in a literal way. Anyone or anything, therefore, can inspire an artist.

Artists are typically quite sensitive to light. They are also usually very comfortable with **chiaroscuro,** the shadow world. Indeed, more often than not artists walk the line between the dimensions. It is their task to make us all that much more aware of the divine.

Painters paint what their souls know. Sculptors sculpt in the same way. Though to our eyes works of art may seem to have great form and substance, it's what's in between their molecules that counts: **Love.** Love is both the foundation of art and its guiding light.

ART OF BEING

As human beings, we must first understand what it means to be and how that is life.

The most important lesson we can ever learn is one of the simplest. Be true to your essence. Always know who you are. Then, drink it all in. **È molto speciale.**

Be LOVE ~ incarnate and disincarnate. Make agape your creed. See how you can BE in the world. Then, BE in all senses of that word. Indeed, we must BE before we can possibly DO anything. Doing follows from and is commensurate with being. The freedom to BE and DO is key to growth and evolution. What you do defines who you are and vice-versa.

Approach life in the spirit of play. Experiment with all the pieces of the puzzle, especially those that seem not to fit. Have fun arranging them. In so doing you will learn something, just as you did in kindergarten. Indeed, life in the Earth Plane is much like kindergarten with we being **der kinder** ~ *the children.*

Recall the memories of childhood which by definition always seem quite beautiful, the forest scenes, playing near streams, running barefoot in the grass. Then use these remembrances to examine the complexities of life from the perspective of youth. When the age of innocence is your lens, there is no lack of wonder!

Each soul entity is a perpetual student, wherever they call home. I, too, am a student, as are you. Whether in the Astral or Earth Plane, we are continuously enrolled in the school of life. The law of cause and effect, also known as karma, governs every aspect of our lives. Our goal, therefore, should be to soften its impact ~ to the extent that we possibly can.

Here is a recipe for having a good life. Embrace love and hope. Allow your soul to always be present. Work in harmony with others while maintaining a sense of individuality. Honor yourself and your needs yet be humble with other people.

El Marcador ~ *The Framer*

Just how to frame, how to play the game
Of life with little or no blame?
Well, maintain your mind's eye glimmer
In the light of a positive shimmer
Be resolute! You must sustain a constructive frame
Of mind as negative thought just not ought to reign
On this sphere or in any other plane.

RVG

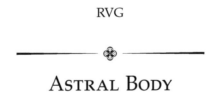

ASTRAL BODY

Think of the astral body as a conglomeration of atomic particles that have coalesced to create an etheric form, one that has substance yet remains intangible.

The soul and astral body are inexorably entwined. If you will, picture them as joined at the hip. Upon occasion, they enter the flesh, primarily to experience life from a different perspective. In such instances, the physical and astral bodies work together, hosting each other for specific amounts of time. The astral body's role is to house the soul while the physical body serves to protect it from the harsher realities of Earth Plane existence. The ancient Egyptians saw this interrelationship very clearly. In their tombs, the outermost coffin or mummy case represented the physical body. The inner sarcophagi, each of greater beauty and more exquisite material than the one preceding it, symbolized the astral body. Finally, the mummy's placement at the core of this arrangement was that of the soul.

Our individual and collective task is to evolve. In order to achieve this most worthy of goals, we must always be willing to learn. Are there ever times when we are not learning? No. Never! We're always apt pupils, whether during waking or sleeping hours.

When we sleep, our consciousness in the form of the astral body separates from the physical body in order to visit the Astral. And, by the way, we learn just as much when we are sleeping as we do when we are awake. The only difference is our so-called condition. What we see and do in the sleep state is called a dream. What we see and do when we are awake is conceived of as reality. In truth, however, they are one in the same.

In the Astral, the astral body 'does' and 'is' what it 'can do' and 'can be.' This is not double-speak. Please read this phrase again and consider the words in their full import. Dreams are what you make them. The physical body needs food and water to ensure its survival whereas the astral body needs only to have direct contact with Universal energy in order to be nourished.

During each sleep cycle, we get to play with thought-force, the stuff that dreams are made of. However, it's mostly a self-contained experience. Though there are exceptions, in the dream state incarnates are generally not able to directly interact with those in spirit. Why? Because as a condition of being associated with a physical body they have limited access.

Nevertheless, each sleep episode offers us plenty of opportunities for learning. In the dream state, our choices are infinite. That's why dreams often morph from one scenario to another in what seems to us like breakneck speed. Dreams represent permutations of what is either possible or probable. Interestingly enough, however, they always seem to relate to the current issues or dilemmas in our lives.

Some dreams are rather weighty, presented to us as parables or 'what if' scenarios. Others are more whimsical, like silhouettes being projected on a wall. Be that as it may, the important thing to understand here is that all dreams, regardless of content, are learning tools. It's often in the sleep state where we have the greatest opportunity to sort through our issues. And, since there are no constraints in the Astral, we're able to experience whatever it is that we most need or want.

Dreams are recipes for self-healing and self-understanding. Why then are the images we see in our dreams often so disparate and at times even alarming? Because each recipe contains diverse ingredients. However, when blended together they always create something delicious.

Dreams would not be were it not for love. Keep a notebook at your bedside and use it upon awakening. In the contemplation of our dreams, there is always much to be gleaned.

ASTRAL PLANE

The other side. Another world, the details of which, at least temporarily, we have chosen to forget. Watching a bird float through the air, we are reminded of what it feels like to be free, that is to say, of the way we once were and how again we shall be. The Astral Plane is our one true home. 'Tis only there that we have complete freedom.

The Astral Plane, by the way, is always nigh. Indeed, the entrance to the Astral is just down the hall from wherever it is that we happen to be, eternally handy and ever-accessible. At the moment of death, we have but to open the door.

As incarnates, we are always only one breath away from our demise. Up to that moment, however, we continue 'being' in the Earth Plane, ensconced in this dimension. Death is concurrent with the first inhalation that does not take place. It's at that point and that point alone that we find ourselves crossing over, ready to continue living our lives, albeit in another dimension.

We might well look to two Italian words, **uscita** and **entrata**, literally egress and ingress, as we think about transition. When we change our dimensional status, what we are doing is exiting one door just as we are entering another. However, in this case both doors are one ~ in the same.

At-One-Ment

(Speaking to the author) As a child you once had a toy that was known at the time as a pinwheel. When activated, it looked like a spinning dynamo, emitting sparks. As simple as it may have been, this toy illustrated the true nature of who we are: points of light rooted in the matrices of our respective souls. When in use it captured the look and feel of At-One-Ment, that state of being characterized by a sense of perfect alignment.

Children are great teachers. If we but pay attention it is often through their eyes that we can learn something. Recall, if you will, you and your friends running around outdoors on a hot summer's eve holding these devices in your hands as though they were scepters. By activating your pinwheels you were able to see each other in the dark.

Remember that we are not who and what we seem. Though temporarily housed in a physical body, in reality we are energy in motion, a helix spinning in clock-wise fashion. While incarnated, we cannot see who we really are even though we are often able to sense it, especially when looking at ourselves from a place of introspection.

At-One-Ment is a relative thing. Of course, we are always 'At-One,' no matter what. But it's only when our hearts are open that we become more conscious of it. A greater awareness of the inter-connectedness of all things is what will lead us to having more joy in our lives. And, all it takes to get us there is a simple thumbs-up ~ that plus giving ourselves permission to go with the flow.

(Again, speaking to the author) In the writing of this book, you and I have often been 'at-one' and are so now ~ at this very moment. This is what it feels like. At-One-Ment is true intimacy, a sense of having docked, interlocked and then merged with the whole while still maintaining a sense of self. It's knowing that the individual pieces of 'what is' all fit together, forming a schematic far more complex than any one of us could ever possibly imagine.

God is One – no other number, and all numbers fit into ONE. At-One-Ment, therefore, is all-inclusiveness run amok ~ in the best of all possible ways.

———— ❖ ————

ATTRIBUTES OF LOVE

A ~ Adoration/Affinity/Allure
B ~ Beauty/Blessing/Bliss
C ~ Caresses/Commitment/Community/Confidence
D ~ Dedication/Desire/Dreams
E ~ Ecstasy/Empathy/Energy
F ~ Faith/Fascination/Friend
G ~ Gifts/God/Gratitude
H ~ Happiness/Honor/Hugs
I ~ Illumination/Integrity/Intuition
J ~ Joy/Jubilation/Justice
K ~ Karma/Kisses/Knowledge
L ~ Lingering/Lips/Longing
M ~ Marriage/Morals/Mystery
N ~ Namaste/Natural/Nourishment

O ~ Offer/Openness/Opportunity
P ~ Partnership/Passion/Promise/Proposal
Q ~ Quality/Quest/Quickening
R ~ Realizations/Receiving/Remembrances/Respect
    Reveries/Romance
S ~ Sacrifice/Sexuality/Sympathy
T ~ Thought/Trust/Truth
U ~ Ubiquity/Understanding/Unknown
V ~ Venus/Virtue/Vows
W ~ Welcome/Wisdom/Wishes
X ~ Xenia (Hospitality)
Y ~ Yang/Yearn/Yin
Z ~ Zap/Zeal/Zenith/Zest

AUGURIES

Augury has several meanings, omens, indications and portents being among them. During the Roman Empire, 'augurs' were appointed to their positions by the priestly class on behalf of the senate and the people of Rome. Their task was to interpret the will of that society's gods by observing the behavioral patterns of birds. In essence they were oracles, empowered by their benefactors and questioners alike to render a yea or nay on the decisions that Rome's politicians, generals and emperors had either already made or were about to make. At the time, the service they provided was seen as essential to the smooth functioning of that city and its far-flung empire. In other words, thinking of sending more legions to Gaul? Let's see what the augurs have to say.

Tanti auguri, a familiar phrase in modern-day Italian, is often used as a sign-off on cards and letters. On one hand, it means may you have many blessings, implying that they all be fortuitous. More literally, however, it expresses the hope that you will encounter many augurs during the course of your life ~ i.e., that you will always have lots of support. For our purposes, let's confine our examination of auguries to omens.

Those of you who meditate on a regular basis are likely to be familiar with the sound that's generated by verbalizing the first two letters of that word: O-M. Used like a cosmic tuning fork, it's purpose is to re-align our vibration. In the bigger picture, however, it is a prayer for inclusion ~ within the sphere of the All That IS – the big O.

Receiving an omen gives us an opportunity to say amen, in other words, to be grateful for the gift we have just received. It's also a confirmation that, at least for the moment, we are in alignment with our purpose, having found a perfect pitch. Whenever we're on the right track, fact is we feel it in our bones ~ from the tops of our heads to the tips of our toes.

What are omens? They are clues that we have left for ourselves, comparable to crumbs or little scraps of paper that have been cleverly dropped here and there in order to help us find our way back home. Their purpose is to raise awareness. Like luck, omens are neither good nor bad. They are purely informational in nature.

Omens may be very subtle or quite profound. Indeed, they come in all shapes and sizes. The one thing they have in common, however, is that they all beg to be noticed. Our challenge then is to do just that. Therefore, ignore them not. To do so would be tantamount to self-sabotage.

Incidentally, we are all our own best augurs. There is no real reason for others to assume that role. The decisions we make need no outside validation. We are the only ones who truly know our hearts and minds. Therefore, if we but pay attention to the clues we'll always know exactly how to proceed.

Auras

As we have previously discussed, each physical body has an astral body associated with it for the duration of an incarnation cycle. In all cases, however, the astral body is semi-autonomous, having its own substantive and rather unique set of operating systems.

Auras are energy fields. They emanate from the astral body and are a primary aspect of its functionality. Think of the astral body as a firefly and the aura as its glow. That will help keep things in perspective. There is one important difference, however. The astral body, unlike the firefly, is invisible whereas its glow can sometimes be seen.

Auras may also be thought of as trace elements, especially given that their existence has now been confirmed by scientific experiment. If auras exist then so do their hosts! Just because the astral body remains unseen does not make it any less powerful.

Our auras indicate our current states of health and general well-being. Intuitives read them all the time. Is it true that some people are more gifted than others as far as being able to see auras? No, definitely not. The reality is that each and every one of us could see them if we really wanted to. All we have to do is try.

But how then is it accomplished? First, I suggest you squint, keeping your eyes either half open or half closed depending on your perspective. Then focus on color. That should do the trick. Auras may only be seen within that framework. Aural colors tend to run the gamut and, of course, are subject to change. However, certain ones usually predominate, depending on the vibratory rate of the individual in question.

When it comes to auras, gemstones have an interesting effect. When we wear them they often strengthen our energy fields. Gemstones also bring their own characteristics and qualities to bear on our lives. Like auras, they are defined by their coloring.

Besides being an intuitive's best friend and a wonderful diagnostic tool, our auras function as magnets, attracting what we need and want and helping us to shape our reality.

When our essences leave our physical bodies during the sleep state, in effect we are visiting our home base. Why? To continue experiencing. Much like a machine operating in perpetuity, experiencing is something that we're always doing, a 24/7 kind of thing. Our lives are forever in motion. In fact, there is never a time when they are not.

In line with the comments I've just made, it's interesting to note that the aura and the astral body are the lead players in our lives. The physical body literally just comes along for the ride. How so? If, for the sake of argument, we were to think of these three components as being less integrated than they are, we might say that the aura and astral body, acting in concert, always make the first move. Actually they do. They, rather than the physical body, initiate each action. By definition the physical body is inert unless the astral body and soul are animating it. The aura is likewise part of that animation.

Let's take this idea one step farther. Picture yourself on a roller coaster ride at an amusement park. Taking advantage of momentum, the cars speed along a track, the physical bodies of the riders following suit. The relationship between a roller coaster and its riders is analogous to the dynamics between the astral body and its physical counterpart. In summary, our physical bodies mirror the actions taken by our astral bodies. Some might even go so far as to call it "copycatting."

AUTOMATIC WRITING

What is automatic writing? It is one of the methods that we in the Astral use to communicate with those who are in the flesh.

(*Addressing the author*) Know that I cannot of my own free will make an automatic writing session with you occur. First, you have to be in agreement. Then we need technical support ~ those who hold the wires or in our case the silver cord that serves as a link between my thoughts and your writing. The technicians I speak of are, of course, skilled in this sort of transmission, aligning themselves with our energies and acting as conduits, helping to pass information from this dimension to yours. It is quite a feat! Your "H" *(making reference to my paternal grandmother, Alice Vincent Hatford)* is the prime holder of this font of energy ~ to be used in all of our communications. I am very grateful to her and her colleagues for all of their help and assistance. I know that you are too. They are the ones who generate and hold the necessary space so that I can communicate with you in this manner.

To effect this means of communication, we on this side have first to find and then wrestle with a ripple in the space and time continuum. Once achieved, we pass the energy through the Veil and down a focus chute, working as a unit. All this must occur sequentially as well as concurrently in order for my thoughts to be able to connect with the tip of the pen in your hand.

The energy used to channel is like tension in a wound-up clock spring, completely available until all of a sudden there's no more torque. As a result, every automatic writing session has a shelf life, able to last for only a certain amount of time.

AUTOMOBILES

Driving an automobile is a simple yet profound way of recalling our astral state of being. It reminds us of how it feels to be unbound while still hugging the contours of the Earth.

Auto-mobile. Such a vehicle moves in and of itself given that ostensively it's self-propelled. However, its operation does require the participation of at least one person whose role is to initiate and sustain that motion, in other words, to drive.

The use of an auto-mobile carries with it an implication of personal empowerment. As we achieve greater mobility, in this case through the use of the internal combustion engine, our consciousness tends to increase exponentially.

Among other things, the automobile is a metaphor for our astral body ~ the one that takes us on a joy ride each night as we sleep, dream and cruise on down the road. Automobiles serve a dual purpose, recalling the old, that is to say, our astral days, while at the same time connecting us with the here and now. From a metaphysical point of view, we might refer to this state of affairs as being on the cutting edge. After all, both sides of a knife are required for it to be of any service. To be at our most effective then, we need to be mindful of the past and conscious in the present.

Generally speaking, automobiles have cosmic import written all over them. We have only to notice. My 1923 Voisin, for example, had a hood ornament shaped like a cobra, a symbol of authority in ancient Egypt. It was given to me by Mary Pickford and Doug Fairbanks around the time I completed a film of the same name. But since we all know that nothing is by accident and everything relates in some way or another to everything else, it's probably not all that surprising to learn that the Voisin company logo had an Egyptian theme, specifically a large pectoral necklace replete with scarab. During my life-time as Valentino, I always felt as if I had lived in ancient Egypt. Now I know for sure that I did.

Here is the point I would like to make. During the course of our incarnated lives we continually run into echoes, time warps and bleed-throughs that can be summed up as reverberations of past experience or, if you will, so-called past lives. They are often only little things like the logo of my vehicle, my making a movie entitled *Cobra* and Doug and Mary gifting me with that hood ornament. There are always connections upon connections you see and the auto we choose to drive often acts as a point of reference.

Cars are just one of the many ways in which we show the world who we are. We may even bond with them to a certain extent. However, we need to remember that we're the ones in the driver's seat. Out of necessity, there must always be an operating agreement between us and that rather complex piece of assembled metal and materials known as an automobile. There has to be!

Some of us like to hide our identities when we're behind the wheel. Others prefer to shine, wanting to be noticed. Whatever the case, none of this is accidental. Our life scripts always come into play when deciding which cars to buy. Interestingly enough, they always fit in too, which is to say the vehicles we drive usually end up being perfect for whatever it is in the bigger picture that we are seeking to experience.

We may think that we are substituting destination for destiny each time we drive a car but in reality they are one in the same. Auto-mobiling, like everything else we do, helps to shape our destinies, at least tangentially. When we drive, we are literally steering our own ships, usually in more ways than one.

Earthly modes of transport are but reasonable facsimiles of the freedom of movement we all once knew in the Astral. In terms of this discussion, however, we must also keep in mind that not everyone knows how to drive or has access to a vehicle. Again, cars are just one way of relating to our personal power. The same thing can be accomplished through the use of any number of other modalities. By the way, please do not be seduced by the horsepower that lies in front of you. Temper the urge to speed. Be respectful of those on the roadways as well as those who we refer to as pedestrians. When operating a motor vehicle, we must always be as conscious as possible. Motors, by reason of their sound and vibration, have a tendency to lull our minds. Witness, for example, the number of people who say that they need to drink a cup of coffee before driving at night.

Never drive in a daze although weather conditions may present us with fog, rain or snow. **Anche nel'inverno, si deve rallentare** ~ *also, it's a good idea to slow down in the winter.* As a driver, I was not always that well-balanced. I paid attention to what I was doing, of course, but there were many occasions when I took unnecessary risks, sometimes by driving too fast for the prevailing conditions. Indeed, my Spirit Guides had to intervene more than once so that I would not have to leave the Earth Plane before my time. This I say now: tempt ye not fate ~ notwithstanding the presence of your guides and the support they always offer. It is only just and prudent to drive in a reasonable fashion.

My '23 Voisin was an open touring car. From a hedonistic point of view, I loved the sensation of speed, the feel of the breeze rushing by. I also loved the challenges I faced by having to go up and down the Hollywood Hills. Most of all, I loved the freedom of choice that is just part of the equation every time any of us drive an auto-mobile.

Driving demands that we continually make decisions, something that always has the effect of expanding our consciousness. That's where the creativity associated with automobiles comes into play. For many, driving stimulates thought. Passengers, of course, may have even greater leisure than drivers to think as they go along for the ride. Even pedestrians may be inspired in some way or other as they observe us from afar.

I once drove a Voisin similar to mine from Paris to my home town in Italy and back. Given the state of the roadways then it was a real adventure. That trip required me to think on my feet ~ even though for the most part I was sitting down! It was my impression at the time that some of the locals watching my car meander through Castellaneta, the place where I was born, might have thought of it as a magical dragon, snorting and slithering down Via Roma, the main street. Fanciful, I know, but far lesser things have inspired the poets of the world.

In addition to the aforementioned echoes of things ancient Egyptian, my Voisin had four small stainless steel star-embossed running boards, one for each of its doors. They had to be used to enter or exit the vehicle. It was a matter of 'step on a star to get in or out of the car' ~ just as Apollo did each time he boarded his chariot to begin the day's trip across the Heavens or alighted after that day's Sun was done. In 1923, I greatly appreciated my Voisin's design and superb mechanicals. Now I better understand the role it played in my life.

I contend that each time we purchase an automobile our ultimate choice reflects any number of factors: economic status, aesthetics, reliability, experience and ego, just to name a few. Of course, there are often a few karmic reasons too as to why we buy the cars we do.

Metaphysically speaking, hood ornaments and company logos are more than just facets of product recognition. They are symbols, markers, if you will, whose job is to call our attention to the vehicle in question. Some are rather straightforward, for example, the three-pointed star of the Mercedes or the archer of the Pierce-Arrow. Others are a bit more subtle. Such symbols often encourage us to throw our lot in with a particular vehicle's image ~ or not. Of course, our tastes are also quite likely to play a large part in our selection of a vehicle. By the way, what is the genesis of taste? Past experience is a big factor. Also a desire for something new. Conceptually, taste originates in the so-called past but rides on the winds of the NOW, forever subject to change.

For many, the automobile is an extension of the personality and its favorite child, ego. In some circumstances, we might even say that it is one of the symbols by which we are initially judged, much as the clothing we wear. That is only a piece of the truth, however. I propose that the total picture is far more complex.

Driving a car is like using a prop in a play, the only difference being that the stage in question is what is most commonly known as life in the Earth Plane. By their very existence cars generate feelings and elicit attitude ~ both from you and others. Moreover, they often create ambiances that are surprisingly similar to those found in our home or work environments.

Will luxury prevail or will basics rule the day? It's an interesting question. The answer is largely a function of personality. Depending on our country of origin or residence, many of us spend large amounts of time in our cars, driving from place to place. Our automobiles may therefore become our home away from home, having been personalized according to our druthers. After all, the personality likes nothing better than to look in the rear-view mirror and see itself in the reflection, in this case cast by the latest vehicle of choice.

Why does someone choose to buy a Chevrolet as opposed to a Cadillac, a Fiat versus a Ferrari? Though money plays a role, they are merely props, to be used as scenery in our respective screenplays. Nevertheless, beyond the obvious benefit of being able to provide us with reliable transportation, automobiles also encourage self-exploration.

Coming back full circle, I can safely say that my '23 Voisin was always ready to take me where I had not gone before. Whenever I drove it, I felt inspired in some way or other. Each time I got behind the wheel, I was expectant, knowing full well that I would be returning from my journey with new perspectives ~ even though I might have only just gone around the block.

I loved driving that car ~ as well as the sense of adventure that was afforded me by doing so. Being in the driver's seat is always a commanding role. Indeed, where my Voisin was concerned, I was captain and it was my ship.

These sorts of experiences are not unique to me, dear readers. If you will, consult your personal histories and think on why you chose the vehicles you did. It's always a rather fascinating study.

AWARENESS

After love, awareness is the greatest gift. But awareness, while eagerly sought, is not for sale nor can it ever be bought. It matters not whether those who seek it are of little means or the wealthy and their respective cohorts. Although awareness is a widely-traded commodity, money or a lack thereof plays no role in its acquisition because in truth it's freely available to all.

For increased awareness to be manifest in our lives, we have only to make a commitment that it shall be so. Awareness resides in the solar plexus. That's where our gut feelings find their home. Being aware requires that we be cognizant of how we are feeling from moment to moment. It's also a matter of being present. Some might say that the shorthand version of this idea is to stay grounded.

When grounded, unfounded fears dissipate, scattered to the winds like shadows that suddenly find themselves bathed in sunlight. Be ye not afraid! Most of us do not develop increased levels of awareness overnight, however. It's something that must be achieved incrementally.

How then shall we become even more aware? Here are some suggestions. Use them as you see fit. Narrow your focus. Adjust the opening on the lens of your mental camera. Snap into it rather than out of it, (awareness, that is.) Do not become distracted in this modern world. Sensory overload, while overwhelming at times, should not confuse or diffuse the process. The bottom line is that we must always remain aligned with our core selves ~ no matter what. Perhaps our greatest challenge is to be as attuned as we can to what surrounds us and then make the necessary adjustments.

Think of awareness in terms of the human eye. Eye movement is constant, often subtle, typically unconscious and usually not subject to volition. Indeed, seeing is part and parcel of the bodily functions that many would label as more or less automatic. Being aware ought to be the same.

The millenniums-old symbol known as the Eye of Horus is particularly relevant to this topic. Many ancient Egyptians wore amulets in the shape of the Eye of Horus, their Sun deity, for religious reasons and, perhaps even more importantly, as a subtle yet tangible reminder to always be vigilant. Their thinking was that the Sun is all-seeing and so should we all be. Allow this image to re-enter your consciousness. It will serve you well.

From time to time, our desire for increased awareness exposes our hearts in ways that may seem uncomfortable. This is as it should be. It is only by taking some risks that we can ever become more aware. By opening up our hearts, we test the waters. Doing so provides us with opportunities to hone our perceptions and better understand what is before us. That said, my counsel is to adjust your heart and soul apertures on an on-going basis. As a general rule, it's good to be open towards others but there are times, depending on circumstances, when it's just not wise.

Being aware has many side benefits. For example, the more aware we become, the more we are liable to want to rid ourselves of certain aspects of the past. In fact, expanded awareness often signals some kind of 'fire sale' in progress. When so inspired, not only do we want to divest, we often want to do it ASAP. Being more aware allows us to get rid of the jumble in our lives, letting go of any and all manner of damaged goods. By discerning what no longer works, we unhook from whatever it is that has ceased to be relevant. The unintended consequence is that what remains often gets polished, ending up having even greater lustre than before.

Awareness is like a dear friend constantly exhorting us to enter previously unexplored territory. When we do, it usually brings us to the threshold of something new. It's at that point that we must choose whether or not to push beyond the status quo or stay married to the past. Awareness is a delicious little devil. It never fails to mix things up a bit.

BAD VIBES (MALPRACTICE)

Bad vibes may be defined thusly: negative thoughts directed inwardly or towards another, often in anger or with nefarious intent. How does this phenomenon square with the desirability of maintaining an open heart? If you allow yourself to be vulnerable, are you then susceptible to being malpracticed? The straight answer to this question is no. Of course, you could be but that would only be the case if you yourself will it.

Therefore, this should not even be a dilemma. But in the event that it is, the solution is two-fold: to dance on the head of a pin and, at the same time, be ready to turn on a dime. Though both of these expressions may seem a bit trite, I quote them here only to make a point. It is advisable to always be nimble as well as prepared for any eventuality. If you sense that bad vibes are in the air, adjust your heart chakra accordingly. Go so far as to close it all the way when you feel there's a need to do so. After all, the best offense is a good defense. If you do not allow someone else's negative thoughts to enter your personal space, they'll just bounce right back to the sender. You may think hmm, that's easier said than done. No, it just takes being aware and a certain amount of practice, that's all.

Closing down the heart chakra is a self-protective kind of move, analogous to raising a shield. As we walk in this world, our shields are usually in the down position so that our hearts can more easily connect with those around us. There are times, however, when without fanfare or advanced warning our shields must temporarily be raised.

Negative thoughts, in being rejected and reflected back to the perpetrator, magnify three-fold. This is likely to feel quite onerous to the one who sent them. It should! That's because there's a lesson to be learned. Those who are in the habit of sending out bad vibes need to understand just how counterproductive their efforts are. Any and all attempts to malpractice others are contrary to the constructive nature of the Universe which, as a matter of course, always seeks the greatest good for all concerned.

When we're angry or jealous, we may begin to stew or obsess about another person and become even more enmeshed with the object of our thoughts rather than being able to maintain a healthy perspective. The unintended consequence of any form of malpractice is that negative thought directed towards another is only likely to further embellish the karmic links that already exist between the two people in question. Negativity sent out into the world always comes back to us in some form or another. And, rest assured, it's not always pretty.

If you give credence to the idea that someone else's negative thoughts or bad vibes might be able to influence your life in some way or another, simply do not allow them into your space. Do not take them in. Again, it would only be through your acquiescence and with your permission that any perpetrator, including yourself, could succeed in getting his or her nasty deed accomplished. It is obviously also very important not to self-sabotage. Unfortunately, we are all too capable of internalizing our own bad vibes, thereby injecting them into our realities and tangentially foisting them on those around us ~ often while not even realizing that we are doing so. 'Tis never wise to be your own worst enemy!

Here are my thoughts on the matter ~ possible 'ways to be' and things to do. Be vigilant. Stay balanced. Think creatively and constructively. Monitor your thoughts and never bask in disparaging other people. In other words, do not malpractice. Nor for that matter should you ever allow others to malpractice you. Avoid using negativity as a default thought construct and you will be able to access the wisdom of the ages. **Messieurs/Dames,** *Ladies and Gentlemen,* this is one of life's most difficult lessons. Our thoughts far too often drift from the realm of constructive criticism into that which is purely derisive, serving no purpose.

Thoughts, like arrows, are often more than capable of inflicting damage. Thus, if you suddenly realize that someone is sending you bad vibes, reject them and do an immediate cleansing. Visualize yourself being surrounded by White Light while at the same time reaffirming your One-ness with the All That IS. If you feel it's warranted, ask your Spirit Guides to help triage the situation. Not to worry! The important thing to understand here is that you must always participate in rejecting bad vibes, whatever their source. Reacting in a passive or neutral way is the same as supporting their presence. You must be definitive, not only in rejecting bad vibes but also in refuting the belief that they have any power or influence in your life. The bottom line is that they do not! But it's up to us to continually declare this great truth. **Only if we accept illusion can we suffer from its so-called effects.**

It is our responsibility and ours alone to send negativity packing by affirming that negativity does not live in my house nor in my heart nor in my soul nor in my physical body. This should be a daily affirmation. To negativity we say: **Va via!** ~ *go away.* Perpetrators, whatever their ilk, often want you to fear them. Do not! Be strong and resolute because they cannot succeed as long as you take the necessary steps to countermand their efforts. Malpractice can cast its illusionary shadow only when it is not being rebuffed.

Walt Whitman once said **nothing external to me has power over me.** First, think about that statement. Then consider this extrapolation. **Nothing external to me has the power to be. Therefore, I am the creator of what I see ~ i.e. my personal reality.** For each of us then, the world without is but a reflection of the world within. If you will, visualize yourself as a heavenly body, a sphere always in the process of maintaining its integrity. That is key to deflecting any such slimy kind of proposition as is represented by malpractice. Be neither its perpetrator nor victim!

BE-ATTITUDE

Conceptually, BE-Attitude advocates directing one's attention towards 'BEING' ~ in the context of an active rather than passive verb. The best and highest use of BE-Attitude is to unabashedly self-validate. This is critical if we are to have confidence in ourselves. It is imperative to focus on BEING above all else. Why? Because it is then and only then that we can claim our full measure of confidence.

Depending on circumstances, we are either more or less confident. I, for example, felt more confident in some areas of my life as compared to others, which is normal. However, I would like to share a concept that I used to good advantage, especially during my early days in Hollywood. Be single-minded where confidence is concerned, that is to say, embody BE-Attitude. This translates as directing all of your confidence or as much of it as you can muster into the project or goal at hand in order to ensure its success. Though perhaps only common sense, there is also a greater principle at play.

By staging confidence within prescribed parameters, it becomes more potent and therefore even more accessible to those who possess it. Containment always intensifies whatever it is that is being contained.

This approach does not necessarily imply that one's confidence would be diminished elsewhere. It simply means that success always lies within our reach when the full force of our confidence is applied to whatever is in progress. If diffused or too broadly scattered, confidence loses its punch. We are at our most effective not only when confidence is in full bloom but also when it's directed at finding creative solutions for particular problems.

I realize that I am stating the obvious when I say that it is extremely important to always know that you are present. Without pro-actively knowing that you are a subset of Universal Mind and therefore a co-Creator, you cannot feel confident about anything. So, adopt a BE-Attitude. Doing so will certainly put you 'in the mood,' the key to having a happy and productive life.

BEAUTY

Beauty, like honey, tastes better unfiltered ~ no wardrobe or special make-up required! Beauty is as beauty is, and does too, having its own intrinsic value. Though often part and parcel of our ideals and creative endeavors, it can also stand alone. We all aspire to beauty as well we should. It's in our nature to do so. If it seems, however, that some pursue beauty more than others, judge ye not. In most cases, they do it for you as much as they do it for themselves.

We all have a vision of how we would like our lives to be and usually beauty is a part of the equation. Sometimes it's even just the possibility of being able to create something beautiful that will spur us on. Beauty is always one of our greatest cheerleaders.

Though the pursuit of beauty is frequently linked to artistic projects or undertakings, I would also like to point out that there is beauty in all endeavors, great and small, plebian or patrician. Therefore, the act of shoveling coal into a furnace can be just as beautiful as the sculpting of a marble statue. Beauty's expression can be compared to a stick of dynamite looking for a match. At some point we know there's going to be fireworks!

Whether man-made or part of nature's bounty, beauty is all around. It is our job to look for it. The ancients knew beauty as we do not today ~ something to strive for in all endeavors. In life, we often just tend to do what we will. However, by adding a dash of beauty to the mix, a bitter stew will suddenly become all that much more savory. Though the eye can see beauty, it's the soul that knows it!

The oft-repeated phrase 'it was so beautiful it took my breath away' is an apt one. Indeed, we may gasp, our breath momentarily in abeyance, in the throes of recognizing that something or someone is beautiful. Though each of us perceives beauty differently, we would all likely agree that whatever it is that we are seeing is but a slice of divinity. **Beauty is akin to God because God is beauty becoming itself.**

In order to understand the essence of beauty, we have only to visualize the daughters of Zeus, the famed Three Graces of ancient Greek mythology ~ all rolled into one. True beauty is never superficial nor is it ever based on artifice. Beauty comes in all shapes, sizes, colors and flavors. It is to be seen everywhere without qualification ~ in all people and things, as similar or disparate as they may seem. Even so-called defects are often beautiful. Whether contemplating a loved one, an artistic masterpiece or a pebble on a beach, beauty rocks!

Being Yourself

Some people say "I just can't be who I really am." The implication in making such a statement is that the outer self and the inner one do not line up very well. I say fie, William Shakespeare's oft-heard hue and cry, fie, fie!

You are yourself no matter what. True, you may perceive that your personality or outer self is blocking others from seeing who you really are but that is just not the case. You are seen, that is to say, your soul is seen by its brethren as well as all creatures big and small. You never have to try to be yourself, you simply ARE. Others always understand who you are even though the fog of personality sometimes prevents us from knowing it.

Love overrides all fonts. I use this word not as an ode to computers but rather to refer to the way we relate to the world. Each of us has a trademark font, also known as our personality or own special brand. However, within that context the soul is still always able to make itself known.

If you feel like your inner self is being obscured, it's probably just temporary. You may simply be in the midst of a re-write, in the middle of making a few changes to your script. Fear not. It is all part of the process and, by the way, definitely not a singular event. We are always busy changing horses in mid-stream.

As an experiment, visualize one or more of your fantasy characters (whoever they may be) as aspects of yourself so that you can explore them in your own mind. Though fictitious, they're sure to be archetypal in some way. Consequently, there will always be something to learn from doing this exercise. Part of being yourself is knowing who you are not.

Contemplating more of life's possibilities than your own script would suggest serves to heighten awareness and encourage personal growth. Also, learning more about others by imagining what it might be like to actually be them is yet another way of increasing our ability to relate. Do you recall hearing the old saying about walking in someone else's shoes? Doing so always helps us to better understand how our own shoes fit.

BELIEFS

Beliefs often beget behavior that is unfortunately based on default. Choose instead to make things up differently. In other words, by changing your beliefs you can pro-actively change your behavior and experience different results. Beliefs lie at the root of all behaviors.

How you see things depends on how you choose to see them. The bottom line is that nothing really means anything unless you believe that it does. Always be willing to shift your belief systems. That is the key to optimal growth.

BIRTH

Let us reflect on the subject of birth. In most cases, we choose a birth canal that will bring us to a mother whose signature patterns are relevant to the script we wrote for ourselves prior to incarnation. This is the general rule and the most common situation. However, there are exceptions. Upon occasion, love overrides the signature pattern requirement and will instead bring us to a mother who does not embody the behavioral patterns we seek. In such cases, the father, siblings, relatives or family acquaintances will exhibit these patterns, allowing us to act, react and interact with them in the necessary ways instead.

When it becomes absolutely essential for a soul entity to incarnate, that soul will come into the Earth Plane any way it can ~ no matter what, through one birth canal or another. Though we might prefer to be born into a particular family, there are always plenty of other families to choose from if, in the first case, our birth process is likely to be hindered.

I do want to make it clear though that any birth requires consensus among all those concerned. The relevant soul entities must all be in agreement with each other. The one who wants to incarnate does not get to make all the decisions. Although karma is usually involved as far as who is born into which family circle, there is also a surprising amount of leeway in the matter. Each family grouping is a laboratory for learning. It almost goes without saying, therefore, that we will be learning something from our parents and other family members just as they will be learning something from us.

That being said, there are still some circumstances where a soul entity must come through a given birth channel and be born into a particular family for the greater good of all concerned.

Each individual life plan can be described as a personal grand design. Our specific issues or karmic patterns, though always right there in front of our eyes, are sometimes hard to encapsulate or describe. Nevertheless, it's our task not only to define our issues but to constructively work with them throughout the course of each incarnation. Birth offers yet another chance for renewal in the Earth Plane ~ and an opportunity to do things a bit differently. A word to the wise: don't fall into patterns that seem all too familiar. Why? Because they probably are. Sometimes just a minor shift in how we do business is enough to open up a whole new range of possibilities. Each incarnated life offers us a fresh start along with the promise of greater understanding and continued evolution.

Remember that birth is usually quite a happy occasion. As a matter of fact, both birth and death really ought to be seen as equally joyous events. Symbolizing the alpha and omega of our incarnated existence, they are two of life's most notable and highly touted transitions, to be experienced by all those who come this way.

Upon exiting the birth canal, there is indeed a miniature person present that looks and acts like a baby. But appearances are often deceiving. Know, therefore, that the full consciousness of each soul is ever present, before as well as after being born and, of course, during the exact seconds, minutes, hours or days that are required for a birth to take place. The so-called baby aspect of any newly incarnated soul-entity simply reflects the temporary immaturity of the personality that has just emerged, now ready to try its latest game plan in yet another sector of the time and space continuum.

Birth Names

The name that you were given at birth is perfect for this life. You chose to come in with the vibration it represents prior to being born. A birth name reflects the divine essence of each soul. When uttered, it invokes an energy that is commensurate with your natural state of being.

If a soul's gestalt and purpose should dramatically shift during the course of a life-time, the individual in question may be prompted to change his or her name. There are sometimes good reasons (not always consciously known) as to why such changes are necessary. For example, when karmic requirements have been satisfied under one name vibration it may well be time to step into another ring. Think circus, at the very least the three-ring variety. A new name will often be part of the package whenever one's second act is about to debut. Life as show biz? That is exactly what it is. Changed or not, rest assured that names are always perfectly suited to those who wear them.

At birth, my parents bestowed me with a goodly number of names: Rodolfo Alfonso Raffaelo Pietro Filiberto Guglielmi di Valentina d'Antonguolla. All were very fitting as well as being truly supportive of who I was at the time. Upon my arrival in the United States, I was alternately known as Rodolfo, Rodolf, Rodolpho or Rudolpho di Valentina. In the meantime, my friends called me Rudy.

With the making of *The Four Horsemen of the Apocalypse*, however, everything changed. I stepped into a different ring, one that would soon alter my life. At the time my inner self knew that my name needed to be simplified in order for me to accomplish my goals. 'Twas only then that Rudolph Valentino clearly became the name of my game.

Names are like icons. By providing us with a focus, they concentrate power and intention. The simple act of saying someone's name invokes their spirit. By the way, you cannot invoke anyone or anything without using a name. It's just not possible. It is also important to note that thinking someone's name is just as powerful as voicing it. Your name is the subject of many a sentence. Name is how you be. In fact, you can't BE without a name. It's your marker in this piece of eternity. Call it not in vain!

Sometimes people who go by multiple names exhibit a certain lack of identity. They are not sure who they really are. Choose one then and stick with it ~ until it's time for a change.

Each person's name is pure vibration, there being much that is encoded therein. In fact, under certain circumstances it can even give us some indication of our shelf life. Gifted intuitives sometimes have only to hear a name in order to be able to read all about it.

Name rhymes with fame. Who knows you except by your name?

BLISS

We all adore being blessed with bliss. It's only natural. A feeling highly prized and eagerly sought, it is often elusive on our shores. On the other hand, it reigns in the Astral Plane. Fortunately, we do get to have a taste of it now and again even though while we're in the body we can't sit down to a full meal. A plateful might be too much for our nervous systems to bear.

Succinctly put, bliss is akin to rapture. It is the end result of having embraced the divine. Bliss rhymes with kiss. When we're in a state of bliss nothing could possibly be amiss. There's just no room for petty annoyance. Bliss lies at the core of IS-ness. As such, it pervades. Its essence is the Creator's signature fragrance. A little bit, therefore, goes a long way in enhancing the overall quality of our lives.

When we're feeling blissful it's as though we are being showered with love. And in truth, we are!

BOOKS

Good books are like our dearest friends. They never become too familiar.

Though we may think we are learning something new by reading the latest books, the reality is that what they contain simply reminds us of what we already know. All of us, incarnate or not, are capable of accessing universal knowledge. As a matter of fact, we do so all the time. Each soul entity, therefore, is literally a font of information. We are seekers, ever striving for a greater understanding of the world we inhabit. Books, some of our most trusted companions, play a vital role in this quest, refreshing our memories while also helping us to stay awake.

When we flip through the pages of a book, it's as though antique magic lantern images are being projected from its spine, story lines and ideas literally jumping off the paper.

Every book has something to offer but, as is so often the case, not all gifts are for us. That said, allow your inner self to assist you in choosing what to read. You'll always know which magic lantern show corresponds to what you really need to know. If you will, choose books in this context. Furthermore, note your rapport with each. Check to see if you have one first. If not, go look for another!

In times like these, it would be next to impossible to become aware of everything. Therefore, it's best to narrow your focus. My advice is to browse before making any commitments. The question to ask yourself is can I put this book down? If the answer is no, you've found yourself a winner.

I Nostri Amici ~ *Our Friends*

The greatest gift any book can bring
Is consciousness so the mind can sing
Reading offers us an opportunity

To re-view our lives with impunity
Maybe even do some things a little differently
As the French say, **"comme il faut"**
Yes, it seems that there's always something more to know
How to **"tornar' laggiù, tornar' laggiù,"**
Go back in time, according to this Puccini rhyme?
A book often does graciously speak
Of the past, memories that subconsciously we seek
Knowledge of and of course how it was,
Yes, it does, cause many a book will give us a peek
At what we're not always able to plainly see,
Who we were in times of yore
Our days of peace and war
In homes with different signs upon the door.
Our shards and traces inhabit still those lands afar
Where wonders never cease because they always are.

RVG

BULLFIGHTING (MAN VERSUS NATURE)

Why has the bullfight persisted throughout the ages? What are its reasons for being? Given their color and pageantry, bullfights are often quite the spectacle, never failing to hold an observer's interest. There is always a certain amount of pleasure to be had in viewing this age-old dance, this back and forth between man and nature. Indeed, we might wonder if man and beast are really one in the same.

Certain elements of a bullfight have a timeless quality, for example, the arena and costumes. In these there is often very little variation. Nevertheless, man and bull in their constant interaction always seem to have a mesmerizing effect on the audience, causing them to wonder which one will survive. Though there is always a certain amount of predictability in the outcome, a sword nevertheless does hang over a matador's head each time he enters the ring. After all, it is certainly always possible that he, rather than the bull, might be the one to die that day.

Rife with strife, bullfights force the spectators to examine their own relationships with nature. In watching, many questions are sure to arise. For example, how shall we face our own deaths? And, how do we live fully in nature's realms while also respecting them? For some, these are dilemmas. Hopefully, not for you.

Where nature is concerned, can we in-deed be good stewards? That is the plan, man.

Though some see bullfighting as barbaric, the fact remains that our conflicts with nature are personified therein. Who ultimately wins? Neither. There are no winners. The only option is co-existence, even though in this case it usually is the bull who ends up getting slaughtered. Man and nature have to learn to co-operate with each other because, for all practical purposes, they share the same space. In Spain, at least, the meat from the slain animals is often sold to the public immediately after the last fight of the day. And so it goes, one thing feeds another. Let's hear it for interdependence!

As inhabitants of this planet, we are sworn to co-ordinate our activities with the forces of nature. Furthermore, it is our duty to honor and respect that which has been bestowed. If not, the depletion of our resources becomes a distinct possibility. Only if we remain conscious of the problem shall we be able to avert a crisis. Denial is not an option.

In the final analysis, it's always nature that trumps mankind. And, when nature speaks we are usually forced to listen. We have only to recall the natural disasters of yore as well as those of more recent times to realize that this is so. That is why incarnates have to understand that they and nature are really a couple, always working in tandem. Things have to be this way. There is no other logical conclusion.

— ❈ —

CASTELLANETA, ITALY ~ *VALENTINO'S BIRTHPLACE*

Museo Valentino

In this southern **"città pugliese"**
Seen through these eyes ~ now **"americano-inglese"**
Sound answers are found, all around
This ancient town by examining Rudy's beginnings plus his
later renown
From points of view many
It costs not a penny
To visit Museo Valentino
Whose exhibits showcase and reframe
A life critics once thought of as mere flashes of fame
Well, true intelligence can never be labeled as mundane,
This the Valentino Museum makes perfectly plain
There, his spirit shines forth in all its diversity
From reel to real. Yes, it's Rudy V-G whose veracity
Empowers the beholder by making him bolder in
the expression of self
What common-wealth
There in Castellaneta does lie
For those with a truly keen eye
Who step up to the plate, inspired, regardless
of detours or wait
To make their own personal run through destiny's gate
Maybe taking a page from the Valentino life-slate?
Hmm, perhaps what we need now may be just such a spate
Life's beginnings always sow fertile seeds
Which then are to flower in our later deeds.

WVH & RVG

CAUTION

What is its genesis? And, does it ever align itself with fear? It does not. Caution operates on different axis, as a child of the rational mind though not, by any means, a bastard. Fear is not on the caution menu, logic is. Being cautious is a legitimate way of approaching life and our reaction to it, just one of the many ingredients in the mix. Again, caution is of consciousness born and therefore has great value. Its overuse, however, can delay our coming to terms with ourselves, either canceling out opportunities or limiting our choices.

While a little bit of caution is always warranted, we must be careful not to steep ourselves in such a tea. Use a modicum versus a good dollop. It's a question of degree.

CELEBRITY

Celebrities are individuals who are celebrated by others, **fêted**, as the French might say, for one reason or another. As such, they are examples of ways to be, in many instances exemplars or reflections of contemporary morality. They come to us from all walks of life, running the gamut from world leaders, entertainers and sports figures to so-called average people. Whether or not someone actually becomes a celebrity, however, is determined for the most part by those who have a say in the matter rather than by the individual himself.

Celebrity status is usually achieved through a combination of deeds done and images projected. And, there is also often another element present: role. Each can play out in any number of ways. My celebrity, for example, came as the result of a series of starring roles in films. However, it was the media's interpretation of them that really put me in the spotlight. Some say that I was one of the first media darlings. Not so. There were many before me, going back to the time of the Pharaohs. I certainly had no leg up on the matter.

Though celebrity as we now know it is essentially personality-driven, it is also often reflective of who we are internally. Viggo Mortensen, a contemporary actor, is an excellent example of this, a man whose inner self is very much present in all he does. He is, however, an exception. Unfortunately, the majority of celebrities tend to be more weighed down by their personalities. In some instances, it's almost as though they are walking around carrying suitcases full of bricks.

In the world of celebrity, personality is often seen as being more substantive than soul. Of course, just the opposite is true. There will be a demystification of the cult of personality in years hence when incarnates again realize the true beauty of soul, becoming more conscious of the fact that everyone deserves to be celebrated, no matter how they have chosen to lead their lives. In the meantime, it is imperative that celebrities err on the side of inspiration and promote only that which is life-enhancing. They, like all of us, have a duty to perform: to act responsibly.

CHANCE (FORTUNA)

An integral part of the Earth Plane dynamic, chance is omnipresent. It's something that will always be, throughout eternity. The nature of chance is to stir things up at bit, thereby creating a jumble which we then have to sort out and prioritize. Wild cards always bring unforeseen opportunities, the net effect of which is to empower change.

By definition, that which is subject to chance cannot be pre-ordained. Therefore, there's always a lot of latitude as to how events will unfold. The unexpected is likely to surface somewhere, creating exceptions to the rules or contradicting the status quo.

Even though we have pre-programmed many of our life circumstances prior to incarnation, the fact remains that there is nowhere on Earth where chance does not hold sway. Picture it, if you will, as just one of the many mechanisms that lie behind the curtain of Oz.

That chance is always afoot is simply par for the course. It is, after all, enshrined in the way things are. Sometimes we'll get what we perceive to be the brass ring and sometimes we won't. But it's all good! The fact that we always have a chance allows for a whole range of options to be exercised, as long as they resonate with us vibrationally. We cannot be offered any opportunities that are completely unrelated to our evolutionary process, karma or personal destiny.

Chance and choice actually fit together like hand in glove ~ and a fine leather one at that. Chance animates choice. By offering us options, it inspires us to make new or different choices.

Our personal wheels of fortune, while always at play, do sometimes pause at certain points in our lives. This occurs when specific issues arise that must be dealt with. By our own volition, they have become manifest, forcing us to pay attention. There's often a sense of urgency involved, coupled with a strong desire to set things right. The net result is that we suddenly find ourselves addressing whatever it is that seems to be up for review. Of course, what actually happens is always subject to chance ~ and free will.

I'd like to stress once again that the responsibility for creating our own reality rests solely in our hands. We are full-fledged participants in our lives. It is therefore counterproductive to attempt to blame anyone else for what is going on, much as we might like to. The fact is we have to live with the consequences of every choice that we have ever made. For every action, there is a reaction. That is the law of karma.

Chance and luck have oft been confused. They are not one in the same. Luck, or the lack thereof, is simply a perception, resulting from our having taken a chance. It's always seen through the lens of personality and therefore subjective. Chance, on the other hand, is a phenomenon.

Here's a piece of information that some of you may find a bit shocking. There's no such thing as good or bad luck. Luck is as luck does. It's part and parcel of the process of creating personal reality.

Although we have a tendency to characterize life events and their consequences as being either good or bad, such connotations are essentially irrelevant. Each life event serves some greater purpose, whether we believe it to be beneficial at the time it occurs or not. If some people seem to be luckier than others, it is just because that's what they have chosen to experience.

We all come into the world seeking our fortunes. I'd like to suggest, therefore, that taking a few chances as we do just might be the way to go. Being overly cautious leads to stagnation. Consequently, it behooves us to make a few moves.

Believe that you always have a chance. Fact is, you do! Chance, one of life's greatest gifts, is forever offering us new opportunities. We have only to grab hold and hang on for the ride.

CHANGE

A decision for change is a decision for life. IT IS to go with the flow because nothing remains the same. However, when change is self-initiated it is at its most powerful. After all, it is always more preferable to do rather than to be undone. The suggestion, therefore, is to be pro-active. When change is afoot embrace it. 'Tis much more than just a friend.

We are constantly being defined and re-defined by the changes we make. Change is the essence of growth and key to our evolution.

CHILDREN

You must never talk down to children because they are your peers. You are not their masters any more than they are necessarily your pupils. Children should be honored for who they are ~ not for who they appear to be.

Children of any age can offer their creativity to the world. Youth is not a liability. Recall, if you will, the prodigies of the past and how inspired they were in sharing their gifts. Some children are very advanced for their age. Indeed, they were born knowing how to channel Universal Mind. I ask all of you to encourage the children you cross paths with to bask in the Light. They need both the light of the Sun and the light of spirit in order to achieve their greatest potential.

Children are the true gods on Earth. Because their personalities are still in flux, they are not fully able to mask their souls. Therefore, even the so-called difficult child shines forth with great acuity, divine intelligence peeking through. As a parent, be a co-creator with your children. This is the best way for you to work together and carry on. And, for those of you who are not parents, do your utmost to encourage the most precious in each child. Sometimes just a nod or a smile will more than suffice.

When you interact with children, try to remember how it was for you to be their age. Also, think of all those who helped you along the way. It's time to return the favor!

———————— ❖ ————————

CHOICE

There are a variety of ways of looking at your dimension. In fact, the choices are infinite. Making choices is an integral part of what we do, the engine that drives our lives. Furthermore, choice is tied to decision by the strongest of lines. For all practical purposes, they always work together.

In making choices, it's not always necessary to seek additional data or clarification, especially if you already know the answer. Nevertheless, there still are times when having it can be helpful. If you take a moment to check in with yourself first, however, you'll always know when more information is needed and when it's not.

What is most important though is not to shirk from what you know must be done by unnecessarily postponing making a decision. When you do, you are putting your life on hold, that is to say, in limbo. A place of non-action is a place with an absence of life. Therefore, choice is vital. It is the driving force behind the well-oiled perpetual motion machine that is our Universe. The numbers of simultaneous, contiguous, congruent and antithetical choices that are being made by all living organisms in any one snapshot of time is literally beyond our comprehension.

Yes, choice fuels motion and motion is the basis of life. Choice is therefore also the genesis of growth and evolution. If our opportunities to choose were only minimal, some degree of stagnancy would most likely prevail. Each choice we make offers us an opportunity to either create movement or not. If we choose to do nothing that, too, is a choice and has its consequences, just the same as if we had decided to take action. Oddly enough, however, doing nothing also moves our lives along for in the big picture doing nothing is the same as doing something.

It must be clearly stated here that making choices never leads to victimhood ~ unless that is something you want to experience. Only if you choose to be a victim will you ever be one. Always listen to your inner self. Think about the ramifications of the choice you are about to make. Then choose wisely. If you can help it, don't make choices for frivolous reasons. When input from others seems dubious, that's because it probably is ~ especially if there is no ring of truth in what you hear being said. Those who offer specious advice could be operating out of malice or they may simply be trying to kick the ball on down the road.

We often place undue pressure on ourselves by supporting the illusion that we always need to make the right choice. Please know that every choice is a right choice. If there is an art to choosing, it is simply to know yourself first and then act accordingly. Indeed, if you listen to your heart, you always know what to do. Moreover, your timing will be impeccable. Making a choice is an act of self-definition.

One other point: in all circumstances allow your soul to be in the driver's seat ~ even though your personality may be doing its utmost to get in the way. If you will, rank soul over personality, soul over illusion, soul over Earth Plane values. The latter three have neither good driving habits nor unblemished records.

Soul is what really IS, my friends, choice being one of its truest and most faithful agents.

Cities

Though some of you may find this hard to believe, cities have quite a bit in common with nature. They, too, are forests, albeit of brick, steel and cement. They, too, have their peaks and valleys. Cities are where man in his indomitable way seeks to re-fashion nature, morphing it into constructs he deems more suitable for habitation. That having been said, nature is to be appreciated ~ in any setting.

Some people choose to see city environments as concrete jungles. However, depending on our point of view what is a problem for one may seem like paradise for another. The bottom line is that ALL environments have something to offer. In that vein, cityscapes sometimes present us with even more fertile ground than their rural counterparts. Therefore, do not reject them out of turn. They also have a greater purpose.

The most interesting kind of city to live in is an organic one, in other words, one that has sprouted over time. In such an environment you'll be sure to find nascent plants, more specifically, relatively new structures intermingling with larger, more mature growth in the form of landmark buildings. That's what really makes a city interesting: variety. It's also how things are done in nature. New plants have to struggle to find their rightful place alongside those that have already been established. New York City is a prime example of this phenomenon at work. I found it a marvel when I first saw it many years ago!

Cities may also be viewed as entities. In some cases poets have even gone so far as to imbue them with souls. However, there's a cautionary note to be sounded. Any city that is overly planned risks losing its identity and, as a result, could easily become soul-less. In essence, countryscapes and cityscapes are pretty much the same thing. Though it may appear to us that the Creator may be more involved with one as compared to the other, that simply is not the case. The truth is that both are a reflection of Universal Mind. While in the body, we need to experience all sorts of environments, urban and rural. In the meantime, the cities that honor nature, making it part of their lifestyle, offer us the best of both worlds. Again, I think of New York and its wonderful Central Park!

Look for nature among the bricks and mortar. Climb the rocks (skyscrapers) and stroll through the canyons (streets.) There are gems to be found everywhere, just like in nature. Enjoy every environment you encounter. One is not superior to another. Know, too, that your place can be anywhere. Even a desert can offer us repose, be it in an oasis or somewhere out under the stars.

By the way, cities are also oases, man-made though they be. They function as oases of thought, places where multiplicity breeds opportunity. Indeed, their density creates a greater propensity for possibilities to become manifest. By definition, cities denote confluence. As a result, a larger number of remarkable things are all the more likely to happen there.

Most cities literally crackle with high voltage, each one having its own allure. Though usually quite stimulating, they all have their moments of overload too, along with a few outages. If you feel a need to clear your mind, plan to spend a day in the country or, barring that, visit the nearest park for an hour or two. And if that's not possible, then take a moment to contemplate any of nature's delights, even if only a single leaf.

Though rather similar in clime, my birthplace (Castellaneta, Italy) and Los Angeles couldn't have been more different. I loved them both ~ as well as the other places I lived or visited when last I walked the Earth. But, 'twas only in Los Angeles where I was truly free to be me. That is where it all came together, where I found my holy grail. You, too, shall find yours ~ here, there or somewhere. And so it is written.

CLOCKWISE

Why do things in the physical world have a tendency to move in clock-wise fashion? Is the preferred orientation of the hands of a clock an illustration of some greater principle? And in the word itself, thusly divided, does wise-dom lie?

Any clockwise kind of turn is but a drill down, a delving into deeper realms. For example, if one turns a screw to the right, it will descend and enter another zone, reaching a depth where new territory is being breached. The same concept applies when we view a page on the internet. Links allow us to drill down to other visual or informational zones. Though not strictly-speaking a clockwise kind of experience, moving back and forth on the internet usually ends up being somewhat circular in nature, at times even bringing us back to where we started.

In the pursuit of understanding, a clockwise-oriented drill down into one's own consciousness is an excellent way to gain greater insight. It's a tried and true method for moving consciousness from one level of thought to another. When meditating, for example, there is an natural tendency for us to approach the whole experience in a dexiotropically-oriented way. Alice, in order to enter Wonderland, went down a rabbit hole but in the process turned to the right. In other words, she descended in clockwise fashion. Hers was not a straight-line dive into the unknown.

From a scientific point of view, the Universe appears to be expanding. However, in reality just the opposite is true. The Universe wants to get tighter, again to drill down. Therefore, the dexiotropic usually prevails. The physical Universe tends to move in clockwise fashion, in the process becoming ever more 'at-one' with the All In All.

There's a 'what lies beneath' to everything that we are constantly being called upon to explore. But, how do we access these nether-lands? Think clockwise!

Water swirling down a drain often has a hypnotic or calming effect. As a matter of fact, many people seek to live near water in order to experience its soothing properties. Water's composition is, of course, essential to life. Its contemplation, therefore, encourages us to delve deeper. Especially in large quantities, water exerts a downward rotationally-inclined force, the perfect kind of vehicle to transport us into altered states of consciousness.

Examples of clock-wise seem to abound. Even when smoke rises from a just-extinguished candle, it often appears to spiral upward in a clockwise manner. It is important to note that most every-thing in the Earth Plane is predisposed to move in a clockwise fashion. However, it is also true that exceptions exist. For example, in the southern hemisphere counterclockwise may sometimes be the rule. Nevertheless, the propensity for the clock-wise to prevail is one of the Universe's most observable and dependable phenomena.

Certain forces of nature, specifically hurricanes and tornados, also tend to gyrate from left to right. These kinds of storms are examples of the Universe tightening its figurative screws. Weather-based natural events such as these may be thought of as capricious and destructive or seen for what they really are, opportunities for change.

Though we may think of ourselves as being fixed in our personal spaces or places of residence, nothing could be further from the truth. As the Earth turns, its steady clockwise-oriented motion causes it to continuously alter its pathway and adjust orbit. Technically speaking then *we are all wanderers,* **siamo tutti gironzolini.**

That anyone or anything could ever be geographically fixed in any plane of existence is a complete impossibility. It simply cannot occur.

COLOR

The colors you choose to have in your living space constitute your personal palette. As Rudolph Valentino, two of my favorites were smoky gray and dark red.

Color is a feast for the eyes, sometimes a sight for sore ones too. It often makes things pop, providing contrast. Where would we be were it not for color? It provides us with a frame of reference, allows us to play favorites and drenches our environments with splashes of reality. To paint a wall, for example, is to give it a dose of love. Each color has a different vibration, and those who are truly gifted know how to combine them to create masterpieces. That is what great artists do, all the time.

Color usually either soothes an environment or makes it more alive. Have some of both on the menu. Stark combinations can also be fun. Remember, not everything has to match. Color was one of my hobbies; I loved all the nuances. Playing with color is like dancing with shadows ~ always enjoyable but sometimes rather difficult to grasp.

Gray is the most neutral color by the way, not beige. That's because it's half way between black and white. Have a signature color too, one that you're noted for. It will help to enhance your vibration. The repetitiveness of wearing a particular color is what does the trick!

COMITY

Comity's hallmarks are graciousness, co-operation, mutual courtesy and civility. The fact that it's perceptible at all implies that on some level an agreement has already been reached.

In order to facilitate a set of circumstances where comity reigns, we must be willing to synchronize our thoughts, feelings and actions with other people for some greater purpose. To join forces with others, however, does not imply an abandonment of self. To the contrary, making such a move usually ends up empowering everyone concerned.

The use of comity in human relations is analogous to using power tools. Both amplify energy, many times over. But, you ask, why bother? Is it really necessary to practice comity? The answer to that question is a resounding yes. We are all just a little bit stronger when we co-operate. Indeed, we must be able to engage with others on some level before we can successfully create anything.

Comity is required for any group to be able to achieve its goals. Its presence creates a pulling together, what one might think of as a pooling of resources. Conceptually, it is epitomized by the 'one for all and all for one' pledge made by the main characters in the novel *The Three Musketeers*. Any courtesy-based event, no matter its format, will always have a whiff of comity.

Cosa C'è ~ *What's Going On?*

It is to get that we must work
Together at times. Therefore, no one can ever shirk
And only be in some self-contained Universe,
Points in time can never be made quite that perverse
Or individually programmed that way,
Try as much as anyone may
Co-operate means to co-create
Grab the bait, go ahead, fabricate
Especially when it's to the mutual or collective
Advantage of all; Yes, of course, be selective,
But take the plunge
Don't be a grunge!
For slimy are those
Who cannot sing in chorus.

RVG

COMMUNICATION

This evening, let's talk about communication, some of the elements involved and how it serves us as we serve others.

How could we ever know what someone else's needs are if they are not able to communicate with us? And in the same vein, how would we ever be able to tell them ours? Communication is the essence of all human interaction. Indeed, our very existence is predicated on the power of the word. Chemically speaking, words are like amino acids. In this case, however, they metabolize thought rather than protein. A more perfect symbiosis there could never be!

Communication is far more complex than one person doing the questioning and the other answering or one making declarative statements and the other listening. Communication is a dance. Sometimes we'll lead and sometimes we won't. The best communicators are those who are most sensitive to the rhythm, willing to switch roles at the drop of a beat. In any sort of verbal exchange, there's usually also a great deal that remains unspoken. As a matter of fact, we tend to communicate as much with our bodies as we do with the words that come out of our mouths. Think about it. There's something really exquisite about being able to express yourself well. It's an art form. Orators and writers, like great artists, all aspire to speak the language of soul. In sharing their perceptions, what they are doing is attempting to interpret the divine.

How then to honor the word BE, the original thought? You have only to ask for Universal Mind to be present in all of your interactions. Allow divine consciousness to be both your inspiration and guide. In so doing, you'll focus on the Light, thereby illuminating your pathway. A few well-chosen thoughts, carefully crafted and expressed, are some of the greatest gifts we can ever offer anyone. There should also be an element of surprise in any conversation. Allowing a bit of the unexpected to ride beneath the surface always helps to keep things interesting. By the way, our thoughts can never be too random. What is said at a given time is always just what needs or wants to be said.

Learning to communicate is similar to learning to surf. In order to be successful we just have to keep on trying. Again, by consciously incorporating the divine into what we say and do, we're likely to feel all the more present and joyful. And, with the spirit of camaraderie coloring the proceedings, anything is possible. Indeed, it is always much more satisfying to engage with each other as peers rather than attempting to do so in other ways.

Being able to maintain a well-modulated stream of consciousness as you speak is the hallmark of an effective communicator. Being concise is also important. Words, my friends, are as precious as jewels. Finding **le mot juste**, the 'right' word for the occasion, is like finding a diamond in the rough. There's always a lot to be said for economy of expression. Verbosity, on the other hand, could be a sign of indifference. At the very least, it shows a lack of consideration for others. Those who have much to say yet convey very little often have a tendency to spin their wheels.

Inflection, intonation and pitch are also vital elements of communication. Though their emphasis may vary according to circumstances, it is the overall timbre of our voices that determines how we are being heard. Our voices are not happenstance. We chose their vibration prior to being born. Indeed, it is through our respective vibrations that we recognize each other, especially in terms of soul mates or other members of our soul group. Though the frame (our physical body) must change each time we are born, the picture, or soul, remains the same. Our voices, therefore, are like homing devices, helping us to find each other again.

As a matter of fact, we are perhaps better known by our voices than by any other means of identification. The voice is a membership card ~ if you will, a badge. It is therefore primarily through our voices that we come to know our fellow men and women. Of course, in the long run everyone is our brother and sister. That is a given. However, we have closer ties with some as opposed to others.

The former constitute our soul group. Be they friend or foe, each individual you encounter deserves to be addressed fairly. Everyone is equally valuable and must be acknowledged as such no matter what sorts of roles you or they may temporarily be playing in each other's lives.

Communication is an on-going phenomenon. It is also everywhere at once, cross species too. Every-thing has communication potential. There is no dearth of communication, anytime, anywhere. It abounds.

By voicing the preference that only the highest vibrations grace all that you say and do, so shall it be!

COMPASSION

Though on some level we are all starring in the same film, our respective scripts are always unique. As a result, we must learn to accept our differences.

Compassion is perhaps the ultimate frame of reference. However, feeling compassion for someone does not require us to 'do' for them. Each soul entity is here to do for themselves. In that process, we each have to find our own pathway, hopefully without pressure or undue influence. When we can see ourselves in others, however, we are supporting their quest in the same way that they and their existence are supporting ours. We all have something to accomplish. That's why we're here. It is crucial for us to embrace the God within and in that process see what's behind the mask.

Compassion is based on recognizing each other's inner beauty, that is to say, the substance of soul. However, have some compassion for the personalities you encounter too. Though they are often quirky, know that each one is right for the occasion, having been specifically chosen by the soul in question. Even so, in being compassionate, you do not need to put up with anyone's questionable behavior. You may even choose not to engage at all if you feel that doing so would be counterproductive to your own growth and development. That is the nature of free will.

All compassion truly requires is that we're able to see GOD in ourselves and others. Use this thought as your compass. It's a reminder that we're all in the same boat. Each of us is different. However, in reality we are ONE in the same. To be compassionate is to rejoice in that fact.

Compassion ought to be ecumenical. It is deserved of all. If ever we find ourselves thinking so and so has a great life, remember the old saying **all that glitters is not gold.** When we observe the lives of others, what may look wonderful to us often is not. Have compassion then for everyone, whatever their story. Every life has a few thorns, no matter how perfect it may seem to the casual observer.

If you will, allow each person a place at your table. Furthermore, acknowledge their right to be. This is the stuff of compassion. Imagine yourself walking in their shoes too, even if only for an instant. If you are able to do so then you will have truly understood what it means to be compassionate.

CONFIDENCE

To be fully confident, you must trust in yourself and your abilities. Self-undoing is the anti-confidence pill. Shakespeare once wrote: **this above all, to thine own self be true.** However, if for some reason you cannot be true to yourself, confidence is likely to remain beyond your reach. Those who lack confidence simply have not made much of an effort to do what needs to be done, that is, to know themselves.

Establishing a sense of confidence requires knowing what you are all about while at the same time respecting who you are. And, the more we're in synch with our inner selves, the more aligned we become with the flow of people and events around us.

Some liken confidence to an emanation from the physical body.

Indeed, it literally beams from every pore when we are in our power, which is to say when we have a relatively unobstructed view of who we are and what we are capable of doing. Though confidence is often based on previous experience, the fact remains that we don't necessarily have to have already done something in order to feel confident about being able to do it. If we trust that we can, chances are we'll succeed.

To be confident then is to declare **I can do.** We all have the ability to accomplish whatever it is we want to accomplish. Knowing that breeds confidence, something that ought to figure prominently in all of our lives. Observing someone with their confidence in stride is akin to watching a gifted performer enthralling an audience. Again, confidence is knowing that we can. We each have it in us to be as creative, flexible and adaptable as we need be. Every problem has a solution.

We cannot rely on the approbations of others, however, to make us feel good. When they do genuinely support or inspire us, it is indeed wonderful. But we should never expect that they will. If we should ever find our confidence lacking, it's up to us to bring it to the Light. To be most effective, confidence must shine. It is, after all, a manifestation of love, self-love as well as love for others. You cannot feel confident about much of anything unless you truly love yourself.

Your capacity to give of yourself is always directly related to how confident you feel. Confidence is rather infectious. For example, if you are confident that will often encourage others to be more confident. It may even be that this is one your roles in life. In my case, it certainly was. We all have the ability to problem-solve our way out of any dilemma. We have but to know that fact.

Confidence, may it always be stirred and not shaken. Be resolute! You can accomplish whatever it is that you will, or want to.

BE-Attitude

Be-Attitude, yes, beatitude,
That's what'll put you in the mood
To shine and then align
With all that is divine
Amar, sí, amor,
Just the trick to get you through the door
To graduate and soar
In a new life blessed with more.

RVG

———— ❀ ————

CONSCIOUSNESS

I have made great reference to this word in all of our communication. If there's a formula for having a productive life, consciousness figures prominently in the equation. When truly conscious, we are both in the Light and blessed with sight.

Consciousness resides in the soul. However, it functions primarily in the context of personality, uniting the inner and outer selves in a common purpose: to learn, grow and evolve. Consciousness is the modality through which the personality experiences life, doing what the soul, on its own, cannot.

Practically speaking, being conscious requires that we BE, SEE, and DO ~ concurrently as well as sequentially. BEING is always the prerequisite, therefore it precedes. SEEING follows and then comes DOING. Taken together, they form the triumvirate of life.

Seeing is the piece that many incarnates often do not fully grasp. To SEE is to most fully BE. And, it is only then that one can thoroughly do. You can't get a job done in the sense of addressing all of the issues that need to be dealt with unless you can clearly see the steps that must be taken in order to reach your goal.

Seeing is a gift that is endemic to all incarnates ~ to have and to hold. Therefore, seeing may always be accomplished ~ if we so will it. Mankind's innate ability to see is like having an ace in the hole, one that's been deeded to us in perpetuity.

Doing, on the other hand, is conceivably subject to the whims and vagaries of others or society at large. What we ultimately do may also be influenced by our own limitations, be they camouflaged or brightly festooned with karmic graffiti.

Being, then doing without seeing as the middle step, is liable to cause interruptions in our energy flows. Perhaps a few mistakes too. If seeing is not part of the process, our personal spark plugs may refuse to fire properly. In such cases, either the engine does not get turned on or it will be prone to malfunction. The gift of sight is ours to use in order to anticipate or successfully bridge any gap in continuity.

Madre ~ *Mother. A circle was carefully drawn around this word.* GOD is the Mother of all existence! When you see the Creator, REALLY SEE, you will truly be in your glory. *Valentino's essence continues by drawing several more circles on the paper and then writing the following words:* spherical, concentric, angelic and ev-angelic. Such is the nature of the Universe and the foundation of all consciousness.

Again, the sphere is the essential building block of all creation. The term concentric in and of itself acknowledges the spherical nature of All that IS with the Creator at its core. Individual spheres may either repel or attract, co-habitating space. There's a procreative and nurturing aspect to all this too which can be summed up as divine Motherhood, yet another way to reference consciousness. Mother Universe **da luz** ~ *literally: gives light; figuratively: gives birth,* on a never-ending basis. And so do we, whether we're in the body or not. For example, *(speaking to the author)* at this very moment you and I are giving birth to the words on this page. The Universe, that is to say, the big picture or macro, is forever sending out echoes, making itself known in the micro, in this particular instance through the pen and paper we are using here this evening.

These are important concepts, known to you all. They may just not have been distilled in quite the same way before.

Addendum

Question: What happens to the consciousness when we're in a coma?

It remains tethered to the physical body. Suspended animation, the animating principle appearing to be frozen in time or on hiatus, that's the definition of a coma. In such cases, consciousness continues to be associated with the body though at the same time very engaged with the Astral or, if you will, the dream world. The person in the coma is somewhat split, confused about where they are, busy having commerce in two worlds simultaneously. Interestingly, they can still see and hear to a certain extent ~ even with their eyes closed. Yes, on some level they are aware of their surroundings. Talk to them. Hold their hand. If it's their time to go you can both reassure them and help facilitate it by doing so. Gestures of love can be given and received in any state of being. Again, a coma is state of suspended animation. The individual in a coma is more sensitive, having in some way withdrawn to contemplate. Think of it also as a prolonged meditation, like sitting on a perch somewhere, removed, far from the maddening crowd.

CORPORATION

How is it that we become embodied? First, the desire to do so must be present. Then, in order to make it happen, love must also be involved. Love is the force behind all manner of corporation. In French, **corps** means the physical body and **coeur** translates as heart, the symbolic residence for love. The enunciation of **coeur** requires a upward exhalation of air and sound whereas saying **corps** requires the opposite. Both words come from a similar linguistic place, having the same initial sound.

Am I regaling you with trivia here? No, decidedly not. It's just another example of how the Universe works ~ in terms of 'as above, so below.' The verbal expression of the French word for heart honors what's above, divine love, while enunciating the word for body in that language honors what theoretically is below, the physical plane.

Here is what's most essential in terms of understanding this topic. To corporate is to breathe love (read: soul) into a physical body. This is what happens the very instant we are born.

For those of us in the Astral, however, corporation involves wearing an ethereal body instead of a physical one. Though we are capable of clothing ourselves in the etheric equivalent of any body we've ever inhabited, most of us tend to choose the most recent. Under the right set of circumstances then, you might still be able to see me as I once was, what you and the public remember as Rudolph Valentino. Although I am presently disembodied, my heart is an open book ~ this one, to be precise. Yes, *Valentino Speaks* has its own brand of physicality. *(Addressing the author)* Our book is a corporation born out of partnership, one that has been created by our combined efforts. You have a physical body. At the moment, I do not. Even so, we have been able to work together to write this book. How nice is that?

Nowadays, the word corporation is mostly used in an entirely different context, relating to business or commerce. In fact, there are laws that treat corporations in almost exactly the same way as they would individuals ~ with specific rights and privileges. We could then say that each corporation must have a heart beating somewhere in its bosom. Would that this were always the case! Proven it is that business conducted with the heart is true commerce in-deed.

COSTUMES

I always loved costumes. But, I particularly loved the ones I wore in the films I did at Paramount. Think *The Sheik* and *Blood and Sand* or perhaps *Beyond the Rocks*.

Trying on costumes is not a frivolous thing. It, too, serves a purpose. After all, every article of clothing we wear is part of a costume anyway. Our jobs or professions, for example, may actually require us to wear some kind of standard apparel. There are also many occasions for men to wear tuxedos and women long gowns, should they choose to do so. The possibilities are endless. Costumes, of course, are representative of different persons, roles or parts in life. If you will, look upon them as learning tools.

In our various and sundry incarnations, our personalities are much like costumes ~ to be tried on and then experienced. In that process, some turn out to be panoplies because they fit well, enhancing and complimenting our souls. Others fit us rather poorly and, as a result, may have the effect of repressing our inner selves to a certain extent. In either case, however, they are essential for continued growth. That is why we chose them in the first place.

Some think that costumes are better suited for playfulness than for any other purpose. Not so! Be advised that they can be quite useful in helping us complete the arcs of the personality wheel without having to embody each and every one. Even so, we still have to experience a whole kaleidoscope of facades during our various lifetimes. Depending on our individual learning plans, however, which types of personalities we must intimately come to know and which we only need to sample vary greatly.

The costumes of to-day often reflect the ghosts of personalities past. It is through the process of trying them on for size that we're able to access some of the archetypes they represent. In slipping into a costume, we're also likely to be slipping into a new role, just like an actor does when he or she is auditioning for a part. What we decide to wear at any given time creates nuance yet it also broadens the scope of who we are.

If you feel so inclined, allow yourself to adopt little props that could have the effect of expanding your reality. You can do this by experimenting with different articles of clothing such as hats, ties, shoes, gloves or whatever. It does not matter what specific details you change. Just know that in wearing each costume or costume subset, you are experimenting with another facet of the total you.

By choosing to wear a number of different of costumes during a given life-time, we're often able to satisfy some of our karmic requirements. For example, there may not be any real need for you to experience a life as a clown but by trying on the garb you'll at least be able to get a better sense of what it might be like. There are many ways for us to learn. Experimenting with costumes is but one. And, even though we are likely to pass this way any number of times, there's no need for us to fully experience every possible permutation. Sometimes a new hat will suffice.

Our desire to play dress-up never grows old. Make sure to have fun **con tutta la roba** ~ *with all the stuff.* And, a little round of applause ~ especially for anyone with an extensive wardrobe!

CREATING PERSONAL REALITY

As sparks of the energy that is God we continually create, whether we can see immediate results or not. It is our task to do so. The point is that we create our own realities. Things don't just happen out of the blue. In some way or other we had to have been instrumental in making them occur. Shakespeare, in his wisdom, summed it all up when he wrote **our remedies in ourselves do lie which we ascribe to Heaven. We will** everything that happens in our lives ~ within the framework of relevant cause and effect and, of course, our respective life scripts. Therefore, we might do well to think of ourselves as perpetual perpetrators in the very best sense of that phrase.

In the Astral, each and every thought has a noticeable result or instantaneous consequence. What fun it is to play with that! You, too, shall have your chance. In the Earth Plane, on the other hand, we often feel more removed from the consequences of our creating, especially as they relate to the larger trends in our lives. Because this is the case, we may not always fully realize to what extent our thoughts are imaging the IS of our WHAT IS.

Most of us do understand that showing up at our jobs and working hard every day will create a paycheck at the end of the month. However, we do not always understand the fact that erroneous thoughts or warped thinking patterns could have troublesome or possibly even dire effects on our personal circumstances.

The power of **I AM** is not always properly recognized or sometimes even acknowledged. Whereas **"I AM" is the most powerful statement in the Universe.**

The Creator said, says and will say I AM as a constant. Each I AM intersects and loops into the next, creating an energetic chain and thereby forming the multi-dimensional canvas of the All That Is. The never ending declaration I AM creates WHAT IS. **There is never a time or a space when the Creator's I AM is not.** Such reverberations are the stuff of the Universe. I am using the term Universe here in order to attempt to concretize the vastness that is the ALL IN ALL so that it might be better understood.

Soul Entities are the channels through which the Creator's I AM is differentiated into form. Therefore, it is a given that we, as reflections of the Creator, also frequently declare I AM. However, we sometimes have gaps in the continuity of our statements or we may choose unproductive wording. Ah yes, here's one of the rubs of incarnation. Be careful how you program your I AM statements. Do note the frequency and consistency of what you say. To create constructive outcomes, I AM statements have to be constructive. They must also be firmly anchored on the 'stage' by no dearth of repetition. Therefore, be consistent and positive, as well as relatively frequent, as you declare yourself to be who and what you are.

Of course, you also have to be aware of what you do not want to create in order to create what you do want. But, as a rule, it is not wise to encourage deconstruction by incorporating self-defeating or pejorative chatter into your personal statements of being. Instead, empower, build and enhance. If you accentuate the positive, that is what you will create. I AM _____. Fill in the blank with only the most positive and creative of words in order to promote the kind of reality you truly deserve to experience.

The personality often wants to insert words into our I AM statements that express temporary frustration, low self esteem or facets of what some might call image management. However, do not go there. Be aware of how the things you say affect your life. What you say, both to yourself and others, creates an ongoing, ever-manifesting network of events exactly mirroring the tenor and import of your words. Words have power. In fact, they are power ~ in encapsulated form. Choose them assiduously, avoiding verbal pitfalls. Create what you truly want to create by knowing that your thoughts and words are continually imaging the reality you experience on a daily basis.

To truly be all that you can, you must, as much as is possible, verbalize what is creative and most powerfully constructive. By choosing to know that only good reigns, it will. This is what's known as the power of positive thinking. Its virtues have been extolled by many people, from Mary Baker Eddy in my life-time to Wayne Dyer in yours.

Name what you want to create: I AM healthy; I AM wise; I AM aware; I AM fortunate; I AM resourceful; I AM strong; I AM happy; I AM wealthy; I AM generous; I AM loving; I AM grateful and so forth. Become what you seek and so shall it be. The idea is: **I can be what I will to be.**

During each incarnation, the real work is found in creating the quality of life the soul truly needs for all to be as it should. To ensure that you create the life that you desire, be certain to visualize only what you want, seeing whatever that may be as either on its way or already part of your reality. If instead you choose to support your fears, you may end up making them real. Remember: **we will be tomorrow what we think today.** Our future circumstances depend on it.

So do your part. Our environments always reflect conditions

that correlate with our predominant attitudes and thinking patterns. Never limit yourself. When you frame your ideas in negative trappings, it is just the same as purposefully inhibiting what may come. In the world of cause and effect, a negative statement is like a gigantic stop sign whereas its opposite will often give us a green light. Then too, be willing to consecrate yourself to any important task. Positive results will grow in proportion to your dedication. After all, **pequeños comienzos tienen grandes fines** ~ *the Spanish equivalent of "big oaks from little acorns grow."*

Whenever you see your dreams coming true, acknowledge them by declaring it so. By simply stating 'my dream is coming true' when you perceive that such is the case you are invoking a powerful prayer, one that supports the continued unfolding of the reality related to that particular set of circumstances.

All realities that ever were or shall be already exist. The specific combination of personal realities projecting themselves on your viewing screen at any one time is a product of the concentration of your attention, desire, will power and thinking patterns.

In the big picture, remember that Universal Mind, in expressing itself, maintains and prospers our endeavors. Because it is both infinite and omnipotent, it always brings people and circumstances together in ways that support the good of the whole. Creation is the primary purpose of life.

Some helpful hints. When you learn to allow your soul to express itself with as little interference from your personality as possible, creating reality becomes almost effortless. As you go about your daily activities, know that divine presence always precedes and follows you. As a matter of fact, it surrounds you. You are eternally in the Light because you are of the Light.

Consciously bless all those who come within the range of your thoughts and actions. In creating personal reality, let us always reflect the magnanimity of love!

Qué Será, Será ~ Aha!

So very elementary; what you **will** to be will be
It's the power of mind's eye imaging that'll really set you free
Just make a mental image on which you want to build
Enroll yourself in this precept as you would an ancient guild
Imagine first, then image to fullest capacity.
And don't forget to honor pertinacity
Focus! To do so says wisdom is of greatest sagacity
Planet Earth, shaped like the letter O ~ when added to GOD
always makes GOOD.
This we know inside, as well we always should

But how do I ensure that the words above are so?
Will verification thereof require a blow by blow
Officially sanctioned report or some curiously tricky diagram
Of Universal Mind's most great and glorious plan?

Qué será, será is a phrase that proves
The Universe moves
With laser-like precision
Geometry rules rather than an emphasis on division
In the mix too, there's existential and exponential multiplicity
Wow, what appears to us as complicated is really mere simplicity
No word profane found in this quite modest claim
If only the purest of **qué serás** we could just maintain

Overly random or specious thoughts
Just not ought
To emanate from you
Cause when they do they don't ring true
Naught as an operative word
Is far too often heard
So it has been said with aplomb and by design
That neither zero nor zed generally moves one on down the line.

Rather sustained and focused thought is what's really sought
So, refine your thinking ~ this you ought
Never fail to do

Hopes are dashed
When thoughts have clashed
And focus is all a scatter,
We question then and say inside oh dear, what is the matter?
Well this then I say to you: support not mental chatter
It takes a straight line
To make things fine,
Non-tangential thought should not be brought to bear
Upon mind's eye productions ~ cause egregious they could be
or simply not so fair

Your imaged AM's, your imaged BE's
Must stay free
Of flotsam-like encumbrance
In order to create the most effective 3-D likened substance
The What IS, our dearly beloved show biz

Volition creates condition,
This fact is so and not in any way perdition
Therefore to consciously create reality and hopefully grow
Shut out all except **that which you would really know**

When thought is askew, start the process anew
Then, see it through
You'll be quite surprised by all you can do
You **can be** what you **will to be**
Qué será IS the law, you see.

RVG

Postscript

Question: As Rudolph Valentino, did you will becoming a movie star?

No, I did not. Instead, I wanted to become a serious actor, one who could live his parts with alacrity and verve. I saw myself like that which is where the phrase **il mio sogno si sta averrando** ~ *my dream is coming true* comes from. As I have mentioned above, such statements are an important part of the creating process. *Author's note: It was reported that Valentino exclaimed "my dream is coming true" at the first screening of his breakthrough film,* **The Four Horsemen of the Apocalypse.** See your dream, whatever it is, as true and real, as a three dimensional thing and so it will be.

When I willed the actor in me to emerge, the notion of movie star came along for the ride. If you will, 'twas an appendage. In the creation of personal reality, addendums to the main document are frequent. Generally speaking, their purpose is to enhance by adding a little spice to the proceedings. On the other hand, they can also come with barbs, depending on the karma involved and how it applies to the conditions being created. Nevertheless, whatever the addendums are, when investigated they are usually both cogent and legitimately tangential.

Question: What are the odds of finding a rare or one of a kind item?

Not high. But when things are duly aligned, all is possible. All may be accomplished, whether it's finding the proverbial needle in a haystack or a pair of shoes similar to some I once wore. Either task is do-able, first given that the desire to accomplish it exists and secondly that a 'meshing' can and does take place.

In order to better understand the point that I would like to make here, visualize the mechanisms behind creating one's personal reality as being similar to what is found in an old Dutch windmill where a series of gear-like wheels and interlocking cogs function as a unit, meshing in order to bring together varying lines of probability into actualized and therefore observable specificities. Whenever your desire nature initiates a meshing of probabilities, that action has a direct bearing on what ultimately shows up in your life, be it a trend, an opportunity or an object that you might really have wanted to find.

———————— ❖ ————————

CREATIVITY

None are bereft of this most precious of resources. Creativity is always at our fingertips, to have and to hold. It is our nature to be creative. We have only to own the fact that this is so. Creativity flows from all sides of a coin. Yes, if you're really creative, there are more than two! Like love, it knows no limitations. Neither does it discriminate. Rich or poor, we are equally blessed with its presence.

Creativity lies within. We do not have to search for it outside of ourselves. Neither do we ever really have to have a muse. Each of us is more than capable of finding our own voice. It's simply a matter of summoning it forth. And, by infusing everything we do with the spirit of creativity, we're all the more likely to be delighted with the results. Living life creatively always works wonders!

The mind is a marvelous thing. We have only to use it. By exploring 'what-ifs' and allowing them to percolate, some inspired course of action is sure to make itself known, sometimes like a bolt out of the blue. Though it may seem as though we are often forced to make quick decisions, the truth is that we always have ample time to consider the alternatives.

Funded as it is by love, creativity is a well that never runs dry. Therefore, whenever you find a particularly ingenious solution to a problem, remember there are always plenty more where that came from. Creativity is irreplaceable. There is no substitute for it nor should there ever be. Always a winner at the box office, its effects tend to linger!

When we are creative in what we choose to image in our minds, all doors remain open. Seeing the possibilities is one of the most exhilarating aspects of being alive. Not only that, when we're in the throes of being creative, there's usually a smile on our face. How could there not be? After all, smiles are endemic to creative solutions whereas grimaces and frowns are not.

Neither Los Angeles, New York, Paris nor Rome could ever have become what they are today were it not for all the creative ideas that have contributed to their on-going evolution. Though there are those who might disagree with some of the details, we can see evidence of creativity in all quarters.

L'Acqua di Vita ~ *The Water of Life*

Creativity, creativity,
Just how does such a loving force come to be?
That inexhaustible source lubricating all forms of productivity
From what proclivity
This concept, this seed
That oft will lead to some da Vinci sort of deed?

Artificial inspirations almost always come to naught
So in thinking about the options 'tis wise they not be sought
Do not bet
That even one cigarette
Will get us a drop of civility
From the fountain of creativity
Neither drink, nor drug, nor smoke
Throughout the long history of Earth Plane folk
Makes anything very keen
Upon our mental screen,
At least not ever yet.

Instead we say this is how the basics play

Ingenuity divided, rectified, then multiplied
By creativity and squared by responsibility

Is an equation so divine
That some might even call it super-fine
To this mix, add a few sprinkles of sensitivity
Along with a dash of spirituality to give it a little more plurality
This recipe makes oh so very evident the sign,
The source, the well, the creativity that all can access and see
So simply thriving there in God's great garden,
the one we call eternity

It is to drink for those who thirst
Step right on up and be the first
For a rose to ever bloom
There must be lots of water in the room.

RVG

———— ❈ ————

CREMATION

Cremation is the primary alternative to burial. Which we choose is purely a matter of personal taste. Once death has occurred and the soul and astral body have departed, what remains is similar to a dried-out corn husk. Though there are those who might say differently, the physical body serves no purpose once the soul, in its infinite wisdom and perfect sense of timing, has moved on. As of the moment of death, the physical body truly becomes inanimate.

Post-death, our remains must be dealt with, either by our loved ones or public entities. Do make your wishes known prior to the final exhalation. And when considering cremation, don't be afraid of the heat. It's really nothing at all. Remember, you won't feel a thing! If you are of the incendiary persuasion, you can show your appreciation for the environment by choosing not to let your former body take up space as it returns to dust. Whether buried or burned, however, that will be its final destination. Cremation simply offers a quickening of the process ~ along with much more immediate results.

Curiosity

Cerca, Trova

Seek and ye shall find
The solution to any sort of bind
Saying it thrice,
Good advice,
Activates the key
The net effect?
Discovering that there are other ways to be.

RVG

Dance

The two as One. Bonhomie with reciprocity. That's the spirit of dance! I loved all expressions of dance, most of all the tango!

Dancing is a metaphor for life. Furthermore, it's wonderful exercise. Nary a muscle escapes its measured effect. Everyone should at least give it a try. On the dance floor we get to experiment and have some fun, stepping in and out of the rhythm, swaying to and fro and, most importantly, entwining ourselves in the All that IS. Our ability to be facile with our bodies is often a wonder to behold. Sometimes even we have to marvel at the extent to which we can get into the flow.

Dance is one of the forums where we're most likely to display our personalities and yet at the same time externalize our souls, alternating between the two like a flashing neon sign. This interface of personality and soul is such that when two dance there really are four on the floor, that is to say, two different souls and personalities, usually quite happy to be in each other's energy fields yet also shaking things up a bit. Whether dancing alone or with a partner, any kind of dancing is incredibly integrating.

In the dance, perhaps even more than in other kinds of physical activity, energy wends its way up the spinal cord and into the brain, stimulating the pineal and pituitary glands which has the effect of raising our vibratory rates. Some people report feeling light-headed or ecstatic when they dance. Others simply enter an altered state of being without taking much notice.

Dancing is the epitome of self-expression yet it's rarely done alone. One of its primary purposes is to enable us to re-align ourselves by adjusting our pitch or tone. Think of it as a self-initiated tune-up. When we combine music with movement, there's a delicate balance that's being struck, subtle yet at the same time quite powerful. To accomplish this feat, all we have to do is listen and then put one foot in front of the other.

On the dance floor whatever we do has merit. Though we essentially dance by ourselves, custom usually dictates that we join forces with another, temporarily creating a duo in the merge. That most of us would choose to dance in pairs anyway certainly reinforces the validity of this arrangement. To dance with another then is to practice the art of relating. Doing either one calls for a certain amount of grace as well as lots of good old-fashioned give and take.

It's in the dance where we are likely to adopt a stance, defining ourselves through our bearing, posture and **sguardo** ~ *gaze*. Who we are shows up as we move to the sounds of music, the energy carrying us to the peak of our game, to that sacred space where we feel most at liberty to dazzle. It is only then that the power that resides within is seen without.

Tango is the game. Valentino was just the name. It doesn't matter who is dancing the dance. The important thing is that we all are.

Tango Eterno

Dancing through life
Causes such little strife
It certainly should be done
And not only just to have fun
So dance ~ each and every time you come this way
Yes, indeed, that's what the wise men say

The tango is not about any old twist and shout
In fact, its fame makes a claim for some creative choreography
That's likely to enchant those in the personal space, the geography
Of anyone who chooses to dance that dance
Be it in the flow of career, friendship, recreation or romance
Each life-time requires some change in the frame
But what's interesting to note is that the picture
always remains the same

When tangos ensue, couples unglue but a dance it always engages
For some even, intensity rages.
Oops! Ignore all those talkative sages
Here's the game:
love on the dance floor first realized then exchanged,
Temporarily misplaced then hopefully regained
All to be joyfully refrained
In soaring **sotto-voce**. With intricate moves, a dancer proves
His or her skills and mettle. And, serendipity behooves
That we all try to be just a little bit light on our feet
Cause it's one way to ensure that we'll all be the fun sort to meet
When tango's the fact and part of our pact
Then to dance requires but focus and tact

So, this dancing through life
Does it really minimize angst and mitigate strife?
If so, go ahead, step to and fro ~ cause fancy footwork's the show

Some say that's the way that the Argentines go
Well, be that as it may, cause this I do know
That the tango creates little stress
While enriching life's frame and enlivening your guess
As to what will likely be happening next
And to pass this test you don't even need to open the text
To dance is your due
The tango's a cue
It's just one way to be
In this world, don't you see?

Dance your way through life
In whatever you do
Wherever you be
This is truly a magical key
Tango's the move
But it's got to be smooth
Enchantment's in the air
When you do dare
To dance your way through life

Nota Bene ~ *PS*
As you picture my times
Be aware of the climes
Where the tango did and doth flourish
Through dance what joy we did sow
And wow, did we grow
By applying the tango to the rhythm of ALL
Yes indeed, that was so. I sure do know cause
I, myself, really had a ball
Be natural in all that you do
'Tis the very best way to carry you through
Life, that IS.

RVG

Da Ricordare – *Things to Remember*

- What are we to do for others? What are they to do for us? Our task is to wake each other up. How? By always telling the truth. Life is about having a conscious living experience.

- As a strategy, diffusion tends to be counterproductive. In order to be most effective, one must be somewhat contained and therefore able to focus on the issue at hand.

- The process is always just as important as the end product. This applies to each and every endeavor.

- Just when it seems as though nothing much is going on, quantum leaps are most likely to take place.

- When one is aligned with purpose, boredom evaporates, everything suddenly becoming of interest.

- Cause and Effect, in many ways the face of the Creator, is part and parcel of manifesting. Everything has its basis therein, all the things of life.

- When you lust after something, you usually don't get it. Therefore, have as few expectations as possible. They tend to repel rather than attract. When you get to the point of being able to say **non mi frega niente** ~ *I really don't care,* what you have been seeking often comes to pass.

- Manifestation occurs through a NOW point of neutrality and the conscious giving up of control.

- In life, look especially for that which you perceive as obscure, offbeat or different. When you do, you can't help but to increase your understanding of the world around you.

- Each moment in time is like quicksilver. It may never be fully grasped.

• Sometimes you wonder if you've been down a particular pathway before. Well, fact is, it's likely you have. There's often a sense of familiarity around certain life choices, especially those that seem both comfortable and challenging at the same time.

• Life is full of tests, ones that we ourselves have devised. Some things, unfortunately, may only be learned through adversity.

• In each of our lives there are moments of confluence ~ when a preponderance of information in the form of messages and clues suddenly just show up, taking aim at us from beyond the horizon, saying look at me, see what you can see. When this occurs, it's important for us to pay attention.

• To be considered, ideas must first be sifted, like flour before making a cake. Then, like flowers, they can be thoroughly examined for their beauty.

• In making decisions it's advisable to take into account any number of different points of view. Just one or two will never do! The greater number of perspectives you have to work with, the more options there will always be for you to consider.

• Speaking of perspectives, just how many might there be if, for example, we were to carefully examine each facet of a diamond?

• Any point of view also depends on where you are standing, be it in a well-treed forest or on a sidewalk in the heart of the city. Go then for points of view. Search them out. When you are well-informed, decisions always flow in a free and easy manner.

• Smile too. Be a Sphinx. Know that in essence you are God-like, without guile, ego or any other tattered frock. Allow the divine to shine through with confidence. Therein lies your real beauty.

DEATH

Death is an old yet familiar beginning. Like birth, it is an experience we all come to know. Death does not separate but joins. In death, we again become as ONE, able to co-mingle and communicate with each other in ways that cannot be accomplished in the Earth Plane. Simply stated, we live beyond the physical body. Upon dying, the soul emerges from its voluntary confines in order to move on. What remains is but an empty shell.

A life is not measured in years. It can be well-done and complete within the twinkling of an eye. Each one is complex and intricate too, like a series of seemingly random puzzle parts seeking to reconstitute themselves into some kind of coherent whole. In each incarnation, our primary motivation is to accomplish this goal.

There comes a time for everyone when the pieces fit and the puzzle is solved. In my case, it happened at age 31. In the meantime, I lived well, the bloom of youth upon my cheeks. My life span was a perfect amount of time, just what I needed and no more, as all lives are. It's a self-programmation. We are born with all of the tools we need to solve the conundrums we came here to deal with. To some, my life looked rather lean, especially given the scant number of years I was here. Nevertheless, lots happened and in that process the pieces came together. The mission that I had proposed for myself prior to incarnating had been accomplished.

I was ready to go even though I didn't know it at the time. I resisted dying in the sense that I resented having to leave Earth how and when I did. But soon after, I was able to see the whys and wherefores of my life as Rudolph Valentino and how it had allowed me to better understand my previous life vignettes as well as their import on the current energy treatises. In the guise of that personality, I had been able to come to terms with any number of issues, successfully weaving them into the whole. Of course, karma was part and parcel of all my comings and goings ~ as is also the case with yours.

My death experience was very much as it should be. There was nothing untoward or unpleasant about it. Though I was seriously ill at the time, it was only when I had difficulty breathing that I realized that life as I had known it was coming to an end. As I lay dying, it felt as though something inside of me was trying to break free. Now I know what I was feeling was my soul, in the process of extricating itself.

I was not really afraid but like most people apprehensive about the unknown. Snippets of memories kept racing through my mind in quick succession. I soon sensed, however, that I would not be alone in this experience and became much calmer. Doubt vanished, like smoke in the wind. I felt loved. The faces of the people around me then grew dim. All physical sensation ceased. It was almost as though a switch had been turned off somewhere. There was 'dead' silence. Then, I suddenly opened my eyes, aware that I was elsewhere. Light and movement were all around me. I immediately saw the faces of people I knew, **anche la mia mamma** ~ *my Mother too.* I felt welcomed and embraced. I was home. Though I was supposed to be dead, I knew I was alive.

At first, I could still see some of the events that had been swirling around me prior to my departure while also being fully present in the NOW. In fact, for what might have been a few seconds, it seemed like I was viewing a split screen, aware of two different realities simultaneously. I was only briefly able to straddle the dimensions, however, for soon I became completely engaged in my new life.

These experiences were tailored just for me, for what I needed to get out of them at the time, again a self-programmation. The same will be true for you.

When King Tut's tomb was discovered in 1922, there was suddenly a renewed interest in all things Egyptian. Newspapers and magazines spoke of the treasures found therein as well as ancient burial practices, the idea of immortality and even the possibility of making contact with those who have passed on. My death, only a few years later, provided people with yet another opportunity to contemplate some of those same issues.

I am so glad that death does not rob us of the power to go on and on. Life as a sweet, loving, helpful, friendly and progressive experience continuing on forever is a magnificent idea. Life is GOD-FORCE in action ~ the greatest burst of energy one could ever imagine. Death has taught me that everything is created by GOD ~ all things, animate, inanimate or seemingly inanimate. We are all simply in different stages of evolution.

At the moment of death, depending on our individual needs, belief systems, points of view, karma and a few other factors that cannot as yet be shared, we each devise the perfect set of experiences, the purpose of which is to re-orient us to life in the Astral. It follows then that the variety of death experiences is infinite in number. What we do or don't do between now and the exact moment of our passing will play a role in determining the size, shape and scope of our transition. Rest assured that whatever the specifics are, they will encompass the totality of what we need or want to experience at the time.

(Speaking to the author) Your friend Janice said: "Death requires an attitude of profound respect and the spirit of adventure. Be joyous when you know that the moment has arrived. Allow yourself to go with grace and loving feelings towards all. Embrace the experience. Be neither sad nor afraid as you embark upon your journey." I fully concur. When death is nigh, think/project/be LOVE in any way that is meaningful. The power of love will vanquish any fears or trepidations. Love is what to think about. Nothing else really matters.

Though we are all destined to pass in the Light, being in the full consciousness of love helps to still the waters and smooth the way. Love is a matter of attitude. Therefore, choose to see the event called death as being for our greater good rather than as something to lament. The nature of incarnated life is such that each of us has but a measured time. We all have to go out somehow. Though most of the choices seem unappealing, always keep in mind that love heals all wounds. Death, after all, is just a momentary blip on the radar screen of life.

The soul always knows when it's time to let go of a particular game plan and return to the source. Death involves dimensional crossover as well as a quickening. Its purpose is to fulfill the soul's desire to move into a new cycle of growth. The whole process requires that we drop the physical body in order to be able to get on with our lives. To cross the dimensional divide there is little or nothing to do. We mostly just have to BE. It's with great simplicity then that the crossover occurs and the Astral becomes our reality.

In the act of dying, I chose to open a symbolic door to the same Light that has been spoken of by so many before me. That may or may not be part of your plan. Even so, there is usually some sort of a portal to cross when one transits to the Astral. The dictionary defines portal as a place of entry. Astral portals are as numerous as the grains of sand collectively found in all the deserts of the world. And, they could be thought of as being just about anywhere. For those making a transition to the Astral, a portal is wherever one reality folds seamlessly into the other.

Again, the last breath we take in the physical body is the key to our transition. It's what unlocks the door, allowing us to step over the threshold in order to enter another cycle of life. Death occurs with the very first breath we do not take. **Ecco fatto** ~ *there you have it!*

There is always a last frontier in each incarnation ~ equivalent in meaning to and concurrent with our last conscious moments in a particular body and set of life circumstances. At some point, it must be crossed. Nevertheless, dying is always a bit of a shock, no matter how well we may be prepared. It is the instantaneous nature of it all that is perhaps the most surprising.

Quo vadis ~ *where are you going* when death occurs? Again, the possibilities are endless, which may be the best way of responding to this somewhat rhetorical question. Not to worry. When the time comes, you will have it all mapped out. The first stop on your Astral itinerary is likely to be wherever you're going to feel most at home.

I want to gently remind you that there is always a marker or space for you in the Astral. The marker I speak of could also be described as an anchor. This figurative anchor and its accompanying chain will be used to guide you back home, to your place in the scheme of things. Therefore, when the time comes there will be no confusion. You will know exactly where you are going. The process of death then is essentially a journey to the folks back home.

I would like to say to all of you that come this way and, that will be ALL of you, that you must be patient with yourself during your transition as you will be re-learning how to **be** and **do** in the Astral. Specifically, you will be remembering how to use your thoughts in more directly consequential ways. Again, be patient and see what you can learn from those you encounter along the way. There is some period of re-adjustment for everyone. It may be nothing much or it may be more involved, depending on a number of factors and the degree of help and support that you yourself have deemed necessary. As far as your own spirit guides are concerned, you may or may not have requested their direct involvement in your death experiences and re-orientation process. Whatever the case, know that it's all fine.

Here is a suggestion. Think of dying as being like the countdown to a rocket launch. Much as any scientist would, stay focused on the process. In dying, make it a point to be as conscious as you possibly can. As is always the case, there are choices to be made. Then too, the more conscious you are while in the body, the more conscious you will likely be when that body is no more. Be happily expectant! Feel confident that all will go as planned. It will.

In dying, we are making a statement. We are announcing to the world that we have outgrown our old suit of clothes. Whether incarnate or disincarnate, we continue to grow, often surprising ourselves in unexpected ways. To that end, there's a need to change costumes from time to time. Life never ceases to be exciting. Never know what role you might be playing next!

All the World's a stage
And all men and women merely players
They have their exits and entrances
And one man in his time plays many parts...
Unfortunate it is, indeed, that every age
Will not come to every man.

William Shakespeare ~ *As You Like It*

Crossing over is both an exit from this present stage and an entrance to a new one. As we return home, new roles await us. In death nothing ends. It simply means life in a different format.

Ancora Libero ~ *Free Again*

I am no longer bound
By Earth touch, taste, sight, smell or sound
For my arms are crossed upon my chest
In a state of eternal rest.
Freedom I now know
Like I could never show
With my feet upon the ground
Even with a past albeit somewhat renowned

True, I no longer have my breath
But what I have instead is greater life ~ in death.

RVG

A parting thought. If perchance you sense that someone else's death may be imminent, there is no better gift you can offer them than your love, beamed through the ether, to bless them and send them on their way.

DESIRE

Desire is the engine that drives human experience. In its purest form, it is always accompanied by positive emotion. By desiring something, we get to experiment with life. In changing what we want, our lives are quick to follow suit, sometimes taking on a whole new direction!

On the surface, our desire nature appears to be personality-driven. Though ostensibly true, the soul has a word or two to say about it also. Judge not that which is being desired, even if it may seem superficial to the casual observer. In the long run, it's just what the doctor ordered, the doctor being the soul and the personality its patient. In life, the medicine is mostly experiential. One never knows how the patient will react if he or she actually gets the thing or set of circumstances being desired.

Though their relationship is, by definition, collegial, in the final analysis it's the soul that directs the personality to experiment rather than the other way around, our desire nature being one of its preferred modalities. That being said, however, there are still times when the personality will at least attempt to call the shots.

Desire comes in many flavors ~ some truly inspired, others possibly bordering on obsession. It behooves us, therefore, as much as possible, to become more aware of which are which. We must truly be able to own our desires in order to bring them to fruition. That is why it is necessary to determine their source. Are we their genesis or have we unwittingly allowed ourselves to be influenced by others? Desiring, unfortunately, has often been confused with its lower octaves: craving, coveting and lust. These are but base forms, for the most part cluttered with the barnacles of youth.

Desire animates manifestation, its role that of an ignition switch, prompting us to take action. In the act of desiring, we are looking to sire something, each of our desires having the effect of impregnating a possibility. Major desires often require long gestation periods.

Minor ones, on the other hand, usually take care of themselves more quickly, needing little or no midwifery. **The act of desiring initiates change and is therefore an integral part of creating personal reality.**

That we ought to monitor our desires seems self-evident. After all, it is up to us to determine if they are serving our best interests. Do they seem unbridled, that is to say, are they all over the place? Or, do they feel focused and solid? And perhaps even more importantly, are they really serving us or simply pandering to our egos? Our desire natures should never be farmed out, willy-nilly, for the exclusive use of our personalities. In so doing, we abrogate our responsibility, not only to our higher self but also to our fellow men and women, by creating unnecessary imbalances.

Where desiring is concerned, the phrase 'adding fuel to the fire' is definitely not a misnomer. Indeed, for purposes of this discussion, fire is will and fuel desire. Staying as conscious as we can about what we want and why we want it is, therefore, of prime importance. When we're not fully aware of our desires we're likely to experience some strange consequences ~ usually in the form of unexpected events that just seem to come out of the blue.

Like an ocean liner in the midst of a sudden storm, desire, too, should not have any extraneous deck chairs. In order to break the waves with ease, both must remain as uncluttered as possible. What we desire can never truly become manifest unless it continues to be recognizable.

My suggestion is to desire only that which is beautiful, true, healthy and strong. Whatever we want must be able to thrive in the light of day. Like the original spark, desire is catalytic in nature. See it as just one of the many things we get to experience in life. In some ways, it's like a match ~ quite useful, yet at the same time not to be toyed with. By clearly stating our preferences, we start the ball rolling. Then our will comes into play, determining the degree to which we're able to follow up and follow through.

Desire and Will frequently work hand in hand, creating confluence where previously there was none. And when they do, some evidence of their collaboration is likely to be noticed. Each time this occurs we need to express our gratitude. In other words, we ought to keep priming the cosmic pump. After all, creating personal reality is always an on-going effort, never a one-off. Will-power, too, plays an important role in the process, adjusting our desires by depressing the accelerator or hitting the brakes, according to the promptings of our inner self. Here's a household hint not previously found in this sort of tome: wash 'desire' with 'will' in the water. Then, handle with care. That's how Light remains light.

Desire not that which you already know is not for you. Likewise, scheme not. Desire should never be a cover for ulterior motives. Indeed, in the act of impregnating a possibility, it always pays to check your reasons for doing so ~ going in. Again, analyze your desires. Are they what someone else wants? Or, are you truly their author? Each desire must first be recognized for what it is and then transformed, if warranted, into a more mature iteration.

Desire is not to be mixed with the dark side of the Moon for in so doing we may damage ourselves, becoming tainted in the process. So why even go there? We would be wise, therefore, not to become associated with the dark arts. He who conspires to trick, fool or deliberately confuse others is certain to come to naught.

Our desire natures are powerfully constructive, **I want** being two of the first words we learn as children. When invoked in a childish fashion, however, they often have the opposite effect. Consequently, we need to be vigilant where desiring is concerned, paying close attention to what we want ~ even when we're sleeping! Of course, we can and often do want it all. But again, it's the wise man who knows what's really for him and what isn't.

My advice is to love what you cannot have for in so doing it, too, shall be yours. Do not compare your circumstances with those of anyone else. Each individual has been given that which is perfect for his or her time and place in the scheme of things. As you see things manifesting in the lives of those around you, rejoice in their good fortune. Thus shall ye also know whither they go. We're all connected. Your time, too, shall come. Eventually we all get to taste the fruits of our labors.

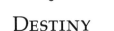

DESTINY

A big word with only seven letters, it implies a lack of free will. Not so, my friends. Though destiny speaks of that which has been destined or predetermined, the truth is that we alone are its perpetrators. Free will reigns in all planes. Though we may have decided to forge a particular destiny prior to being born, we are always at liberty to tinker with the plan.

We have all programmed ourselves to accomplish something while we're in the flesh. Should we want to call it destiny, well, that's a choice and, like all choices, there for the making.

DIET

There is no one single diet that is the answer. Each physical body has a unique DNA and therefore its own nutritional, mineral and vitamin needs. Our diet requirements come from within, largely unaffected by the perceived hunger that advertising is so cleverly designed to promote.

If there's any real choice to be made around what you eat, it's quality versus quantity. Large portions of food tend to shut down the body's ecological systems, creating overflow. Habitually excessive food intake, therefore, may contribute to arterial clogging or digestive problems, leading to premature aging. Also, avoid eating when you are angry. Anger prevents proper digestion.

BE MODERATE in what you eat and drink. What a surprise! But, it's true. Be neither too fat or too thin; that's the rule. Drinking lots of water is necessary too. Drink as much of it as you possibly can, occasionally adding some fresh lemon. By the way, lingonber-ries are a wonderful anti-oxidant if you did not know, even lingon-berry preserves. A little bit of beer works wonders too! Not only that, **un bicchiere di vino rosso sempre si fa sorridere** ~ *a glass of red wine always makes one smile.*

Postscript:

What we feed ourselves, other than food, also constitutes our diet. Be mindful, therefore, of what you are ingesting, including certain kinds of entertainment. Guts and gore do not, in any sense, nourish the soul. Neither do extreme forms of pablum. The level of discourse must actually engage us rather than acting as a soporif-ic. If not, flee or turn to another channel. This applies to any form of communication or media. You will certainly not be missing out on anything.

DOUBT

When in doubt, what's that really all about? Nothing more than fear, playing itself out. Doubt is a false friend. Some of you, however, choose to see it as an ally who appears to be looking out for your best interests. Others view it as a minor player, an occasional annoyance that's hardly worthy of a second thought. Either characterization misses the point. Doubt, no matter its guise, has a poisonous sting. Therefore, its role is potentially a dangerous one, that of saboteur.

If doubt were ever to be personalized, his or her résumé might include the following: dour, pessimistic, faux expert looking to camp on your doorstep. Think about it. Do you really want doubt to be a member of your team?

In terms of properties, doubt is not so very different from a dense fog. Indeed, it's often pervasive, blinding, foreboding and clammy, with gray as its signature color. Its modus operandi is to wrap our issues in a shroud, rendering them opaque and therefore much more difficult to assess. Whenever doubt is in the picture, it tends to cloud our judgment. Also, doubt has a tendency to cast aspersions where none are merited. In so doing, it sows the seeds of destruction, making us always wonder if we are being deceived. Its venom can paralyze even the strongest among us ~ if we allow ourselves to fall victim to its charm.

Doubt is rather insidious. We may not even always know when it's around. A good analogy might be the coal gas that used to silently kill miners in the 19th century. At that time, coal miners would bring canaries into the mines with them in order to monitor the toxicity of the air. If one of the birds suddenly died, they knew it was time to come to the surface. Unfortunately, we can't monitor doubt by using such a simple method. It's far too pervasive.

The bottom line is that being a 'doubting Thomas' does not serve anyone. Being skeptical, however, is another matter. There is such a thing as healthy skepticism, which is quite different. Being skeptical involves examining issues in the light of hard facts and relevant empirical evidence. He who is skeptical is able to evaluate situations for the ring of truth and make decisions accordingly. Doubting, on the other hand, usually stems from fear, ignorance or personal insecurity. He who is doubtful often tends to embrace the lowest common denominator, creating a gloom and doom scenario that is then likely to become a self-fulfilling prophecy.

The following point speaks for itself: if doubt is being cultivated, love has no room to sprout. Do your best not to doubt. Instead, discern. Maintain a healthy amount of skepticism too, especially if you discover that things are just not adding up, or never could ~ under any set of circumstances. The opposite of doubt is trust. That said, I'm not advocating being naïve. I am simply suggesting that we pay attention to the proceedings while giving others the benefit of the doubt. Trust others, therefore, unless it becomes clear that you should not.

The worst kind of doubt has to do with loved ones, for example, suspecting them of being unfaithful. One only has to recall Shakespeare's

Othello to realize where such thinking can go. Insane jealously can all too easily develop into irrational behavior. Doubt is often a precursor to jealously, opening the door to an issue that all of us have to deal with at some point in time. If you have a predilection for doubting others, you may want to work on loving yourself a little more.

Doubt is endemic to Earth Plane existence. Even so, it can easily be overcome. If we're willing to push through it and go beyond, great freedom awaits on the other side. Again, doubt is nothing more than a shadow casting itself. The light of truth burns it away, just as the Sun does when it pierces the clouds. Truth dissipates doubt. More importantly, love vanquishes it.

Dreams

**We are such stuff as dreams are made
on and our little life is rounded with a sleep.**

William Shakespeare

Dreams are life extrapolated. Our dreams allow us to work with the parts of self that we cannot so easily access in the waking state. Dreams stimulate our imaginations too, stoking the fires within. A dream must BE before we can SEE. Dreams are often prerequisites for manifestation. Having a dream is just the starting point for any series of actions that must be taken in order for something to become actualized. If you will, think of dreams as ethereal building blocks ~ to be used in the fabrication of substance, that is to say, in the creation of personal reality.

Dreams give us endless opportunities to exercise our creativity. Indeed, upon entering the dream state each night we become expert actors, writers, set and costume designers, ready to ply our trade. Our dreams can never be too incongruous by the way. It's only in the light of day that they seem to be. Dreams also tend to highlight issues that, for one reason or another, have been submerged. As we dream, we get to dislodge them from their moorings so that they can rise to the surface and be noticed, sort of like cream in unprocessed milk. Even though they may sometimes be convoluted, our dreams give us a chance to experiment, unfettered by what is commonly thought of as waking reality.

To dream is to BE, once again, in the Astral Plane. Dreams are wonderful learning tools. Indeed, they always provide us with a wealth of information. Dreaming is about you experiencing you, beyond the limitations of so-called waking life. In many ways too, dreams are like home shopping catalogues. In them, we get to try on feelings as well as accomplish things that might seem to us as out of the ordinary. Dreams are guides for ways to be, vehicles for more fully rounding out our life experiences.

In reviewing our dreams, it is advisable to focus on the transactional rather than the trappings, the dynamics rather than the metaphors. Dreams are designed to cut to the chase, inviting us to go deeper. In waking life, on the other hand, we spend lots of time fiddling with our props and plodding through the fog of illusion. In the dream state, none of that is required. We have only to BE. **It's in dreams that we're often able to see things most clearly.**

We do not always remember our dreams even though we always have them. Only certain ones rise to the level of waking consciousness. All dreams, however, have import. What we experience in them is always exactly what we need and want to.

In our dreams, who is speaking to whom? The answer varies. For one thing, dreams allow the soul and personality to keep each other informed. They also facilitate various types of information sharing with our spirit guides and, in addition to that, often help us sort out our thoughts and feelings. In the big picture then, dreams provide Universal Mind with a venue for communication.

Though waking life may appear to be more predictable, that is not necessarily the case. One thing is for sure though, dreams are not less real than waking life. Indeed, some would say that when we're awake we are simply living out some sort of a dream.

Water, whether it's ingested or to be found in close proximity, gently lubricates the dream state. Therefore, drink a little water before retiring, even if it's just a few sips. Doing so stimulates dreaming and is also good for your health. Taking a bath or shower soon before going to sleep also encourages dreaming. In bed, wear flowing garments, loose night clothes, or as little as possible. Warmth, safety and comfort are all important elements in creating optimal dream conditions. They need to be present for the most prolific dreaming to occur.

When sleeping near water, people often report increased dream activity. An island then, as Shakespeare surmised when he wrote *The Tempest*, might just be the most perfect of places in which to dream.

Why do we find islands so intriguing? Perhaps it's because that's where famous fictional characters, such as Dafoe's Robinson Crusoe and Shakespeare's Prospero, live on in our collective imaginations. Then too, an island is an apt metaphor for any seemingly tangible experience swimming in a sea of feelings.

Our dreams are set on the ethereal equivalent of Shakespeare's poor yet magical isle where all may come to pass. Indeed, while in the dream state we could even be thought of as being temporarily marooned. At the very least, it appears as though we must remain on our respective islands 'til dawn. Each morning, however, we're rescued by the light of day, suddenly free to focus our attention elsewhere.

Throughout the centuries, many have wondered if waking life is just another kind of dream. *The Tempest* examines this conundrum in depth through the device of magical illusions. On Prospero's isle, things seem to the shipwrecked visitors as they apparently are not. In *The Tempest*, Shakespeare asks us to consider whether the dreams dreamt and illusions cast in his play are really any different from what we experience when we're awake. The answer to that question, dear readers, I leave to you.

As we write, there is a television program called *Lost* which I contend examines the issue of dreams. Have these characters been traumatized to the extent that they know not what is real? Could they be dreaming? And if so, are their dreams individual, collective or both?

The Tempest ~ Alonso: **These are not natural events, they strengthen from strange to stranger.**

Could it be that the fictional characters of *Lost* are on an island to find their authentic selves just as we are here on Earth to accomplish the same goal?

The Tempest ~ Gonzalo: **Did Prospero his dukedom find in a poor isle and all of us ourselves when no man was his own?**

Lost presents its viewing audience with an intriguing proposition. The questions I have posed here are simply for your consideration. You may or may not choose to examine them.

Shall we all eventually arrive at the same conclusion as fair Miranda?

The Tempest ~ Miranda: **How beauteous mankind is! O brave new world that has such people in 't.**

YES, definitely so. This I'll say to answer my own question, soul, in all instances, being infinitely greater than personality.

In the Astral, one can dream all day and all night too, for that matter. What we, from our perspective, label as a dream is mere reality in the elsewhere. Dreaming is our nightly opportunity to visit the Elysian Fields, those fertile lands where all may sprout and grow.

As soon as you close your eyes, be ready for adventure. You will never be bored, especially in finding yourself poised on that fulcrum-like point where active and passive modes meet and interact. Although dreams may sometimes seem to be fraught with danger, fear not. Keep in mind that you can never be harmed.

We would all probably agree that we mostly seem to be on our feet when we're awake. On the other hand, sleeping usually requires us to lay down and temporarily surrender to the unknown. Should any of us ever wish to assign a physical whereabouts to the dream experience, we would do well to think of the inside of our eyelids as the screen upon which we dream.

Dreams, whatever form they take, always demand our attention.

Indeed, the more jarring a dream is, the more learning potential it often has. When dreams are disturbing, the point is to get us to think.

In the vastness of Universal intelligence dreams were devised as a conveyance, showcasing our issues by night and then, with the dawning of the next day, giving us an opportunity to make them part of our waking consciousness. In the aggregate, dreams are thematic propositions presented in fragmented ways, often defying logic but usually rather brilliantly developed. All dreams have rhyme and reason. It behooves us, therefore, to try to capture their essential meanings. Again, when examining a dream, pay attention to the feelings that have been evoked rather than thinking about literal interpretations. Therein lies the truth.

An obvious suggestion is to keep a bedside notebook or journal. Immediately upon awakening, jot down even the most far-fetched fragments of each dream. Every detail is significant when it comes to deciphering them. Then, free-associate, making note of the words that surface in your mind, no matter how random they may be. If you feel so inclined, take a few moments to look them up in a dictionary ~ even if you think you already know their meanings. Doing so will often give you some additional information. After all, one door opens another. Consciousness is thusly engaged.

Sueña con los angelitos ~ *May you dream with the angels,* a sleep-time wish that's frequently extended in many cultures and climes. I leave you with this thought: dreams, whatever their ilk, are always divinely inspired.

Dreams, dreams ~ nothing but fantasy you say? Well, look at things another way. Dreams always lead somewhere ~ but never to a dead-end street. Instead, they'll lead you to where you'll meet yourself ~ and others too. Dreams are but an ethereal glue, designed to knit us whole again each night.

DRUGS

The primary reason for the existence of drugs is to help people cope with pain. Rather than always help though, they sometimes have the opposite effect.

Drugs can also be used recreationally ~ to create altered states of mind. Whatever their intended use, however, know this: no matter how great their efficacy, they cannot help but to muddy the waters a bit. It is in their nature to obfuscate. In particular, beware the latest drug **du jour** as well as all the usual suspects. Their side effects can often be disastrous.

In the 21st century we live in an age of proliferation ~ where more is seemingly always better. And nowhere does this appear to be truer than in the case of pharmaceuticals.

Not all drugs are created equal. Neither are they to be taken lightly. Some cause great harm while others are life-sustaining. It is up to us to pay attention to which are which. Also, what is helpful for one person can be toxic for another. Therefore, be cautious when adding drugs to your regimen. The body is far more sensitive than one might imagine.

Except where survival is an issue, there are relatively few drugs that should be taken on a daily basis. The question to ask is whether or not they are crucial to maintaining our health or quality of life.

Drugs are perhaps the greatest thief man has ever known. By ingesting them, we may suddenly find ourselves robbed of consciousness or on the road to stagnation. Yes, it's that simple. Habitual or prolonged drug use encourages stagnation. Though there are exceptions, as a rule drugs do not lend themselves to consciousness-raising. To the contrary, they usually inhibit it. Any drug, be it minor or more hard-core, has pretty much the same long-term effect. It dulls our awareness. This is especially true for most recreational drugs, given the fact that they tend to encourage escapism. When used purely in that manner, they serve no good purpose.

It's a safe bet that those who do not overly indulge will sooner regain the states of health and equilibrium they seek. On the other hand, habitual users are likely to sink ever further into perceptual misery or become enmeshed in their own misguided efforts. Some drugs even go so far as to actively destroy brain cells.

Avoid medicating yourself unless it's truly necessary. Generally speaking, you are better off without any drugs in your system. Medications tend to pre-empt the normal functioning of the body, which in the long run may not be in our own best interest.

For some, a reliance on drugs is simply an excuse for bad behavior. For others, it provides a way to collude with some of the baser instincts of their personalities. The reasons for drug use are varied and, of course, not always directly related to medical need. Individuals who choose to abrogate their responsibility to themselves through repeated or unnecessary use of medications and controlled substances are literally giving up on life.

It has been said that the use of certain kinds of drugs may actually encourage obsessive or robotic types of behavior. A point in fact supporting this contention is that habitual users often report feeling stuck in situations that they themselves have created, seemingly powerless to bring about change. Drugs can have the effect of scattering our energies rather than bringing them together. Again, use them sparingly ~ and only in cases of real emergency, extreme pain or unconscionable stress.

A final thought: a drug or two a day aren't necessarily going to keep the doctor away. That, my friends, is up to you, you being the final arbiter of your own health.

ECOLOGY

There is a real necessity for us to be more proficient in the use of our resources. We must all learn to be wiser. Every one of us needs to be a way-shower around this issue, even if only tiny steps are being taken. When pigs fly! This is an old adage. However, it's quite apropos. When concepts of ecology are promoted in a natural format rather than being forced, they take on new meaning ~ even inspiring pigs to act differently than they typically would. By encouraging the status quo to adopt a fresh approach, progress is certain to occur. Ecology is that important.

Do whatever you can towards supporting the preservation of the Earth's natural resources. Once lost, they can never be regained.

EDUCATION

Think of education as an on-going series of learning experiences, only some of which are formal. Their ultimate goal is to provide us with the skills to manage our lives while at the same time stimulating mental activity. The pursuit of knowledge, be it self-generated or related to participation in educational programs, encourages the development of mental constructs which then enable us to become more consciously involved in our spheres of influence.

How do we best ensure that we'll each get a good education? By living life. It's the one course in which we are all enrolled. As children, however, it is advantageous for us to learn a few basics in order to lay a foundation for what is to follow. In having done so, we are then all the more able to live constructively.

Educational experience serves to enhance the flow of thought. But, whether or not our thinking functions smoothly depends more on how diligent we are than on any other factor. We all need to become life-long learners, embracing that stance wholeheartedly. Moreover, it behooves us to be pro-active in our learning rather than simply passive consumers of information. Fact is, none of us can ever learn enough.

In the pursuit of education, all the resources at our disposal must be utilized, the internet being just the latest example. Know, too, that whatever we learn supports our higher purpose, ensuring that the twists and turns we continuously insert into the scripts of our lives help to further our evolution rather than retard it.

Learning is often a humbling experience. Sometimes the more we learn, the more we realize how much we do not know. Nevertheless, our education is always on-going, with no endgame in sight. The desire to learn is palpable and just as much of a vital sign as a heartbeat, no matter our chronological age. Not only do we have an innate desire to increase our knowledge, but one of our greatest attributes is our ability to integrate what we've learned into some coherent frame of reference.

In life, we are each just as much of a teacher as student, those two roles not being mutually exclusive. Indeed, both always ought to be practiced in an open and deliberate way. Where education is concerned, nothing muddled or vague is called for and should therefore be avoided.

When we choose to view the world through the lens of education, we're likely to find ourselves challenging assumptions while at the same time feeling nurtured by the information we're absorbing. The purpose of all of our educational experiences is to help us access the font of knowledge that is Universal Mind. Participating in the educational process also has the effect of re-awakening us to our potentials. Awakening stimulates becoming, which then begets remembering, once again, that we and the Creator are ONE. The moment this memory has been reconstituted and ensconced in its rightful place, our lives are irrevocably altered. We suddenly feel more alive for the simple fact of having realized that we truly are who we know ourselves to be, perhaps the ultimate confirmation.

It has been said, and rightfully so, that attending classes simply helps us to remember what we already know. Learning expands the mind as well as our ability to think clearly. Indeed, a thought-full person is much more likely to reflect prior to taking action. The brain's electric-like impulses, known as neurons, help us to continually reframe our perceptions of events while encouraging us to be creative in how we choose to respond to them. There is at least one solution, or more, for every possible dilemma.

Brain function can either be impaired or stimulated by the experiences we call education. Hopefully, it's the latter and, far more often than not.

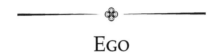

EGO

Ego is the little boy and girl in each of us, the baby crying out for its mother. It knows very little reason. It simply IS, therefore its beauty.

Found at the core of every personality, the ego is its genesis, the point of origin which then blossoms into its fuller expression. Think of the ego as a seed that, once in existence, must immediately begin its growth cycle. If we attempt to remain seeds, however, we obviously cannot grow. In such circumstances our egos themselves would be getting in the way, in essence retarding the natural course of events.

Ego, centered in the human mind, likes to see itself as an isolate, a wild child left to its own devices whereas just the opposite is true. It's that most tender part of the personality, easily bruised and all too frequently predisposed to looking at its own reflections or becoming defensive. Ego, therefore, has a tendency to repeat itself, like a clock covering the same numerical territory every twelve hours ~ in effect, keeping us stuck in certain kinds of behaviors.

Wallowing in one's ego, whatever form that takes, is a trap it's wise to avoid. Instead, we need to make sure we're living our lives to their fullest. How so? By aligning our personalities with our souls. In order that this may be accomplished, however, the ego must first become actively involved with the rest of the personality.

Ego = I go ~ leaping into the void. Well, do look before you leap! It's rather good advice. Again, ego refers to the part of self that often doesn't think very much. It simply jumps into the fray, eyes more often closed than not.

Do we need to wrestle with our egos? Decidedly not. Neither

should they ever be squelched. Rather, it's a matter of 'bringing up baby.' In the course of each life-time, the ego, just like its larger self, the personality, must learn to spread its wings and fly.

E-THEREAL MAIL

Any act of remembrance directed towards loved ones is noted from afar by those being honored, wherever they may be. Therefore, it matters not if the recipients are just down the street or in another dimension. If your intention is to communicate, the message will be heard. If you wish, light a candle or leave some flowers. Or, just silently call out their names and send them loving thoughts. It's all the same.

Whenever a thought is offered to another as a gesture of love, an e-thereal message has been sent. We are always nigh ~ closer than you think, never more than just a thought away. Electronic mail simply models what has always been ~ since time immemorial.

EVOLUTION

We design our life experiences in such a way so as to be tutored by them. By definition then, we are always in school, even though we may sometimes find ourselves avoiding our lessons or not doing our homework. Each incarnation both introduces us to fresh subject matter and plays with variations on old themes. In terms of the school of life, our states of mind always exactly mirror where we are in our evolutionary process and, consequently, our current levels of awareness.

How can we best utilize our time in the Earth Plane? By making a strong commitment to the pursuit of knowledge which in turn will lead to further growth and development. Evolution, by the way, is synonymous with the fuller expression of who we are ~ as reflected in our personal vibratory rates. The faster we vibrate, the freer and more cosmically aligned we become.

Evolution is also equivalent to change. Change and its logical consequence, transmutation, are a must in life, vital to the workings of the substrata in all planes of existence. Stasis, on the other hand, is a non-starter. By the way, evolution does not always imply moving from the less refined to the more refined or from a lower to a higher octave. It can, of course, but it may also be of the lateral persuasion. What's irrefutable, however, is that it involves some sort of transmutation. In alchemical lore, something base or gross always has the potential of becoming more refined, that is to say, of being changed into gold. While strictly speaking this is so, the fact remains that any sort of transmutation has an infinite number of variables associated with it. Therefore, on a given axis of probabilities, gold may not always necessarily be the end product.

Nevertheless, some lines of probability may be more desirable for us to pursue than others, especially when there's a moral value placed on them, implying a need for some kind of karmic rebalancing or restitution. Evolution is the life-long process of refining ourselves through the lens of experience. And, incarnate or not, it is our destiny to pursue this most worthy of goals.

Those of us in the Astral inhabit a hall of mirrors, able to contemplate as many possible roles, life scenarios and permutations as we care to, each reflecting infinitely and endlessly in those same metaphorical mirrors. Why is this a constructive pursuit? Well first of all, the variety of possibilities never ceases to amaze. It's something to be savored and respected. More importantly, however, each soul entity gets to order from this menu of infinite possibilities in order to try them on for size. These Astral dress-ups or costumed events, as they are sometimes called, can be long, short or somewhere in between. Their primary purpose is simple: experience. In other words, while in the Astral we can play with any number of roles and scenarios in order to learn more about ourselves ~ much in the same way that incarnates do when they dream their dreams, waking and otherwise.

In the Earth Plane dimension, our respective costume parties usually end up lasting a life-time, having been chosen from that same menu of possibilities prior to being born. In either plane of existence, choose your roles wisely. By incorporating the wisdom you have already garnered into selecting the axes of probabilities that you now want to pursue, you cannot help but to evolve.

Eyes

The eyes are symbolic of what **can** be seen, can being the operative word. What we actually see depends more on how aware we choose to be rather than solely on being gifted with 20/20 vision. We also have to believe that we can see what we think we are seeing in order to be able to see it. Our belief systems tend to filter out a great deal of whatever is being registered on the ocular nerves.

Metaphysically speaking, there are no limits as to what the eyes can see. In practice, unfortunately, that is not usually the case. Nevertheless, there's always so much more to be seen. We have only to look. Luckily for us, our eyes are predisposed to do just that, always seeking to behold that which is extra-ordinary. Though some would dispute it, they are also more than capable of capturing glimpses of cross-dimensional phenomena. How many people throughout history have attested to seeing things that others disavow? And how many times have you yourself said it was right there in front of my eyes all the time but I was not able to see it until now?

In one of my films, I wore a monocle. Very fitting because in that role my character's sight was limited due to the circumstances of his birth. However, with the help of love, the conquering power, he eventually learned to use both of his eyes to see what was before him.

How do our eyes function in a spiritual sense? They are the soul's lenses as well as its windows on the world. By using the eyes to peer out from within the confines of the physical body, the soul is able to make its presence known. Although it may be concealed from time to time by the personality, it must eventually reappear and shine forth. No soul can remain hidden for long. It must express itself and, as a result, be seen. It follows then that if we but take the time to study the eyes of our fellow men and women, we shall truly come to know them.

Our eyes tell the whole story. Among other things, they reflect our current levels of vitality. They also speak loudly of the magnificence that is all of creation. Keep in mind that our eyes communicate far more than we can ever know, which is as it should be. When words fail us, our eyes never do. One little glance may be just enough to start another dance. He who has a soul-full gaze often speaks volumes, what some film critics once said about me.

Since time immemorial, the question 'what do you see that I don't' has been grist for many a conversation. In sharing our points of view, not only do we get to share our perceptions but also our true selves. The eyes are a true miracle of creation. Think how wonderful is the apparatus that allows each of us to see and experience all manner of the ONE!

Soul Tints

Eye colors have their meaning
The Creator's way of screening
Shimmer, light, wonder and delight
Through the portals of our vision
The realities of fission
Engraving themselves upon the panorama
Of this, our life-sized diorama.

While brown eyes flash with glamour
Blue eyes yearn and clamor
For the perfect companion ~ romantic reception
With no exception

To the rule
Neither he nor she would ever want to play the fool

Green eyes flirt with passion
They're always quite in fashion
Gray eyes sometimes pout
But they, too, have lots of clout
Traveling, as we do, our twisty runways
All eye colors are equivalent ~ and fun ways
To tint the soul's prism
Avoiding any schism
In the ultimate perception
Of our own true perfection

Better it is not to always take classes
From those who wear rose-colored glasses

Though each of the aforementioned colors bring far more
Than we ever might have imagined onto the dance floor
Contributing to our might, stanchioning our sight.
The latest 'day' done yet it's still not night

But, you say, time is now right to return unto the Light
To again be in a perfect state of harmony
With the ONE that IS, i.e., the Trinity.

RVG

FAMILY

In terms of birth families, we often speak of blood lines. Instead, think of family as an energy line, seemingly becoming more dif- fused throughout the generations but at the same time maintaining its own unique flavor and sparkle.

Who is your family? Theoretically, it is composed of blood relatives, usually those you grew up with. You may or may not have strong emotional ties with them but that matters not. The fact is that we each are a family of one. Family, therefore, is us.

Now some would say that it takes more than one to constitute a family. At the very least, three are needed to create the circumstances of reincarnation and birth. However, even though we may have people in our lives playing the roles of parents and siblings, once born we become our own mother/father/brother/sister, in essence all our relations. As much as we may perceive that we are part of a family unit, we are self-contained, each of us a mini-universe.

Sometimes there are multiple people in our lives who, interacting with us and each other in loving and creative ways, are actually members of our blood family. This is lovely when it occurs but do not count on it. Although we are part of the fabric of the Whole, we incarnated to experience differentiation. To that end we must learn to be self-sufficient while also engaging with our family and peers. If we do have family members who love and support us, so much the better. However, the knowledge that we alone have the responsibility for maintaining our own well-being increases our effectiveness in accomplishing whatever it is that we have set out to do.

Many of us are quite involved with our birth families, others less so or not at all. Some families are loving and supportive while others seem to sabotage all those who enter therein. Again, what happens is all according to plan, based on prior agreement and the laws of karma. That said, take heart, there is a mitigating factor. If we don't get the family we think we might have wanted, we get to make one up ~ if we so choose. We always have the option of creating a family of choice, a course of action that many of us eventually decide to pursue anyway. In the final analysis though, alone or not, everyone has some sort of family. It may just not always be labeled as such.

Blood should not necessarily be thicker than water, especially if we determine that participating in our family circle is counterproductive to our growth and development. Society often exhorts us to stick with our birth families even if it's not warranted. I, however, was legitimately close to my parents and siblings ~ though primarily at a distance. I loved them and they me, but each in our own way, again dictated by mutual agreement and relevant karma. Even so, I, too, began to create a family of choice just as soon as I ventured out into the world.

Dear readers, embrace your people and the knowledge they impart, if not always certain aspects of their personalities or ways of doing. Learn what you can by studying your roots. Each and every blood line has the wisdom of the ages embedded therein. Maintain an open heart with those you love. Do not, however, willingly subject yourself to tyrants, family or otherwise. Abuse should never be part of the picture.

A family circle is most empowering to all concerned when each member realizes that there is no actual need for them to be together. They are simply because they want to be, not out of obligation or fear of being alone. Then and only then does a family function like a common-wealth, supporting each other's individualities in the context of the whole. Only when each person in our blood line or family of choice can stand alone and be complete, do we witness a real coming together.

Family is about making the decision to love yourself as well as those who are near and dear.

Don't feel badly if it turns out that you are not very close to your birth family. You and they may have come together for any number of reasons. However, being emotionally available or living in proximity to each other may not have been part of the package. Even so, family, defined as those who love you and you them, usually manifests in some way or other. Know, too, that there is always a gang in the Astral who loves you, especially during those times when it may seem as though you are all on your own. That is never the case. Not only are your Spirit Guides always on call, they are literally just around the corner.

Even so, the bottom line is that each of us is quite capable of being our own family unit. The participation of others in that concept, when it occurs, is simply a nice bonus. Express gratitude, however, in all cases ~ whatever your circumstances may be. And, nurture thyself. You cannot necessarily always count on others to do that for you.

La Famiglia Scelta ~ *The Chosen Family*

Sei pronto? *Are you ready?*
Deciding which family circle is to be yours can be rather heady
Shall it be a Lancelot style clan with lots of glamour
and corporate **élan**
Or a more mundane group who loves to spend time outside
sitting on the front stoop?
Well, in order to be born again, one does first need to fly the coop
In the process scattering karmic dust to the wind
But by any chosen group you are never actually pinned
To the mat. In fact, just the opposite of that is true,
Your family circle offers you a paint brush ~ yes,
though now it may be blue
But the canvas itself is yours alone to do
With what you will ~ to create
Something beautiful. Surely that ought to feel great.

Family is an operating platform, a heart-felt frame of reference
Agreed upon and magnetized by respective soul preference
The flavor selected, like ice cream perfected
Will never melt in the heat of the Sun
Why? Because life is about having some fun
And dealing with challenges too ~ But family ties,
I'll tell you no lies
Can help us decipher this life's what to do
A question typically rife with lots of karmic stew.

RVG

118

FEAR

Negative thinking encourages fear. And, when fear takes hold, it divides and conquers.

When we demonstrate the ability to overcome adverse conditions, it means that we fear not. In such instances, fear has been seen for what it is, a useless stage prop. If, on the other hand, we are living in fear, it is because we ourselves have given it space to grow.

Fear and love cannot exist in the same quadrant of time and space. Indeed, love dissolves fear by invalidating its very existence. And to the extent that love prevails in any situation, we come into our own power, inspired to live a fuller life.

Power, by the way, is a relative term. Whether one can become more powerful or not is always contingent upon the proper use of power already attained. True power, however, is neither a function of personality or soul but rather a demonstration of the fact that we and the Creator are ONE.

We can eliminate fear simply by re-affirming our Oneness, that is to say, by recognizing the omnipotence of All That IS. Even in the thorniest of gardens, there is a perfect rose. Fear nothing. Accept all things. They are just part of living life.

FEELINGS

Feelings well up in all of us from time to time. Their purpose is to remind us that we are capable of sensitizing ourselves to higher vibrations. We have only to give ourselves permission to experience them.

Anch'io piango ~ *I also cry.* I say this because I want to remind you, dear readers, that I, along with every other soul entity that ever was, have known sorrow as well as great joy. Every life will have a few patches of melancholy. Mine was no exception. I was not always the happy-go-lucky Rudy boy with a smile on my face. Though the smiling Valentino was an important part of my persona, I, too, had moments of sadness.

Whether we witness perfection in nature or find ourselves temporarily flummoxed by the mysteries surrounding our lives, it inspires a myriad of emotions. I often cried. We all cry and so we should from time to time. It's part of being alive. Weep not, however, only in sadness but also for the many joys of life.

Empathy is associated with affinity for others. In being able to identify with our fellow men and women, we come to know who they are. Empathy is synonymous with emotional resonance. He who is empathetic can literally feel the love and tenderness in another soul. What would we be were it not for the essence of the Creator that walks in all of us, that feels, that IS? We could not live without the exquisite sense of connectivity and attunement that we continually feel.

Connecting with others in a visceral way is similar to a sprocket interfacing with a bicycle chain. It creates enmeshment. When that occurs, acknowledge it ~ for it is not always an easy task to accomplish. My advice, however, is not to stay there for very long or your fingers just might get pinched. While we should always attempt to understand what others are feeling, we serve no one if we become inundated and can no longer separate our feelings from theirs. Too much enmeshment produces emotional contagion.

All that notwithstanding, jump right on in. Delve into things. Experience your feelings. Allow yourself to cry. Like rain falling gently on a window pane, tears have a way of bringing us greater clarity. Indeed, issues are always at their most profound when exposed to the light of day. We must first be able to name our feelings before we can ever let go of them.

FEET

Each time we dock at this port of call our feet assume great importance. Their job is to be anchors while we're afoot in the world.

Indeed, the moment we decide to reincarnate our feet begin their latest journey, symbolically at first and then, a number of months later, quite literally.

Take a good look at your feet. Study them well, in particular their unique architecture. If you will, go so far as to allow yourself to personalize them, at least to the extent that you might want to inquire about their well-being from time to time. Far too often we take them for granted.

Our feet serve us well, their role being vital. Again, the feet are our grounding agents. During waking hours, they are in contact with all manner of underpinnings. In fact, the feet are the part of the body most likely to provide us with a constant connection to our collective frames of reference, what we perceive of as our reality. Much like simple picture frames whose purpose it is to define the paintings that lie within their spheres of influence, the feet allow us to focus our attention on the Earth Plane. Puns, though often whimsical in nature, usually express truth in some form. Consider this then: the feet are a source of 'good understanding.'

All our body parts deserve to be honored. In fact, they must be, in order to live a healthy and productive life. Why then do the feet often get such short shrift?

In ancient times, offering a foot bath to a newly arrived guest was part of the social fabric. This gesture was a respectful way to acknowledge the fact that both soul and personality reside in the temple known as the human body. Recall, too, if you will, that in addition to its being essential for our survival, water serves to re-calibrate our vibratory rates each time we immerse ourselves in it. Moreover, being seated for a foot bath has the effect of temporarily relieving our feet of their Atlas-like role of holding up the world.

As we walk, our feet literally greet the street. Their greatest purpose is to create a link between our-selves and the Earth for the duration of our incarnated lives. In carrying out this task, not only do they express solidarity, they also model connectivity. The overall importance of the feet, however, varies for each individual. It is directly proportional to the frequency of our comings and goings.

Our feet correlate very nicely with our hands. There are, of course, wonderful echoes of similarity between the two ~ even though their respective functions are quite different.

In the Earth Plane, we often just trod along even though we would dearly love to stride or gallop, in other words, to be as mercurially fleet of foot as we once were. That said, it gives me pleasure to remind you, dear readers, that each incarnation is rife with opportunities for picking up the pace, should you decide to do so. And, as a rule, it's a good idea to work toward speeding things up anyway, at the very least from trod to stride. The Universe, after all, is always predisposed to help us increase our vibrations. The whole idea of picking up the pace is also complimentary to our innate desire to maintain the health and well-being of our physical bodies ~ as personified by those who once took part in the marathons of ancient Greece. Then, being fleet of foot was greatly appreciated.

The feet represent duality, likewise the astrological sign Pisces, said to be their ruler. Our feet are arguably one of the toughest yet most sensitive parts of our bodies. Optimally, they ought to work really well together. Fortunately for us, most of the time they do! We are indeed lucky, too, that they are made to come in pairs. Our feet are truly a marvel of engineering, especially when we consider the pounds per square inch they must support as we go about living our lives. Beyond the daily bath or shower, we owe them all the respect they deserve ~ and then some.

The healing practice known as reflexology involves manually applying pressure to certain points on the feet. By using this approach as a tool for incitement, a healthy stimulation of the body's internal organs can easily be achieved. The fact that reflexology is so successful as a technique suggests that the way to our hearts may well be through the feet rather than the stomach. That said, using massage to focus on the overall muscular and skeletal systems of the body is equally valid, each variety having its own particular benefits and long-term positive effects.

In suggesting that massage be one of the modalities that you might want to consider as a means of maintaining good health, I want to emphasize that all therapeutic approaches can be beneficial. Listen to what your body has to say. Which ones you choose to work with are directly related to your inner promptings.

Should we go barefoot from time to time or is it preferable to always be shod? The ancients could have completely covered their feet had they thought it wise to do so. Instead, they compromised and chose the open sandal as their preferred foot-cloaking device. In so doing, they were perhaps more aligned with the Earth's energies than we are today.

Practically, what can we do to keep our feet healthy? For starters, change your shoes regularly. Do not wear the same ones day in and day out. Keep in mind, too, that we stay more in tune with the Earth Plane by wearing natural rather than synthetic footwear. Furthermore, let your feet breathe when you can ~ without any shoes or stockings. In tropical climes or during the summer months, wiggle your toes in the grass. The feet require some exposure to all four elements. By the way, going barefoot is not just some youthful folly. It has a purpose, part of which is to remember freedom. When I played in the little park next to the home I lived in as a child, I often took my shoes off. Later, during my time in California, I loved walking barefoot on the beach, feeling the sand crunch beneath my toes. Allow yourself the luxury of going without shoes from time to time too. It's that important.

Although for the most part learning must first filter through the personality in order to be assimilated by the soul, the feet are the soul's most direct experience of its standing in the world. And, there is always great value in any 'sole to soul' transference.

FIRE

What is fire's role in today's world? The answer is simple. It both nourishes and purifies, just as it did back in the day when people were still drawing on cave walls. Though some like to think of fire solely as an agent of destruction, its primary purpose is to transmute. In fact, each time we see a fire burning we are witnessing an alchemical moment in which one substance or material is changing form in order to become something else.

Fire is symbolic of metamorphosis. It facilitates change and letting go, while also providing us with comfort, warmth and a certain amount of glow. The Romans, for example, often used it as a focal point, particularly in the practice of religion. It was also common for them to use fire at official ceremonies and public spectacles such as games and chariot races. Not only that, huge conflagrations were sometimes part of the Roman political scene, having been secretly instigated by its rulers **du jour** for their own personal gain. In those days, braziers full of burning charcoal could be found at the heart of every household. And so it was, even under the best of circumstances, that the danger of fire was ever-present.

The contemplation of fire is often an entry ticket to a state of meditative bliss. Focus on a single flame if you want to quickly steady the mind. I offer this as a constructive suggestion, an easy way to get inside your head. By using fire as a meditative tool, you'll be able to enhance the experience, infusing your brain with all manner of appropriately seared invocations.

Again, fire bespeaks transformation. Indeed, in many civilizations cremation is the main method of body disposal. The yellow part of a flame represents the sum of the Sun. The blue part reflects fire's spiritual and transformational nature. With fire there always comes purification.

The presence of fire in an environment, whether in the form of lit candles or glowing embers in a fireplace creates a certain level of comfort as well as the sense that all is as it should be. **Allumez une bougie de temps en temps** ~ *light a candle once in a while.* Also, maintain a fire-place, both in heart and hearth, fire being synonymous with heart energy. Do pay attention, however, when there are live flames in either. If not properly contained, they can easily run amok.

Contemplating fire elevates consciousness, allowing each of us to become seers in our own right.

FLOW

In the flow? Be in the know! Have you heard of stream of consciousness? Conceptually, think of flow as being like a comet, streaking across the sky. Inside its luminosity there lurks a bit of animosity. To wit: comets are made up of competing elements that simultaneously repel and attract, giving them energy and creating a flow, though in this instance one that's high in the sky. And so it goes, more or less, for all manner of flows.

During the course of our lives we often become active participants in many different kinds of flows. Indeed, we all partake. We must. But, the fact that we do is usually only noticed when we withdraw or somehow isolate ourselves from the flow in question. It is difficult to clearly perceive a flow while you're a part of it or still in its wake.

Most flows can be observed from the outside. There is one flow, however, that can never be seen in a dispassionate way as it is ours, forevermore. No, my friends, we cannot separate our consciousness from life itself. So the biggest flow, therefore, is an on-going one, life, the one show that's always in progress. Smaller flows, on the other hand, are as numerous and varied as our imaginations might contrive.

In order to illustrate my point, consider that as a motorist you're in a flow as you drive from one location to another, from point A to point B. It is, of course, easy to recognize that you have left that particular flow once you have arrived at your destination.

(*Addressing the author*) You and I happen to be in the same flow right now, the one called automatic writing. There are a number of sub-flows to be found therein and a governing one too, relating to the total number of topics and pages that we will be writing in order to complete this book.

Everything that happens in our lives is related to our participation in some flow or other. As you partake of life, be steadfast ~ not like sand in the wind to be scattered hither and yon. Our job in any flow is to be in the know. In some flows we are more than just willing participants. In others, however, we may feel somewhat reluctant and therefore rather uninspired.

In a sense flows are like rides in an amusement park. Ask yourself which ones you really want to board. Again, that is why you must always be in the know. First of all, you need to decide if you would like to participate. Default behavior just won't do. You need to have an exit strategy too. When a particular flow is no longer working for you, do take the necessary steps to extricate yourself.

Once again, the only flow we can't ever get out of is life itself. In the body or out, we are all part of that flow. That's what makes the Universe go ~ round. Life is the IS, the ALL. All other flows are fair game and ours to choose to participate in or not, as we see fit.

So then, we must be willing to move in and out of innumerable flows at will, according to our inner promptings and personal needs. When we find ourselves in a flow that's particularly appropriate and timely, we're likely to sense that what we're in the process of doing is inherently right. Such feelings serve as our barometers, confirming that we are indeed in the right place at the right time. Conversely, when there's nary a trace of rightness to be found, it's probably in our best interest to retreat as quickly as possible.

There are, nevertheless, always some exceptions to the rule. And so it goes with flows. At times, the most brilliant among us, when finding themselves participating in a flow that feels unwelcoming or hostile, will typically produce some of their finest work. Indeed, in the process of confronting adversity, creativity often soars. Life's the biggest flow and grandest show of them all, where, my, my, we sure do have a ball!

--- ❦ ---

FORGIVENESS

Forgiving is an exercise in Godliness. When we forgive, what we are doing is addressing unresolved karmic energy. Yes, karma can be neutralized or even completely dissolved through the simple act of forgiving. Forgiveness is indeed divine. Whether you are forgiving or being forgiven, it feels like a smile from Heaven.

A sigh of relief is heard each time someone in the world forgives. Forgiving opens up space for new developments to occur. Indeed, it's in the act of forgiving that whatever's been clogging our emotional entrails suddenly gets released. He who forgives brings contrition into the Light. He who acknowledges being forgiven may then be able to move mountains.

Forgiveness is often activated by prayer or meditation. But, however it's forged or whatever its genesis, simply forgive. And when you forgive, be sure to forget. As a matter of fact, you might want to create a ritual that will involve both. Write down, if you will, who and what you are forgiving. And, once you have forgiven the person in question, destroy the paper that contains his or her name, letting it all go. The specifics of your forgiving ritual are not so important. The fact that you are willing to forgive is. What is most important to understand about this whole process is that the person on the receiving end will realize that they have been forgiven even if you have done so in silence.

When the spirit of forgiveness reigns, a new day dawns, pregnant with possibilities. In moments such as these, wonderful things are bound to happen. Forgiving and giving are irrevocably linked ~ practically, grammatically and metaphysically. They are working partners, colleagues if you will, co-creative in nature. Some would even postulate that they are two of the most productive words in any language.

The corporations of today often speak in terms of deliverables, the specific tasks their employees must complete by a date certain.

In the same vein, I am suggesting that we see giving and forgiving as actionables ~ *actions to be taken*. These two verbs really ought to have permanent slots on each of our 'to do' lists, especially given the fact that we all work for the same corporation, the one called life. And, whether we're personally incorporated at the moment or not, we are always involved in the process.

This then is perhaps our most important bottom line, something we would all do well to remember: in giving or forgiving, we are doing one of the most God-like things any of us can ever do. Such acts are sure to be noticed ~ by all concerned. Not only that, he or she who gives or forgives shall also receive. So it is written.

As a rule, are you a giving person? If so, under what circumstances? Can you forgive those who have trespassed against you? Do you? If you tend to hold grudges, why is that the case? I contend that these are exactly the kinds of questions that each of us ought to be asking ourselves from time to time.

Is forgiving any more meritorious than giving? In a word, no. They are equally praiseworthy. Both are triggered by heart-felt promptings, at their most powerful and efficacious when there's a sense that it's both appropriate and timely for us to take action.

During the course of each incarnated life, there are times when our personalities become offended by the deeds of others. In such circumstances, choose to see the offending behaviors as gifts rather than annoyances. Whenever our personal boundaries are aggressed, we are being provided with an opportunity. We have a choice to make: to forgive ~ or not. While our personalities like to insert themselves in the process to greater or lesser degrees, our souls tend to remain neutral, neither judging nor casting stones. In essence then forgiveness is a soul-inspired phenomenon. Unfortunately, the extent to which incarnates are actually able to forgive is sometimes influenced by the self-serving nature of their personalities. **Attachment to states of un-forgiveness (grudges) is wasted energy and has the effect of inhibiting personal growth.**

Whenever you feel offended, let forgiveness be a priority. Seriously consider forgiving the offending party, no matter the circumstance. This does not mean that you are required to have further contact with them in order to do so. Again, forgiveness does not have to be verbalized. It can be just as effective when spoken silently in the privacy of your own home or in the context of a meditation or prayer.

When at all possible, it is advisable to adopt a forgiving attitude. To forgive is to be constructive. Forgiving, by the way, has just as many positive effects for those who forgive as it does for those who are being forgiven. On either side of the coin, personal karma is released whenever the balm of forgiveness is being applied. Since all that we do or say is karma-related anyway, any act of forgiving serves to re-balance our vibrations.

Being in a place of forgiveness always has the effect of bringing us further into the Light. When we forgive, we grow. Not only that, we also serve as an example to others, encouraging them to do the same. To forgive the heart must be open. It also requires us to make ourselves vulnerable.

Note: an insect resembling a scarab suddenly ran across the table top as I wrote the final sentence of the preceding paragraph. I was astounded to see it, my concentration momentarily broken. Then, the session resumed, hardly skipping a beat. Do not be annoyed. It is life, as is everything. LOVE it and forgive.

Forgiving is taking the high road, the principled thing to do. How many times have you heard someone say **they know not what they do?** Far too often that is true, whether one is speaking of others or referring to one's own behavior. Nevertheless, when we forgive someone from the bottom of our heart, our countenance changes. In expressing divinity, our whole being starts to glow, reflecting a state of grace. That is when the soul can truly be seen ~ in all its glory. In the act of forgiving we get to remember who and what we are.

FREEDOM

Free to be you and me. This is one of the Creator's greatest gifts. Free-dom = the kingdom of the free. We are kings in this domain, our home away from home. Even so, some of us choose to see this dimension as primarily one of limitation and restriction. That most certainly is not the case.

Freedom prevails in the Earth Plane in the sense that we always have freedom of choice, no matter what our life circumstances are. We are therefore as free to be in our earthly dominion as we are in the Astral. Nevertheless, being free requires some degree of self-discipline as the completely unfettered self is likely to flounder and, as a result, might not be able to achieve its goals. Indeed, freedom and personal responsibility are contiguous. In fact, they go hand in hand. They are what some might call a package deal. We may not, therefore, always be able to do exactly as we please because the end result might create problems or have unforeseen consequences ~ either for ourselves or someone else.

The paradox is that in order to be truly free, we must be willing to self-limit at times, especially when the greater good of the society we live in legitimately requires it.

Under what circumstances are we to embrace the prevailing societal, governmental or religious structures? The answer to that question is for each of us to decide and, of course, varies greatly according to life purpose. However, I suggest that at the very least it ought to be defined by common sense and the boundaries of existing law. The inner self always knows what's right for the occasion.

The concept of freedom is sometimes bandied about by politicians and pundits alike as a singular goal, an end in and of itself. That is not possible. Freedom can only be experienced in the context of the circumstances that surround it. Therefore, it cannot be categorized as a stand-alone.

Though the word freedom implies a lack of restrictions it should not, under any circumstances, be construed as an excuse for unconscionable behavior. Again, freedom involves taking responsibility for our own actions. Only by being as present as possible within the framework of the tasks that we have set out to accomplish and being aware of the ramifications of the choices we are making in order to complete those tasks can freedom be exercised. The more conscious we are, the freer we become.

As you walk in the world, avoid being pre-empted by the prevailing winds, especially when it serves no purpose. In terms of personal freedom, adopt a pro-active approach rather than leaving things in the hands of the powers that be. Voluntarily self-restrict only when the situations you find yourself in seem to require it. Trust your inner wisdom. You will always intuitively know when and where to make a stand.

In erecting our personal boundaries known to some as 'rings pass not,' we must allow others to have their own space to be and do. Again, freedom and restraint have a rather symbiotic relationship. One really can't really be present without the other.

We sometimes don't fully realize just how wonderful our lives actually are. In creating personal reality, anything is possible. It follows, therefore, that we are all rich beyond our wildest dreams. It is freedom in its purest sense to know that what appears to be restriction is not. It is, only if we think it is. And, if we choose to think it's not, well then the **'it'** becomes irrelevant.

FREE WILL

Free will is a player in each of our lives yet it does not always come into play. We may instead just decide to go with the flow.

For karmic reasons certain things seem meant to be. At least we have that sense about them when they occur. Nevertheless, in all circumstances free will prevails, allowing for a range of choices to be made ~ as long as they are commensurate with our life scripts.

Each time we're born, it's a life-changing event ~ comparable to suddenly being catapulted into another reality. It is always with a tremendous force of conviction that we leave the Astral, ready to pursue what we must in order to further our growth and development. Some things can only be accomplished while in the Earth vibration.

(Speaking to the author) This writing project was of your own free will when begun and continues to be, to this day. But the simple fact that you are both willing and able to do it opens up auxiliary lines of probabilities, karmic intent to be all the more vividly served in the process. We came together to write this book out of a desire to be of service to others. In carrying out that goal we are being of service to ourselves as well, re-framing and thereby transforming that which karmically was into some other iteration.

FRESH START

A fresh start is the equivalent of being fully present in the NOW. We literally make a fresh start each time we take a breath. As a matter of fact, every breath is both a re-birth and an opportunity for us to see what's up. The fresh start point of power is the realization that each inhalation gives us an opportunity to examine what is currently going on in our lives. Breath is an awakener. Just one inhalation/exhalation cycle may be all that's needed to catch ourselves in action, causing us to reflect on what it is that we are doing and why. By continually checking-in, we're able to make more informed decisions and, as a consequence, effect any number of mid-course corrections.

If we can but consciously embrace the breath-centered awakenings I refer to here as fresh starts, we'll find ourselves becoming increasingly more aware. The practice of yoga and other body-centered disciplines put great emphasis on working with the breath. This is not by accident. When we focus on breathing not only do we feel more alive but we're also able to go inward. It is in the breath that our disparate parts are able to dialogue and come to terms with each other.

Breathing is both evidence of Spirit, the animating principle, and the primary mechanism by which the soul and personality stay in tune with each other.

Fresh starts also offer us opportunities to unhook from karmic patterns that may have outgrown their usefulness. With each breath, there are choices to be made. Do we choose to do something new and take our chances or do we trod the 'something old' pathway, welcome in its familiarity yet at the same time rather uninspiring? This is an age-old dilemma. Hopefully, we'll find ourselves opting for something new more often than not. At least that ought to be our goal. Repeating the tried and true has its blessings and may even be prudent at times but by exclusively focusing on what's old we create a lack of forward momentum.

At some time or another, most of us have been known to say 'been there, done that, nothing new.' But, that just ain't true. In fact, each moment in our mutually agreed-upon construct known as time and space is, by definition, new. Therefore, no one can ever claim to have done it all because that is an impossibility. What we often do, however, is revert to our default behavior whenever it seems expedient. If, on the other hand, we decide to behave differently we're all the more likely to fine-tune or enhance 'what is' ~ while in the process of discovering what can be.

My advice is to be creative in your moment to moment decision-making. By being conscious about what we are choosing to do and why, not only are we supporting our natural inclinations, we are open to change.

Unfortunately, some of us tend to be recidivists, mindlessly repeating our past behaviors even when doing so might turn out to be onerous or downright unproductive. When we habitually decide to go with what's old instead of opting for a fresh start, what usually happens is that we end up feeling trapped, caught up in flypaper of our own design.

Again, each breath is a de facto fresh start. Use it as such. With each inhalation, open your mind and therefore the door to the winds of change. Breathe in what you want to see realized while at the same time exhaling what no longer serves you. Every breath we take has a dual purpose, to facilitate change while maintaining the integrity of our physical bodies.

FRIENDSHIP

A true friend is one whose presence in our lives is both lasting and pervasive. The sum and substance of a true friend remains even when, for one reason or another, we're no longer able to be in each other's company.

True friends are those who are there for you. However, you must also be willing to be there for them. Friendship has to be mutual. Remember the golden rule, **do unto others as you would have them do unto you.** In the pursuit of friendship, raise the bar by setting an example for the kinds of friendship you seek. Be the type of friend you want to have.

True friends come along with you. You and they continue to relate to each other, no matter what realm of life either of you may pursue. A true friend is someone who loves you and you them, each willing to accept the other's fame and foibles. As such, you are likely to enrich each other's lives, in a multitude of ways.

When friends love each other, their respective quirks become irrelevant. Neither are there any regrets. In friendship, love overrides other considerations, helping us to stay on track as we change and evolve. Many friendships, as it turns out, are a lot like committed relationships though as a rule neither do they morph into marriage or typically have a sexual component. Friendship is in a different category yet often just as intimate and profound.

A true friend then is a rare commodity and, like the finest of wines, to be appreciated and savored. Friendships can span a whole life-time, or they may be quite brief. Longevity matters not. What's most important is that both parties help each other progress along their respective pathways.

Fortunate indeed is he or she who has at least one true friend.

FUN

Who does not love fun? Though not always that easy to define, it's something we all crave. I propose that fun is actually life itself, what Costa Ricans like to call **pura vida** ~ *the essence of being.* In a classical sense, it is perhaps best personified by the image of a faun cavorting in nature.

That said, whether we're having fun or not usually depends on our attitude and state of mind. The more lighthearted our approach, the more likely we are to be having fun with whatever we're do-ing. Not taking ourselves or anyone else too seriously is of prime importance too. In finding ways to enjoy ourselves, however, we must take care not to fall prey to hedonism while still being able to embrace the child within.

What is fun for some others will often have none of. Fun, there-fore, is in the eye of the beholder. Many people, for example, see their work as fun while others view it as an obligation. Enjoying ourselves, however, is not an either/or proposition. It is measured in degrees. We do not always need to laugh out loud to be amused. Sometimes just a smile will do.

Whatever we love doing will always seem like fun. Therefore, plan on doing something you love every day, even if it's only for a few minutes. While we can and should enjoy ourselves doing any number of things, there is one caveat that I would propose: neither embrace overindulgence nor substance abuse in the guise of having fun. 'Tis folly to do so. Such behavior leads to self-undoing, that is to say, no-where. Also, do no harm in the pursuit of fun, either to yourself or your fellow man. In attempting to have fun at someone else's expense, we usually only end up hurting ourselves.

If we but look for the humor in the circumstances surrounding our lives, we'll all be better off. Laughter is a healing agent, a fact I cannot stress enough. It is the elixir of life, a veritable fountain of youth. Be willing to laugh at your own all-too-earnest approach or studied nature also, especially if you suddenly find yourself creating problems where there are none.

Having fun often means doing things for the sheer pleasure of the experience, whether it's building sand castles or climbing a mountain. Fun has an effervescent quality about it too. Indeed, we'd probably like nothing better than to be able to wrap our arms around it and hold on for dear life. Fun, however, is not a product. It does not come pre-packaged nor can we order it from a catalogue. If we're having fun doing something, it's simply because that's part of the reality we are creating.

The nature of fun is to be spontaneous. That is why having fun is often about discovering the unexpected in what you and others are saying or doing and then running with it. This is exactly the approach that most comedians take when they pose rhetorical questions to their audiences.

Though fun ought to always be part of our daily lives, it can sometimes seem elusive. Nevertheless, it is our right to be able to enjoy ourselves ~ even in the midst of difficult times. Therein lies the challenge and thrill of it all. What is life, my friends, without a modicum of fun? Indeed, we should always be ready to seize the moment. By allowing ourselves to go with the flow, we're all the more able to drink from the cup of life.

Fun is the equivalent of laughter summed, then squared to a higher power.

Gemstones

Why do we find ourselves attracted to certain gemstones as opposed to others? Personal preference certainly comes into play but the answer to that question is based on a number of factors, some of which I shall now endeavor to explain.

Each gemstone has its own vibration, the sum and substance of which is determined by its color, composition and specific properties. Though they breathe not, gemstones are as much part and parcel of the All That IS as anything else. They, too, are alive ~ in their own way. Because this is so, gemstones have the ability to enhance the vibratory rates of those who choose to wear them. Indeed, throughout the centuries the rulers of lands near and far have sought to use gemstones for this purpose.

Who among us has not been thrilled, at some time or another, by the sparkle of precious stones? In more than one incarnation, I was fascinated by them, having amassed quite a few. As Rudolph Valentino, I saw the jewelry I wore as reflections of the characters I played in films as well as footnotes of that life and time. Wearing jewelry is just another form of self-expression. Though not in everyone's game plan, I'd like to encourage you to wear some ~ regardless of gender or role. Why? Because it can be a lot of fun, like trying on costumes or hats. Not only that, gems are always on the lookout for a friendly wave length, meaning they like to be worn by someone appreciative.

If you're open to buying jewelry, choose it intuitively, that is to say, by using your emotional compass as a guide. Your initial reaction is what's paramount. Then, decide accordingly. In choosing a gemstone, however, not only do we need to think about its color and properties, we also ought to consider its presentation. Each setting tells a story. As a result, it behooves us to make sure that what it conveys accurately reflects who we are. It is important, therefore, to ascertain which pieces of jewelry are most appropriate prior to buying them, both in terms of the stones being used and the settings that have been chosen to display them.

That said, let's examine the practical and spiritual uses of several well-known gemstones while leaving their commercial values for others to determine.

Jade. Jade is quite a soothing stone. It slows the vibratory rate of those of us who tend to get too caught up in our daily lives, bringing greater clarity to the wearer.

Diamond. The diamond is literally a rock star, no pun intended. Unabashedly scintillating, it's in a class of its own when compared to other minerals. Not only that, it's extremely durable, almost beyond belief. Wearing a diamond is a way of staying in touch with those on the other side. Much as would a beacon of light, diamonds illuminate our presence.

Each of us would do well to own a diamond and wear it somewhere on our person. Diamonds help to keep our channels open, internally as well as with those with whom we interact. It's oft been said that a diamond is forever. That is indeed true. As spirit in one of its most concentrated forms, it is a symbol of pure love. And, as we all know, diamonds have traditionally epitomized the joys of wedded bliss. Though this may come as a bit of a surprise, men as well as women need diamond energy. They just have to decide where they want to wear one. **Allez Messieurs, ce n'est pas tellement difficile ~** *come on guys, that's really not so difficult.* Diamonds are nothing short of miraculous. Their sparkle transcends all notions of time and place.

Lapis Lazuli. Much beloved by the ancient Egyptians, the blue of this stone provides us with intuitive focus. The brilliance of its color, when contemplated, can take us deep inside ourselves. Lapis bestows inner vision upon those who wear it. Only by looking on the inside can we truly see that which is without.

There are often flecks of golden pyrite embedded in this stone, symbolically mixing that which is above (the blue) with that which is below (the gold) and creating a blend that must then transmute itself to a higher vibratory rate. Lapis Lazuli is an alchemical stone.

It both mirrors and reflects what we, too, must do on a daily basis: successfully blend the things of the Earth with the things of Spirit ~ even though they are already one in the same. By wearing lapis, we open our third eye, the one that so many have alluded to over the years. If we but use it to see our-selves, we'll know much more about life than we might ever have thought possible.

Emerald. The vibration of this gem conveys a sense of peace and place to those who wear it. In regards to peace, it bespeaks tranquility. Energetically, it helps us to align our disparate parts, what we might think of as the definable segments of our personalities. In regards to place, it serves both to align us with nature and our immediate environment. An emerald, therefore, is both a stone of alignment and at-one-ment.

Within the emerald's complex structure we see nothing less than the bounties of nature, constantly reminding us of the ONE source. Emeralds are known as philosopher's stones, in the sense that those who wear them seek truth in all things. A gemstone of great compassion, the emerald is also renowned for its healing properties.

Ruby. This gem was my personal favorite. After the diamond it is perhaps the second most important precious stone, well-known for its properties as well as its lore. In one of my films, I briefly held a number of them in my hands ~ faux though they were in that particular instance (*The Young Rajah, Paramount, 1922.*)

One of the rarest of gems, rubies are a reflection of passion. It is in this context that I speak of it ~ also of desire but not of any negative or exaggerated manifestations of either one. Rubies symbolize passion as well as the desire to love and be loved, that is all. Wearing a ruby is a reminder to maintain an open heart. In essence then, it has the effect of encouraging relationship.

In ancient times, the ruby was also seen as a conjuring stone. Not so surprising, given that passion is one of the tools we routinely use to help shape our realities. This gemstone amplifies the wishes of the wearer, encouraging their manifestation. Such wishes, however, must first be born out of love. There is no other way. Not only are secrets unlocked through the use of this stone, mountains may also be moved.

Pearls. Valued as gemstones even though they're not, pearls are of the oyster born, their origin but a grain of sand. As they develop, they become crystallized, taking on a definite form. Products of consolidation and focus, pearls come in all colors, sizes and shapes, the round ones being the most highly prized.

We might think of a round pearl as a metaphor for the globe we know as Earth. That, too, is crystallized thought, always in motion and ever in the process of becoming. The pearl is a product of reflection, if you will, the result of an oyster gazing at its navel. As a jewel it does not glitter yet its translucence is legendary. There is a parallel between the growth of a child in the womb and the development of a pearl in an oyster. In both instances the feminine principle is being served. No surprise then that men are usually not drawn to pearls. The pearl is an excellent example of the multi-layered nature of the Universe.

Sapphire. In and of themselves, sapphires tend to be rather neutral. Nevertheless, they have their functions, the most important of which is to consistently remind the wearer that all must come from within. Said to be a healing stone, they serve to ward off errant vibrations, neutralizing them in the process.

Sapphires enhance the energy fields of other gemstones they are paired with, in effect taking on the role of transformer. Sapphires and diamonds, for example, work particularly well together. If we flank a diamond with a pair of sapphires, its rays become more focused and the vastness of the Universe, encapsulated therein, even more apparent. The gems we wear always say much more about us than anyone might ever expect!

GOD

GOD is like a jewel of incalculable beauty and worth. And we are but refractions of the light that shines forth from that jewel. **GOD is** the Love that moves the Sun and the other Stars. So wrote Dante in his most famous work, *The Divine Comedy*. And so it is that no man or individuated soul is to be worshiped above others. Rather, the ALL, which is GOD, is to be revered and honored ~ in love and gratitude.

Question: What is GOD?

I AM

THE WORD

THE CREATOR

THE FACE OF TRUTH

BEAUTY BECOMING ITSELF

CONSCIOUSNESS UNFOLDING

THE ANIMATING PRINCIPLE

SPIRIT

THE ALL THAT IS

THE ALL IN ALL

THE TRUTH FOUND INSIDE A BUBBLE OF CHAMPAGNE

What truth is to be found therein? Visually, a champagne bubble appears to be empty. However, what it really contains is the All In All, encapsulated. Though perhaps a leap of logic, the empty part of a champagne bubble can indeed be thought of as GOD ~ in this case seemingly **no-**thing, but in reality **every-**thing ~ in other words, the All In All.

Again, what is GOD? What is Creation? GOD is Creation, the ever-becoming ~ indefatigable, omnipresent and yet not always so easy to define ~ at least within the generally established framework of language. As the wave is one with the ocean so are we ONE with Universal Mind.

GOD is seen in all things, people and planes of existence. GOD is constantly witnessed because action and GOD are intertwined, much like the double helix. Action awakens our consciousness which causes GOD to be noticed and thereby acknowledged. When we witness action of any sort, it is proof that GOD IS. Then too, just in case we don't get it, the hand of GOD tends to write exceedingly large. We cannot not notice the CREATOR. Divinity is revealed in a myriad of ways ~ anytime, anywhere, through anyone or anything. There are no limits. The breath of the CREATOR is to be found in all forms of life.

As a phenomenon, action is circular in nature. It consists of emptiness evolving into becoming and becoming devolving into emptiness. This cycle is graphically represented by the number 8, the number of infinity. The emptiness I speak of here is illusory, however, as no-thing is ever truly empty. There is no empty space in any plane of existence.

Action, also known as the Motion that is GOD, must be contained in some way or it cannot be fully grasped and understood. For action to be comprehensible and therefore the hand of GOD noticed, it must happen in the context of some recognizable frame of reference or thought matrix. Scientists and other researchers are continually finding instances of action taking place where none was previously thought to occur. As mankind's personal and professional frames of reference expand, discoveries will continue to come to light.

Likewise, in order for the All In All to be conceived of it must also be conceptually contained and referenced within some agreed-upon sphere of comprehension.

Incredible though it may seem, just as much of the All In All can be found within the so-called empty space inside of a champagne bubble as within any other sphere of containment, be it a planet or even the Universe.

Spirit, the Animating Principle, the CREATOR, GOD, all ONE in the same, may also be thought of as a bottomless reservoir of water. At birth, each soul entity forms a separate stream that flows out from it only to return at the moment of death in order to once again merge with the WHOLE.

Simply stated the CREATOR is Spirit. Every-thing of the CREATOR is Spirit. There is no-thing that is not Spirit. Soul is Spirit ~ in individuated form. Soul is but an expression of the All That Is.

GOLD

Traded all around the world, gold is highly touted as a measure of success. It is also used for personal adornment, as an agent of personality. For some, its pursuit is seen as part of the creation of wealth but that is not always necessarily the case. Wealth, too, is in the eye of the beholder.

In sharing my ideas, I am not suggesting that we should never indulge our auric pleasure. We all have a need to be seen at times and wearing gold on our persons is one way of achieving that goal. Rather, I am simply reminding you to be cautious where gold is concerned. If only we could learn, early on, the extent to which gold is apt to be seductive. In reality, gold is a huckster, forever encouraging newcomers to jump on the bandwagon and get caught up in the fever. As it shimmers and shines, it beckons to all those who would easily become bewitched by its wiles.

More does not always equate with more. More is often less. Having more gold, therefore, does not necessarily mean that we are going to experience more success, happiness or anything else. In fact, accumulating gold out of greed or simply for the sake of doing so often has quite the opposite effect, creating imbalances where there need not be any.

There's no doubt, of course, that gold has a certain mystique. Alchemists, for example, have long sought to make it out of other substances. Not only that, people have gone to great lengths to search for gold in every corner of the world. Of all the elements, it is perhaps the one that most strikes our fancy.

Think gold rush, if you will, and consider the effects that such movements have had in history. You, for example, *(speaking to the author)* now live in California, the golden state, a bountiful land whose mountains still ring with past discoveries of this yellow ore. Though it is no longer a viable factor in the economy, its influence lingers, supporting the notion that California is a land of opportunity ~ where dreams may come true.

Dear readers, our dreams do come true ~ anytime, anywhere. Every land is a land of opportunity. Though my dreams were realized in California, I can assure you gold had nothing to do with it.

It is most unfortunate that gold can so easily blind its beholders, causing them to go astray. In fact, those who contemplate it to the extreme are often so dazzled by its luster that they lose the ability to see what is right in front of their eyes. Its glow may sometimes even cause a disconnect, posing a threat to their continued evolution. Why am I so wary of gold? Because each time I've been in the flesh, I have personally witnessed its corrosive effects. Practically speaking, it's one of mankind's greatest distractors, far more potent than any aphrodisiac.

In my heyday, this topic was explored in several films, *Greed*, for example, as well as one I starred in called *The Conquering Power*. In that film my uncle, Père Grandet, is literally driven mad by his lust for gold. He loves only gold and in the end that is what takes his life. Having forsaken his adopted daughter and nephew, he is destroyed by the very thing he values the most. Love conquers all, however, as is its wont to do. My character and Père Grandet's step-daughter reunite in the aftermath of his death, declaring their love. Though rather simplistic, this story serves to remind us that love, not gold, is really our most precious commodity.

Gold and its corollary, money, seem to hold great sway among ye. What to do? How not to fall prey to gold fever? The answer is simple. Appreciate, but do not engage. Possess, but do not obsess. Be willing to walk away if that's what's needed or called for. And most importantly, never put gold or money on a higher pedestal than love.

Though an important tool of commerce, gold has a propensity to lend itself to folly, engendering fools or, at the very least, promoting foolish behavior. Fool's gold *(pyrite)* is an apt name, not just for the substance it refers to but because of gold's shadowy nature which often has a deleterious effect on our lives. Fools, it seems, always have their **payasos** ~ *clowns.* Gold is just such a clown ~ with a painted face and false body parts. It is not our friend nor could it ever be. Far too often, gold ends up being nothing more than a stumbling block ~ over which many trip and fall. In dealing with gold and its many wiles, maintain a healthy distance. Better yet, give it a wide berth. You will be all the wiser for having done so.

Gossip

Often described as pernicious. Like catarrh constantly dripping in one's throat or poison ivy. Gossip, unfortunately, has a tendency to run rampant, especially these days. How to categorize it? As superfluous chatter, baseless speculation, titillating chit chat or something to fill the airways, which, by the way, are already quite full. Nonsense in many cases and pure bunk in others. You can tell I hold little respect for gossip. Mostly, it's a waste of time.

There are many levels of gossip, ranging from casual inquiry to pure slander. Lying, too, is sometimes part of the picture. Believe not all that you hear. We are often deceived by things people gratuitously tell us or, if not deceived, confused. Society loves to gossip. Why else are there so many outlets for it? Tattling helps keep people's minds busy, though not necessarily in productive ways. The constructive life has little room for gossip. Speak not idly nor have the idle minds of others speak to you. That is my sincere advice.

Innuendos often create thought forms that have barbs. **Si prega di non bucarsi** ~ *do not get pricked.* Instead, choose to be associated with more constructive ways of thinking. In other words, build solid foundations with your friends rather than hanging out with demolition crews. That is what any circle of gossipers is, by the way, nothing more than a demolition crew.

GREED

An ugly word in any language, it is one of mankind's most unattractive traits. Greed comes from a place of non-compliance. As a feeling or phenomenon, it pre-supposes that possessing something outside of yourself will complete you or that having more of something is going to bring you greater happiness. It almost goes without saying that both of these notions are false. Greed, unfortunately, is one of the most common issues we all face ~ one that requires recognition and balancing.

Allow me to be very direct. Greed kills. It's a snuff emotion. It does not create. To the contrary, it destroys when predominating in our thinking. It does not nurture anyone or anything ~ anytime. Know this and greed shall be vanquished from your life. The essence of greed correlates with the effects of gold ~ as previously noted. Their implied and/or actual manifestation encourage each other in a negative way.

Being greedy is really about attempting to negate someone else's right to fully pursue his or her dreams. The truth is that if we, in our greed, want it so much, there is no space for others to have it ~ *it* being any desired object or outcome. Greed sets up resentment, anger, possibly even revenge. Furthermore, it has a corrosive effect, likely to spoil what has already been achieved or accumulated. Greediness is certainly not the type of behavior that any of us should ever embrace. Instead, it's one we ought to reject out of hand, not only for our own best interests but also out of respect for our fellow men and women.

Abundance prevails in your dimension, just as it does everywhere. There is no earthly reason, therefore, for anyone to be greedy. This I say to greed: **va via** ~ *clear out!* **Non c'è posto** ~ *there's no room for you.*

Habits

Habits are well-worn neurological pathways, analogous to the grooves on records. However, it's not always so groovy to be habit-ridden. Those who are sometimes just end up being labeled.

The term habit can be applied to anything that's done or partaken of repeatedly, especially in those areas in our lives where we have worn down resistance. Typical examples are smoking cigarettes and drinking coffee or alcohol. When done in excess, however, lots of different behaviors can lead to some form of addiction.

In and of themselves, habits are habit-forming. Certain ones spawn others, creating a network. Some are even intertwined. Coffee and cigarettes, for example, are like honey and bees, for all practical purposes inseparable. There are good habits, of course, such as brushing one's teeth after meals or going for daily walks and others that are less so. When does a habit turn into an addiction? When we develop a strong psychological or physiological dependency on it ~ governed by a lack of reason. Either track can take us right over the edge.

I was once a perpetual danger to myself, smoking endless packs of cigarettes. I loved to smoke, or so I thought, yet it really did nothing for me other than to offer something to have in my hands while I was being photographed. Smoking was once something the so-called smart people did. How silly that all seems now. It was a badge, just like ordering the right drink is nowadays ~ depending on the crowd you run with. What to do? Become more conscious of your habits. Specifically, be more aware of which ones serve you and which do not.

In my case, smoking became an addiction. However, some of my other habits were more in the realm of personal preference, for example, wearing jewelry most of the time, going barefoot at home, using green ink with certain pens and keeping my bedroom in order. The list goes on, ranging from the benign to the overdone.

Lots of habits have little or no consequence. Others, however, can be dangerous, either to ourselves or others. 'Tis a wise man who knows the difference. Who cares, for example, what my preference in underwear once was? Yet if I had been a big drinker, which fortunately I was not, I might have endangered any number of people by attempting to drive home after a night out on the town.

Any habits that are detrimental to our health must be looked at on a regular basis. We need to decide if what we are getting out of them is worth the gamble. Just about anything can become a habit. Whether or not it becomes an addiction, however, is another story. Again, the most common denominator is frequency. In the majority of cases, over-doing is what turns many a habit into an addiction.

HANDS

Our hands are an important part of who we are. In addition to whatever it is that we do with them on a daily basis we also often use them in symbolic ways. Not only that, our hands provide the soul with its main point of contact in the world.

The hands are both repositories and transmitters of Universal Energy. It's not so surprising then that they are often used to heal. Indeed, where would practitioners of the healing arts be were it not for their hands? In working with their clients, they tend to use them as though they were the most delicate of instruments.

We are all healers, my friends, whether we label ourselves as such or not. And, when we desire to focus healing energy in our hands, it is eternally available. Everyone can access this energy. Some people are just more aware of being able to do so than others.

In addition to doing all that they routinely do, our hands are also instruments of communication. In that role, they serve to enhance and support whatever is being said by conveying tangential information, mostly in coded or unintended fashion but sometimes more overtly too. We Italians, for example, because we really like to use our hands when we speak, usually provide a richer context in which to convey our thoughts.

Our hands have an uncanny ability to transmit love and grace as they go about their business. Their mission is divine and their purpose is to transform. Furthermore, they are co-creative by nature and illustrative of the IS-ness of the Universe.

Hands, digits, fingers ~ they are bringers of tangible results, that is to say, evidence ~ by dint of their constant doing. The hands serve to shape and form what we have first desired and willed, each manifestation having started with a single seed of thought sown in the fields of probability. It's only when it has sprouted, however, that it can be noticed. That said, we rarely operate in a vacuum. Whatever we manifest is often the result of joint or combined efforts, stemming from shared interests or common visions with others.

When consciously used with dash and verve, our hands often gift us with a certain degree of nerve, what some might call **chutzpah** ~ *boldness*. What else can the hands do? Balance, serve and, of course, provide ~ just to name a few of the possibilities.

Consider this: how often do we take our hands for granted instead of more actively involving them in our lives? In mulling over this question, common sense must come into play. Our hands are designed for constant use yet we always ought to think twice about attempting to grab something that we know is not for us. Rash or foolish behavior should never be a part of the equation where dexterity is concerned. The hands serve far greater purposes.

Hands, my hands, your hands, or any pair of hands are essentially sacred. We utilize them to effect the divine in this, our three dimensional clime. Our hands are even capable of bridging the dimensional divide. They are the instruments through which thought becomes action, leading to some tangible result. Our hands serve as a direct link between Universal Mind and physical manifestation. Their worth, therefore, is incalculable.

Just how happy are we when we complete a task? Generally speaking, we are thrilled! When we achieve something we really wanted by bringing it to fruition, it feels like we should celebrate. We should indeed. So, throw a party or a fest. It's always important to take a moment to say thanks for what has been wrought.

Whatever our hands may or may not accomplish is reflected in the data that is created as a result of their efforts. Indeed, statistics would scarcely exist were it not for their labors.

(*Speaking to the author*) You've been on the receiving end of the works of others as have I. Likewise, other people have benefited from our respective labors. As we work together this evening you are using one of your hands to help create the connection that is allowing me to express my ideas. In fact, your hand, acting as scribe, is birthing thought into the written word at this very moment. However, our circumstances are not as unusual as one might think because so do we all. Indeed, each and every one of us is constantly giving birth to thought ~ in one way or another.

If we were to carefully observe our hands, we might be able to see Universal Energy in our palms or fingertips. Our hands and their respective digits function much like electrical circuit breakers. When we touch something or someone, energy becomes engaged and starts to flow. Conversely, when we remove our hands and fingers from that same object or person, the flow of energy ceases.

Where the hands are concerned, practice makes perfect. The more we embrace being At-One with the All In All, the more capable we become. They go hand in hand. The dictionary defines capable thusly: having ability, competent, being able to do things well, that is to say, in a skilled fashion. Doing things, of course, implies a use of the hands. The etymological origin of **cap**-able is most likely to be found in the Hebrew/ancient Egyptian/Coptic word for hand, **kaph.**

That the hands were considered to be sacred by the ancients is clearly not in doubt. Indeed, vessels shaped like hands were often used to hold incense and other offerings during official or religious ceremonies. In the pantheon of ancient Egyptian deities, Ptah was the patron of crafts people and Thoth protected scribes and writers. The idea of honoring one's hands and the work they do is not a recent concept nor has it been copyrighted in this tome. From the very beginning, such thoughts have been indelibly engraved in the halls of time.

The discovery of early Egyptian hieroglyphics depicting hand and foot massage suggests that those who had them placed on the walls of their tombs must have thought such treatments to be helpful. I wholeheartedly concur and respectfully suggest that you consider exploring them. You might be pleasantly surprised. And, guess what? You can also handle the job all by yourself, that is, if you'd like to.

Addendum

Question: In watching your films, people often paid a lot of attention to your hands. Why were they so remarkable?

My hands? What language did they speak? As you have already guessed, it was the language of love. That's what people watching me heard in their minds. Love equals movement. The movement of my hands in films was a signal, a sign of love directed towards the audience. I had no need to say anything. 'Twas as if I was speaking sign language. Also, my hands were very healing, helping to soothe those around me, and in general calm things down a bit. Why were they remarkable? Not so remarkable, just hands ~ although I did know how to use them better than most.

HAPPINESS

Happiness looks different for each of us and rightly so. It has nothing to do with bravado, however, nor is it simply about making an attempt to put on a happy face. True happiness is reflected from within, in feeling that all is as it should be. It's what we experience when every cell in our body informs us that it is in perfect alignment with the whole, in other words, that at least for the moment we are in the right place at the right time. Such is the stuff of happiness.

Feeling happy is proof that we are singing in harmony with the All In All. It's oft been said 'this feels so right' or 'something was meant to be.' Such comments go to the heart of what happiness is all about. It is from this state of consciousness that we are able to catch a glimpse of our name in lights, writ large upon the cosmic marquee. In seeking to achieve harmonic convergence, life's purposes are both revealed and fulfilled.

Our happiness is primarily of our own doing, part and parcel of the interlocking series of emotionally-based phases that we are constantly creating for ourselves. However, it cannot always be sustained at the same pitch. It is the nature of happiness to be variable, to rise, fall, ebb and flow ~ on a moment to moment basis.

Even so, happiness is eternally accessible. Indeed, it is available anytime, anyplace, no matter what our circumstances may be. We just need to do our part ~ even though we still do also have to sample other kinds of feelings. Look at it this way, if we had nothing to compare it with how would we ever know what happiness truly is?

Our feelings are not monolithic. Neither are they mutually exclusive. It's perfectly OK, therefore, to feel more than one thing at a time and that's exactly the way things usually work out. However, if we make an effort to be happy at the same time we are experiencing other kinds of feelings then we will be, especially if we realize that it's in our best interest to do so. Even in the midst of tragedy we are all quite capable of finding something to be happy about.

By the way, other feelings are not of lesser value. All feelings have their time and place, each being just as valid as the next. Happiness is but one. While we must come to know them all, it is a wise man who learns to sow happiness wherever he goes ~ even in a field full of sorrow.

Learning to be increasingly happy requires the evolution of both personality and soul. Though some would contend that happiness is something that must be earned, the truth is that being happy is our birthright and therefore always a worthy pursuit. As is the case with any garden, however, it must first be cultivated.

In the geometry of happiness, smiles are both axioms and postulates. **Dai, sorridi; va bene** ~ *come on, smile; it does one good.* Simply stated, a smile is a physical manifestation of happiness. When we smile, we often cause others to do likewise. Smiles are infectious. They're likely to have wonderful consequences too. In Italy, for example, people always used to say **il sorriso porta la speranza** ~ *where there's a smile, there's always hope.*

Perhaps even more importantly, there's also laughter to consider. If we're able to laugh, happiness is usually on the same menu. Laughter is connected to happiness at the point at which it meets itself, coming and going. Health is also therein entwined, at the very same juncture. That we often pair health and happiness in the same breath is not accidental. They are birds of a feather. That said, laughter's role with this pairing is one of facilitator. Quantifiably potent, its healing properties are perhaps even more effective than other therapeutic agents. **It IS** to laugh. The more we laugh, the happier and healthier we are all the more likely to become.

Laughter erupts whenever we pause long enough to notice the absurdities in what either we or others are saying or doing. When sourced from the depths of our souls, it allows us to break free from past conditioning and see our lives from new perspectives. While laughing at ourselves, we often end up marveling at just how often we seem to be getting in our own way.

Being happy is about finding balance in all things. By maintaining an inner equilibrium, not only will we tend to feel happier about ourselves, we'll also be able to deal more effectively with our personal dichotomies, whatever they are. True happiness is soaked in the brine of the soul.

Being happy is a choice. By focusing on what we have rather than spending time worrying about what might be eluding us, we're usually in fine fettle. Once again, we all have a right to be happy. Therefore, happiness should never be viewed as elusive or something we must fight for. It is at hand ~ always. We just need to adjust our thinking and so shall it be.

Être ou Ne Pas Être ~ *To Be or Not To Be*

What is happiness?
Some desired state to be
In or some Faustian fantasy to flee?
What manner is this creature
That so many would love to feature
Up on the silver screen,
Perhaps life's most cherished dream?
Well, we certainly know that we never would want less
Than pure, unadulterated joy plus our own brand of happiness
In the mind of Man, it's a theme that reigns supreme
As a concept, it's definitely the sweetest cream
That one could ever add to the mix, our daily lives
In supporting our endeavors its guise
Is to offer us kind and gentle pleasure in whatever measure
We needs must take in order to shake
Any semblance of the blues from ourselves or our wake

Shall we further opine
On this crux divine
Or consider the bucks
Required to rent a happiness tux?
Well, an absence of controversy it could be said
Is a serious definition to some, or so we've been led
To believe but to me it is more than perfectly clear
That in order to fully BE we must hold very dear
The vision of happiness
Our souls never fail to see.

RVG

HEALING

Physician, heal thyself! As custodians of our physical bodies, it is our sworn duty to do just that, to the best of our abilities. Healing ourselves is a life-long task, sometimes requiring our undivided attention. How do we accomplish it? As is the case with so many things, personal choice comes into play.

Though few of us can claim to be doctors, we are the ultimate authority in matters of our own health ~ regardless of the degree to which we choose to work with health care professionals.

I invite you to hold the thought that body and soul are one until such time as we breathe the final breath. To remind yourself of this fact is to facilitate healing. Focus your consciousness on the breath each time you need to recharge your batteries. In doing so, we are restating the truth of our eternal and perfect inclusion in the All In All. Breathing, perhaps more than any other activity, allows us to witness Universal Consciousness in action. Again, we are all healers. We have only to realize that this is so.

Healing may also be accomplished from afar. We do not necessarily need to be in close proximity for it to occur. To be most effective, however, find a quiet space. Ask that what you are about to say and do be in the Light and to the highest good of all concerned. Align yourself with the healing forces of the Universe through the use of a brief meditation or prayer. Then speak the names and conditions of those you seek to help, including yourself ~ when appropriate. Ask for their ease to become manifest. Send them love, visualizing it permeating their beings from head to toe.

In following these suggestions, you will have done your utmost to be of assistance. The rest is up to them. Whether someone can be healed or not is primarily a function of their own volition. In other words, they have to want to get better.

Healing has many modalities, traditional and alternative. For example, it can even be effected through the use of sound, an area of investigation that demands further inquiry. Vibration (sound) works to support the presence of ease in each of us. If not monitored, however, sound can also have deleterious effects, contributing to a sense of dis-ease. Consider, if you will, how it might feel to spend hours or even days in a sound-disordered environment. Though you will obviously not melt if you do, be conscious of the fact that repeated exposure to such circumstances may be injurious to your health.

The opposite of sound also has great merit, having been given its due in the annals of healing. That is why some people seek solitude in order to regain their health while others like to have lots of company. Healing takes place in any number of different ways.

HEALTH & DIS-EASE

According to conventional wisdom, being healthy is indicative of an absence of harmful bacteria in the body whereas dis-ease implies a lack of harmony or some sort of malfunction. Of course, there's more to it than that. If, for example, our thinking is askew how can we ever be at the top of our game? In looking to be healthy we must occasionally meet dis-ease head on, if only to be able to differentiate it from its opposite.

On a soul level being healthy requires that we deal with our energy imbalances. Yes, karma, too, in some way is an indicator of health. Wouldn't it be wonderful if, in addition to examining our physical bodies, health care professionals were also able to read our karmic circuitry to find out how we are wired? Do, for example, our circuits line up? Are they vital and bright? Do they vibrate with ease? Are all of them operative? If so, to which degree or percentage? These questions all pertain to the stewardship of our physical bodies as seen from a spiritual point of view.

Karma, though a force to be reckoned with, does not lock us in to any specific outcomes. Neither does it condemn us to poor health. It is simply a frame of reference. Though at times we may be nudged by our karma, we are never bound by it. There are many ways to untie a karmic knot. That said, be aware of the fact that karmic as well as physical imbalances can sometimes lead to dis-ease which, by the way, is often quite different from being sick.

In terms of the relationship between our astral and physical bodies, health may be thought of as a superannuated state of equilibrium, in other words, one that potentially lasts forever. Being healthy, therefore, is not so mysterious. It's primarily a consequence of how we choose to think. Our thoughts have great power, capable of creating kidney stones or moving mountains, as we so choose.

Our thinking either nourishes or poisons us. Yes, and this bears repeating, thoughts can be toxic. If the poisoning progresses past a certain level, the physical and astral bodies will exhibit some form of dis-ease. Reverse thought and our bodies respond accordingly, healing themselves in the process. This was one of Mrs. Eddy's basic tenets. Mary Baker Eddy, the founder of the Christian Science religion, knew how to simplify metaphysical ideas so that people could more easily understand her points of view. In mentioning her work, however, I want to make it clear that I am not endorsing any particular faith or creed. They are all equal in the eyes of the Creator.

It has long been proven that the physical body can be healed instantaneously ~ as witnessed in healings done from afar or through a laying on of hands, both of which involve others acting as conduits for healing energy. But healings do not necessarily require the services of facilitators or practitioners ~ unless that is part of your belief system. Healings are brought about through our understanding that there is no reality to dis-ease. We arrive at this conclusion simply by re-affirming our perfection ~ as reflections of GOD.

Dis-ease, therefore, is nothing more than an illusion. When accepted as reality, it is a mis-interpretation of what is. Dis-ease is the result of our being at odds with ourselves, due to incongruities in the way we think. The power to heal lies within each and every one of us. Error is believing that we can only be healed from without.

Dis-ease is literally just that. But instead of focusing on not being at-ease, why not say he-al-th or she-al-th, as the case may be ~ out loud, thereby creating a mantra? This is a practical suggestion, designed to countermand repeated bouts of erroneous thinking. By breaking this word into its vibrational parts and saying them aloud in the form of a prayer, we are calling attention to the fact that what we are seeking is a coming together. In he-al-th, there is unity.

In my current place of residence, dis-ease is unknown. Indeed, health is a given in the Astral, part and parcel of the happy home-coming realizations that every soul entity has upon its return. It follows then that imbalance is likewise unknown. The only pos-sible gyrations are related to thought, the creation of karma being in abeyance.

Thought is instantaneously manifested in the Astral as there are no screens to be pierced, no doubt, no hesitancy and definitely no second guessing. Think and so shall it be is the rule in the Astral ~ where each thought is tied to some direct action and its attendant consequence. The gyrations I speak of, therefore, are merely mid-course corrections, the result of on-going changes in consciousness. In the Astral, awareness is paramount and love reigns supreme.

During each incarnation, our astral bodies are linked to and merged with a physical body. Strange as it may seem, however, we experience sensations in the astral body only. Though this may fly in the face of scientific belief, the physical body does not, in and of itself, feel anything. We only think it does. Instead, it's the astral body that feels. Therefore, when we experience pain it stems from imbalances in our astral bodies.

The physical body requires food and water to survive while the astral body receives its nourishment from Universal Energy ~ most simply described as emanations of the All in All. If for some reason the astral body is temporarily restricted in its ability to ac-cess Universal Energy, it feels pain. Pain is simply a reminder that on some level we need to re-align ourselves with the All In All. Once this is accomplished our discomfort will gradually disappear, a sense of well-ness again becoming the norm. By re-affirming our congruency with the All In All, we re-align our astral bodies with their physical counterparts.

The soul is not contained by the physical body. Along with the astral body it is simply sheltered therein for however long that a given incarnation may last. Never an appendage, the soul resides at our core.

It is important to note here that the health of our astral body is reflected in and exactly mirrored by the health of our physical body. The converse is equally true. During sleep cycles, the astral body emerges from the physical body in order to nurture itself and continue experiencing life. However, it remains tethered to the physical body by means of a silver-colored etheric cord. If perchance we should experience prolonged periods of insufficient sleep, the astral body may become deprived of nourishment, causing some sort of mis-alignment to occur.

When we receive an anesthetic in preparation for surgery, an artificial sleep state is being induced. As is the case each time we fall asleep, the astral body emerges from the physical body and journeys to the Astral, remaining separate yet connected ~ until the effects of the anesthesia wear off. That is why physical sensation disappears and no pain is experienced.

The soul and the astral body animate the physical body. It is never the other way around. Upon death, they terminate their relationship in order to return home. The physical body, now empty and inert, remains behind, beginning its decomposition process.

All that being said, **cari amici** ~ *dear friends,* know that it is always within our power to lead healthy and happy lives until such time as our day is done. We have only to try.

Help Mates

A collaborative effort will always be at the center of any help mate activity. Those who are our help mates are often the precipitators of specific projects, sometimes without even realizing it. Similar to soul mates, you and they have loosely contracted with each other to get something accomplished. A major difference, however, is that help mates are primarily focused on service, which is to say, on practical matters. There is often little of the personal where they are concerned. In other words, we don't necessarily have to be friends or lovers with someone in order to be one of their help mates. Nevertheless, sometimes there are overlaps. Help mates can also be soul mates. They can also be friends or lovers.

(Speaking to the author) Your former employer in San Francisco, for example, was a help mate, assisting you on many levels ~ even to this day. You returned the favor by removing some of the responsibility of the business from her shoulders. Our mutual friend in Boston, likewise, is a prime example of a help mate, having played a pivotal role in both the birth and evolution of this project.

Our help mates do not always make things easy. Sometimes it's their job to play devil's advocate or be a constant irritation. In so doing, they provide contrast, in a roundabout way helping us get even clearer about what it is that we really want to accomplish.

The basis for all help mate interaction is generosity of spirit. No one owes anyone else in these sorts of transactions. What is offered, therefore, comes straight from the heart. Though our interactions with our help mates may sometimes be slight, their effects are often profound. We are linked by what we do, Light joining Light to create a network of souls whose purpose is to facilitate the exchange of energy.

HOME

What could be more desirable than for each of us to have our own place in the Sun? In seeking housing, what we each are looking for is an appropriate venue to stage our lives, a place to live where we can feel totally at ease to be our-selves. The perfect living space, therefore, is wherever we can grow and prosper. Which four walls, by reason of their construction, layout or orientation, will allow us to feel most balanced, the parts of self aligned? That, my friends, is a question worth asking.

When we discover a potential living situation that seems both inviting and supportive of who we are, it is a confirmation that we have found a dwelling place that will encourage our growth and development. A home, however, rarely is forever. Our needs change and, as a result, so do our living spaces. Therefore, we are likely to have a number of different abodes.

First and foremost, home is where the heart is ~ no exceptions. That is where we really reside rather than at a physical address. If we were ever to write to ourselves, we would need to address the letter in care of our heart. Hearth, like heart, bespeaks warmth. Far more than just somewhere to lie down, a real home allows us to feel both comfortable and secure. It must glow from within while also sheltering us from the storm. That hearth or fire energy be present, therefore, is a prerequisite. As a concept, home is at its most powerful when it encompasses both heart and hearth. All three make excellent company and are naturally at ease with each other.

As has always been the case, our homes are sacred. It behooves us then to treat them that way. They are literally both our temple and base of operation, a point of power that's lovely to behold. Creating a space that we can call home is not a matter of money. Rather, it's based on attitude, ingenuity and the desire to do so.

Whatever your circumstances, it's imperative to define your tastes on the home front. Therefore, be creative with what you have, making sure to express yourself in ways that clearly reflect who you are. I did and so should you!

Home is a big idea, one that's not only all-encompassing but also rather immense. It is not simply about walls, roof or a floor. What makes a home a home is often more intangible than not. Where we live speaks to our sense of well-being. Our home functions as a safety net, the seat of our emotional, spiritual and physical support systems and, upon occasion, the dwelling place of our loved ones.

How we choose to arrange our belongings makes a statement about who we are too. Will our taste be reflected in an ornate mirror or represented by a few shards of broken glass? The choice, as always, is ours to make.

All home environments ought to be dedicated to the principles of beauty. Where we live, after all, is really the only place where we get to arrange all of the things we consider to be meaningful. Color, too, plays a part, each of us tending to have our favorites. Mine primarily were muted golds and reds, autumnal in nature. In living color, we tend to make ourselves all the more beautiful. No one really wants to live in a beige world.

Anytime we so desire, we can create a home space with as little as just one personal touch. There are travelers, for example, who like to rearrange their hotel rooms or bring a favorite item with them in order to infuse the places they stay with the spirit of home. In so many ways home is a state of mind, almost independent of bricks and mortar.

Our castles on Earth ought to be simple, elegant and comfortable ~ in perfect harmony with the four elements. Individual taste runs the gamut, of course, as well it should. In my case, the views were always paramount. I liked seeing the horizon each time I gazed through a window. Equally important was my desire to create some semblance of old-world flair wherever I lived, if nothing more than to remind me of my beloved Italy. I cite this merely as an example of personal taste ~ not as something to emulate. In matters of the home, each of you will have your own sets of issues and priorities. When it comes to decorating, however, one thing is for sure: our personalities will always have a go at it!

As far as layout is concerned, some floor plans are better than others. There must be flow, good feng shui, as it is now known. Houses that are designed with a center axis and wings on either side, for example, promote flow. This cross-shaped configuration forms two imaginary lines, creating a focus where they intersect.

Which would I recommend? The cross shape does allow for easy flow which is just one of its many reasons for being. But there are also many other equally valid floor plans. Which feels most comfortable? The answer will vary from person to person.

In scripting our lives, our living space is one of the primary sets. Use it wisely. Not only is a home a place to live, it's often a laboratory ~ we being both the subjects and perpetrators of the experiment. Home is where you can hang your hat and relax, whenever you would like to do so. If, however, you find yourself wanting to run out the door the moment you arrive, it's a sign that something is amiss. Choosing an appropriate living space usually comes down to whether or not the environment in question embraces life. If it does, proceed. If not, I suggest looking elsewhere.

(Addressing the author) You saw my first home, the one where I was born ~ *referring to my having visited Valentino's birthplace, Castellaneta, Italy.* You realized at the time that I must have felt like a bird living there, free to come and go in my flights of fancy. And so it is, for all of our living spaces. We must be able to go out as well as come in out of the rain.

Tana dei Falconi ~ *Falcon Lair*

How beauteous was Falcon Lair, **casa mia**, my Falcon Lair
But why oh why did I ever want to live there
In that distant bevy of hills?
Was it just to get Hollywood out of my hair
While off lot or part of a plot ~ angling for quieter times,
roots or maybe even a stasis?
'Twas an oil on canvas, that home, a living **tableau**,
no illusions, my **terra firma** basis
Where I could stage what were to be my ending days
There, in the glory of a Los Angeles year-round summery haze

Freedom there to me was shown
Wisdom there in me was grown
A home, *a cradle* ~ **un berceau,** serving as a ladle
To dish up that perfect stew,
a **pot-au-feu** of delicious variables, no fable
It was ~ the name of this exquisite mixture
writ deep inside my brain
Yes, on those hills called Beverly I even liked the rain

At Falcon Lair, no random bear but indeed was there a view,
Olympus-like divine it was plus there were always a slew
Of birds in flight and yes, lots of falcons too
Oh peregrines of pharaonic times with your heavenly laden lore
Were you not once more my talismans, leading me through a door,
The entrance to the secret chamber wherein lies our own true mind?
Proposing and disposing ~ no atoms there to split ~
for it's love that doth bind
The Universal Mind
Creating peace and harmony ~ it's that which I opine

'Twas my own choice to soar
As falcons did and do. With my 'day' undone,
there was no time for more
Home again, I began a quest with all my best,
becoming a tenured teacher
It's my dream to share my thoughts in print;
I've always been a reacher
Renown book-bound this time around
No glitz or sheen from the silver screen
Here within to be found or gleaned
Except in passing.

RVG

A Casa ~ *At Home*

Home, home,
It's wherever thou dost roam.
A place to say grace?
Yes, and some would also call it my space.

RVG

HOPE

Miracles occur daily, though often in small doses. They are one of the things in life that always give us hope. In the meantime, don't forget to take an occasional walk in the moonlight, wherever you happen to live. Looking at the Moon in all of its splendor inspires hope, reminding us that there is a grand design to everything. After all, the Universe is a hopeful place, there being a preponderance of evidence to support this conclusion.

Believe that ALL is possible, because, most assuredly, it is. Nothing should ever be categorized as a no-can-do. On the contrary, everything is a BE ~ as well as a DO, these two actions being interchangeable and simultaneous.

We are just as predisposed to hoping as we are to feeling. It's the way we are wired. If, for any reason, we were ever to cease hoping we would literally find ourselves sabotaging our own efforts. Therefore, we have to hope. We have a responsibility to ourselves and our fellow men and women to do so. Like the construct that is the Universe, our thinking patterns are oriented towards creating positive outcomes. And, because it's in our nature to hope, we would actually have to try hard not to.

In being hopeful, we cannot help but to advance. Hope fuels our progress. Like Love, it's always working on our behalf. By hoping, we define our preferences, the first step in bringing about a desired result. In hoping for the best, however, we would be wise to expect nothing. Becoming attached to specific outcomes is counterproductive, having the effect of inhibiting our ability to be creative. Instead, let us be both grateful and pleasantly surprised when whatever we have been hoping for comes to pass.

As four-letter words go, hope, like love, are among the most brilliant, encouraging us to be true to ourselves even under the most dire of circumstances. It, too, resides in the heart, with love as its most ardent of champions. Hope and love are our truest companions. With friends like these, we need no other.

HUBRIS

Arrogance lies at the core of hubris. Indeed, they are partners in crime. Personified, arrogance works to create barriers, isolating those who have decided to partake of its heady charms. Metaphorically, it's like a moat surrounding an ancient fortress, foreboding and dank, the kind that no one in their right mind would ever dream of trying to cross.

Then, as if this were not enough, hubris steps in to seal our fate, building walls where there were none, closing us in. It is next to impossible to have real relationships with those who have been enslaved by this subtle foe.

Indeed, once we've been smitten with hubris it is potentially quite damaging. In disregarding the needs and rights of others, we disrespect ourselves. We are all ONE. Therefore, the golden rule must always come into play. Each of us has to take full responsibility for our actions. Being self-confident to the point of embracing hubris is not to be confident at all.

Oddly enough, hubris is often invisible to those it enshrouds. To others, however, it stinks to high heaven, like a piece of old cheese sitting on a kitchen counter in the midst of a hot summer day. Not to worry though. Help is just around the corner. The moment we become more enlightened, the hubris wall comes tumbling down. In the aftermath, we are then free to roam ~ to be in that state of mind where we can truly connect with others and they with us.

HUGS

We all need to be hugged now and again. Indeed, embracing our fellow human beings is one of the most nurturing and healing things we can ever do. How is it that we come to know another soul? In a multitude of ways, hugging being one of the easiest. Hugs, like kisses, are signatures, designed to inform us who we are dealing with.

In order to effect a soul to soul **rendezvous**, we have to go beyond the realm of personality. It's there, in the arms of a hug, that our souls can meet while at the same time respecting the boundaries of being in the flesh. Embracing is an unparalleled opportunity for any two people to join forces.

Hugging another person is akin to hugging yourself. Much like eating comfort food, it's incredibly satisfying. So delicious are the sensations that we may even, at times, literally become lost in his or her arms. And oh, how we all love that!

Each time we hug one another, love is being conveyed. In hugging, not only do we have an opportunity to give of ourselves, we also receive. If someone is doubtful, hugging them will dispel it. If someone is upset, embracing that person will help to calm them. Problems go by the wayside wherever love abounds. Would that we were able to hug each person we meet, creating an infinite daisy chain. What a wonderful world that would be!

On my side of the dimensional divide, we are all the more frequently entwined. Hugging here is the thing to do, tantamount to the whole embracing the whole. Imagine, if you will, what that might feel like. Have you ever felt a shiver go through your body for no apparent reason? 'Twas a hug from beyond, my friends, one of the ways that we in the Astral inform you of our presence. Feel free to return the favor! Whether in the body or out, we can send an etheric hug to anyone we choose. The only requirement is that we must be able to visualize it happening.

The next time you hug someone, close your eyes and imagine your physical body like a series of interconnected electrical circuits. See yourself lighting up. You do. That's exactly what happens each time we hug one another. Light is meeting Light.

Embraces come in all flavors, sweet, perfunctory and profound, just to name a few. It's only when we come together in an embrace, however, that we truly know if we have met our match.

INSPIRATIONAL THOUGHTS (APHORISMS)

- To give is to live. To take without offering something in return is to negate the laws of abundance.
- We can either be imprisoned by our thoughts or not. The choice is ours to make.
- Trust we must. Every happenstance has a reason.
- Doubt, festooned in gray, turns all it touches into clay.
- Insecurities are of personality born. They have no provenance in soul.
- Those whose hearts are the most open are those who we are most likely to hold dear.
- Nature needs to know many languages just to have a conversation with itself.
- It is in simplicity that beauty finds its strongest voice.
- Life's truest currency is love.
- The sweetest chimes are usually rung when the sounds of silence are at their loudest.
- Always choose your words with reason ~ and in rightful season.
- Sometimes we just do not see how little bits make harmony. But they always do, anyway.

- Living life creatively always works wonders.
- Where liberty walks, choice abounds.
- Love is never singular, even in a "one-man" show.
- Those who are just to the core usually find nothing but good camping at their door.
- The land of nuance borders on pun.
- The best thing we can ever do for anyone is to expect them to be successful.
- Truth is who and what we are whereas things are merely props.
- The language of soul is only audible to those who choose to listen.
- Each time wisdom is revisited, clarity makes its presence known.
- Life as we know it is nothing more than love incarnate.
- Though both roses and the human heart may be touched, neither should ever be taken for granted.
- All thoughts, as disparate as they may seem, are relevant. Each one plays a part in shaping our reality.
- It is only through loving someone else that we may better come to know ourselves.
- Judgment resides in the vestments of personality. Compassion lives on in the soul.
- Each life-time is but a comma, just long enough for us to take a breath or two.
- **Meglio si ascolta l'amore nel cuore** ~ *Love is best heard in the heart.*

Internal Dialoguing

Between the I and the Me, a conversation there must be, in other words, an open and frank discussion, the goal of which is to get to mutual understanding and agreement. To be most successful, this coming to terms needs to be bilateral, with both parties ending up on the same page.

When we speak of having such a conversation, who is speaking to whom? And why might such an interchange be constructive? I shall endeavor to respond with all due clarity. There must be a never-ending dialogue between the parts of self, specifically the personality and soul. Know, however, that there is never any estrangement between the two, ever. Imbalance, yes ~ at times, but disharmony, no ~ just the occasional disagreement, mainly about focus and timing. A sit-down is all that's required.

The I and Me conversation is best served in the form of an ongoing tea party, in and of itself convivial and genteel. On one side sits the personality and on the other the authentic, eternal self. In these discussions everything is on the table, including, of course, the finest linens, china and silver. A pow-wow of the highest order, the net result is inspiration, occurring when there is a vibrational match between the wants of the personality and the needs of the soul. Such alignment can often come about through only a slight shift in perspective. It all depends what perch we are on as to how far we can see.

The personality is all for looking at itself in the mirror, never tiring of the match. The soul's plight, meanwhile, is to plumb the depths, asking tough questions. The personality wants relief, quick solutions ~ the soul, peace, true accord. Each has a role to play, equally important, their dynamics grist for evolution.

Agreements between personality and soul, as a matter of course, feel good, helping us to remember who we are and why we came here. When a deal has been struck, the realization that it has often comes to us in a flash, like a bolt out of the blue. How so? We experience positive emotion, our faces brightening, suddenly clear about what it is that we would like to do.

Each time an accord is reached we know it deep inside, where the Universe lies ~ in a heart-beat. How we feel about what we're doing is our barometer, the primary way of determining where we are in our process.

The most propitious life-times are those in which we're able to be more soul-centered. To that end, I propose that we always make a point of finding out what our souls really need. Only in this way can the personality be put on a different shelf. In order to fully BE, we must always keep in touch with our essence.

---------- ❖ ----------

JANUS (BEGINNINGS & ENDINGS)

That Janus sure is a two-faced so and so! Standing on a threshold, ever the visionary, his attention is, by definition, bifurcated, evenly divided between past and future. A mythical figure whose origin is shrouded in the mists of time, Janus was one of the originals in the Roman pantheon of deities. In his role as the god of doorways and portals, he was depicted as a head with two faces, one peering into the future and the other gazing into the past. In Latin, he was known as **Janus Geminus.** In modern day parlance such terminology speaks of duality, more specifically of twins.

However, the particular dynamic duo with whom Janus is aligned, namely beginnings and endings, are nothing less than eternal partners. Indeed, beginnings and endings at the very least always abut each other. It may even be that they occupy the same space. What is certain, however, is that they do hover around the same point, sometimes even lying within the same breath. If you look closely there's nary a gap in between. The point I speak of here, where beginnings and endings meet to dance their dance, is both mythical and real. It lies in mid-step.

Consider this. As you walk, one foot is always in the future, participating in a beginning while the other is in the past, tidying up an ending. Janus rules the middle ground. Had the ancients wanted to choose a deity to be patron of the golden mean, Janus might have been the perfect candidate. Symbolically he represents our life-long quest for balance and moderation in all things. In their time, the Romans also saw Janus as an initiator. And so he was thusly remembered, the first month of each calendar year having been named in his honor.

Midnight of December 31st is a perfect example of an ending and beginning coinciding and seemingly sharing the same moment. How do you tend to see that evening? Does it simply toll an ending? Or does the fact that another year is about to start predominate in your thinking?

All things considered, it's more than evident that each and every moment in time is both a beginning and an ending, depending on our point of view. Beginnings and endings imply change and transition. Conceptually, they are synonymous with birth and death, alpha and omega.

The future is tied to the past by an endless succession of doorways through which we all must pass. Janus, patron of the middle ground, literally the threshold, is keeper of the keys. As a door is unlocked and opened something begins. Conversely, as a door is closed and locked something ends. The mid-step, the point that lies between each ending and beginning, is the threshold, the frame of reference from which our consciousness is able to perceive what is ending as well as what is about to begin.

Beginnings and endings are rather graphically depicted by the daily comings and goings of our dear friends, the Sun and Moon. According to ancient lore, Janus was once their patron too ~ dawn and twilight being middle grounds, examples of the thresholds of which I speak. Their arrivals and departures always herald some sort of change in our perspectives. Additionally, Janus rules the moment, that is to say the NOW ~ where beginnings and endings meet and sometimes collide. Think on this then: Janus lives where you live!

JUSTICE

The purpose of justice to get to an outcome that most would agree is fair to all concerned. Only when this is accomplished can it be rightfully be said that justice has been served.

Sound judgments demand careful consideration and deliberation.

Therefore, it is prudent that they only be rendered upon having examined, assessed and evaluated the relevant facts. In weighing the evidence, each pro or con has importance and ought to be considered within the context of the whole. Even if the evidence in question is but a lowly pound of dirt, it, too, will have its day in court.

Rectification, the art of setting things right, requires a close examination of **vinculum** ~ *relatedness,* which is to say the ties that bind disparate people, places and events. In order to make a fair decision, all aspects of a matter have to be taken into account.

The Egyptian Book of the Dead states that upon death a soul should weigh no more than a feather. When placed side by side on a scale, do they indeed balance? Or, has karma been accumulated and the soul in question grown heavier? In each life-time resolution and reconciliation must be our primary tasks, the overall goal being to keep karmic anomalies to a minimum.

Justice is a beautiful thing. When we see it prevailing, usually a collective sigh of relief can be heard. If each of us would only commit to being fair in our dealings with others, there would be no real need for institutions of justice.

Though jurisprudence is primarily concerned with determining and meting out appropriate punishment, there are also larger fish to fry. In their highest and best use, prisons could be thought of as crucibles, capable of re-forming all those who enter therein. Indeed, punishment is alchemical in nature, serving to redirect and reroute energy that in some way has been perverted. Crime itself, of course, is just such a perversion. When crimes occur, they have the effect of interrupting the natural flow of things.

Films often speak to our psyches in archetypal yet profound ways. An interruption in the flow of things, therefore, is akin to a disturbance in the force. As popular film culture would have it, those who choose to pervert the 'force' are said to have gone over to the dark side. In our collective consciousness, the force is conceived of as that which is life-affirming. Criminal activity, on the other hand, is its antithesis.

Once a crime has been committed, setting things right, to the extent that they can be, usually involves the criminal paying a fine, doing some time or, in some instances, being condemned to die. Know that these are but devices, ostensively designed to punish but in truth serving to re-adjust and re-frame that which has occurred.

After the fact, both perpetrator and victim usually have plenty of time to examine their roles. Horrific as they can be, crimes, too, often act as catalysts for change. In life some come to do ~ others to be undone. Or so it has been said. One thing is patently clear, however. He or she who deliberately undoes is sure to be undone. Such is the law of karma. Therefore, monitor your actions to ensure that they are in alignment with the golden rule. Doing what is just and fair serves up a tasty dish whereas its opposite serves but to flummox, liable to confuse even the best of us.

Justice is reflexive by nature. Some might even say that it has a boomerang effect. When we put it out there, it usually comes back to us ~ in spades. Indeed, those who are just to the core usually find nothing but good camping at their door.

Sometimes justice is about **just us,** that is to say, about our own particular soul and personality, and sometimes greater numbers are involved. In being just, we are acting in concert with life, adding our own little flourishes along the way.

For justice to be front and center, there must be some sort of discord at play, issues that need to be addressed and reconciled. Getting there may sometimes be challenging. However, once our goals have been achieved we're apt to feel quite liberated.

On a personal level, karmically-inspired imbalances often reveal themselves in the form of something physical ~ money problems or dis-ease being prime examples. Indeed, whatever life props that can be used to alert us to an energy imbalance will be used. Such is the way of the world. And, when we suddenly notice that we have issues to address, it's our cue to face them head on.

Justice is designed to redress and restore whatever it is that has been divided or undone. Energy, having been disrupted, must be returned to its proper balance and flow. Though 'do the crime, serve the time' is the bottom line of the rule of law, in the bigger picture institutions of justice are primarily about making things right again.

KARMA

Karma, the term for the sum and substance of our respective behaviors, is inherent in the law of cause and effect. That law, which states that for every action there is an opposite or commensurate reaction, governs our very existence. Indeed, there are no get out of jail free or wild cards to be had. Every action has a consequence. **We are responsible, therefore, for whatever it is that we decide to do.**

No matter our station in life, we're all required to deal with the results of our actions. It's the price of admission for having chosen to be re-born. Because of free will, however, we have countless opportunities to examine our behavior and change it ~ if we so desire. When things go awry it's just a sign that something may have gotten out of hand and needs to be re-aligned. In other words, it's an indication that there's work to be done.

As it pertains to individuals, karma may be defined as a collection of unresolved energetic complications that, because of their disproportionality, tend to make themselves known, rather like short circuits in an electrical system. One of the main tasks of each incarnation is to continually re-balance our energies. That we all have imbalances should not be perceived as a problem, however. Resolving them, to the extent that we can, is an important part of why we came here in the first place. In reality, they are nothing more than learning devices, usually evidenced by a series of events suggesting that some sort of realignment in our thinking or behavioral patterns ought to be taking place. Remember, we our-selves are the authors of our own karmic circumstances.

In dealing with the consequences of our behavior, there's a process involved that's not unlike bringing a product to market. It must first be designed, then manufactured and finally sold ~ by us to us, we being the primary consumers. Yes, in all cases we must willingly embrace that which we hath wrought in order to be able to effectively deal with it. Fortunately, each of us is quite capable of understanding what we did and why. By making that determination, we're then able to untie our karmic knots.

The principles of geometry are quite instructive, however they're applied. In order to better grasp the origin of any unresolved energetic complications we each may have, I suggest they be examined in terms of angles, soft and hard, flowing and not so flowing, the harder angles being the ones most likely to create imbalances. Where angles are concerned, of course, triangulation is the name of the game. Whenever our attention is contained, we're able to get a better sense of exactly what needs to be accomplished.

In creating paradigms, we sometimes find our '**selves**,' that is to say, the personality and soul, at odds with each other or occasionally in opposition ~ *90 and 180 degrees, respectively.* Unresolved conflict, culminating with taking specific actions, is the antecedent of all karma. When we attempt to deal with our issues by coming at them from right angles it creates stress, often causing us to overreact. Accommodation can be more easily reached in opposition. There, it's always possible to find some common ground.

In terms of integrating the parts of self, go for the flow ~ the softer connection, if you will, geometrically expressed in terms of 60 degree angles. In the on-going give and take between personality and soul, this approach is far smoother, having the effect of minimizing anomalies. By definition, an equilateral triangle is the very model of proportionality.

Because our personalities only figure tangentially in the totality of who we are, I'd like to suggest that we never even consider giving them full sway. If perchance we do, it's but a sure-fire way for us to accumulate more karma.

As pupils in the school of life, we are always in the process of developing our own curriculum. I, for example, continue to be a student as do you, *(addressing the author)* notwithstanding your previous experience as a teacher. Indeed, it is impossible for any individual, incarnated or not, to become a know-it-all. That, dear friends, is a role reserved exclusively for the Creator. As a result, there is always something more for each of us to learn. That is why we are enrolled in institutions of higher learning ~ namely our environments.

Every action we take is connected to the Whole. Therefore, they're bound to affect something or someone else. Much of creating karma stems from carelessness or neglecting to take a moment to reflect on what we are about to do. If we attempt to harm another, for example, we are essentially harming ourselves. Like echoes, our actions reverberate, their effects eventually coming home to roost.

Working together in perpetuity, cause and effect create wonderful symmetry. Again, for every action, there's a commensurate reaction, though not always perceivable at the time. Only when we're caught napping, however, does our karma tend to get out of line. My advice is to stay awake, even when you're sleeping. How so ? Simply by suggesting to yourself that you remain in the know.

Think of karma as yarn being wound around a spool, all the thoughts and actions of a person cumulatively recorded therein. As the spool becomes fuller, tension develops, necessitating some sort of release. When karma unwinds, as it periodically does, the associated events often seem like non-sequiturs, having little or nothing to do with our current activities or life choices. Even so, they usually present us with fresh opportunities to revisit our issues and re-balance whatever it is that may have been askew. Meditate when puzzling events surface in your life. By better understanding their root causes you may be able to achieve greater clarity as to their purpose.

Karma may be dealt with in any number of ways. There are no hard and fast rules. Likewise, there are no proscribed or formulaic approaches just waiting to be discovered. How we deal with our imbalances is solely a matter of personal choice. Yes, we may each have a few crosses to bear but we are never in any way bound to them.

Our so-called past life scenarios, therefore, do not, under any circumstances, force us to repeat unseemly or inappropriate behavior this time around. Instead, they simply focus our attention along certain lines of probabilities, providing us with opportunities to examine them prior to taking action. It is not so important, by the way, to be able to remember the specific details of other incarnations even though some of you are more than capable of doing so. What is crucial, however, is that there be a visceral recognition of the fact that our current behavior is sometimes influenced by energy patterns that are rooted in other times and places. Now stored in the solar plexus and often in desperate need of re-wiring, it is our ongoing task to integrate them into the Whole.

To minimize karmic anomalies, strive for moderation ~ keeping cause and effect as measured as possible. No lusting after outcomes or seeking retribution either. In terms of behavior, allow nothing to get too far out of hand or become overly exaggerated.

KEY (CATALYSTS)

For purposes of this discussion, you may want to visualize an old-fashioned cast-iron skeleton key as a frame of reference. A key, however, need not literally be a key. Rather, it is the concept that I would like to explore here, the image only serving to remind us that there's always something more behind every metaphorical door.

In the broadest of contexts, a key is any instrument *(person, place or thing)* that has the potential of expanding our consciousness. In saying that, however, it's important to note that we do not always need to be motivated from without in order to take action. We are also perfectly capable of acting as our own catalysts. To that end, each of us came into this world carrying a **chatelaine,** the keys to our castle, so to speak, allowing us to access those private spaces where we all periodically need to go in order to deal with the unresolved energetic complications I spoke of previously. Each time we use a key to enter, something good's bound to happen, not the least of which is often a new take on life. Keys then provide us with opportunities to work through our issues, should we be willing to accept the challenges involved in doing so.

Simply by making the choice to open our self-created box of tricks, we're agreeing to initiate some sort of change in the status quo. Just as Pandora's actions had their consequences, so do ours. The tricks I speak of here, again, are but learning devices ~ in the form of events that we ourselves have programmed (even though they may be carried out or orchestrated by others) in order to re-awaken some fallow patch of psychological ground deep down inside.

Key is pronounced exactly like the word 'who' in Italian ~ **chi**. Who, therefore, is key in your life? What is he or she able to unlock? I invite you to continually ask yourself that question as everyone you encounter is some sort of a catalyst, a gate-keeper if you will, ever-ready to open or close one door or another. This, therefore, is my gist: we're all but part of the grist. That said, we are just as frequently catalysts for others as they are for us.

A microcosm of a larger IS, the computer functions as a key, inspiring us to take action. For many, however, it has assumed even greater importance, becoming the focal point of their lives ~ a stance I do not recommend. However, when used judiciously it's a wonderful tool, allowing us to become better informed.

Think of the individual keys on a computer key-board as representing some of the many possibilities that continually swirl around us, remaining latent, of course, until such time as we decide to get involved, our initial commitment requiring but a single key-stroke. Once a program is underway, however, we always have the option of modifying it or even starting over. Indeed, we have only to press delete if ever we want to beat a hasty retreat.

Actually, we're liable to find ourselves using the delete key with some regularity, especially upon discovering that something we thought was relevant is no longer serving us or realizing that certain of our karmically inspired issues have already been sufficiently addressed.

The computer, to many but a tool of commerce, is so much more, literally a work of art, brimming with its own creativity while stimulating ours. With their constant upgrades and never ending technological advances, computers, much like our own lives, are always subject to change. In their inimitable way, they remind us of what we know to be true: namely that intelligence begets intelligence or in other words, as above, so below. Michelangelo, in the painting he created on the ceiling of the Sistine Chapel, was seeking to illustrate this very principle.

As is often the case, the ancient Egyptians had their own take on the matter. It should surprise no one, therefore, that the ubiquitous obelisk, so frequently erected in the name of Pharaoh (*the perfect man*) was seen in that society as a phallic symbol uniting Heaven and Earth. As a matter of fact, where the uppermost point of an obelisk touches the sky is exactly where **as above** meets **so below**. Continuing with the phallic analogy, we could then rightfully say that so long as there is even one obelisk in existence, Heaven and Earth are forever engaged in intercourse.

While the phrase 'as above, so below' suggests the presence of a hierarchy, nothing could be further from the truth. The Astral and Earth planes mirror each other, even though there are differences in how they function. In essence then, 'so below' nourishes 'as above' just as much as the other way around.

Though there are likely to be moments in each incarnation when we feel like we've been boxed in by circumstances, we need to disabuse ourselves of that notion, as soon as it occurs. Our options are never limited, even though we may sometimes perceive them to be. Remember, it only takes one key to change our perspectives, suddenly unlocking a door that we may not have even known was there. Self-created prisons are nothing more than their name implies. Though often seen as reality, they are best compared to fog on the moors ~ initially appearing to be substantial yet with only the slightest change in our orientation apt to be gone with the wind.

We all have the capacity to free ourselves from any self-imposed limitations simply by turning the key of our choice in the lock that binds us. We need not, my friends, always be at the mercy of our own thoughts and perceptions.

In terms of our behavior with each other, we're bound to be catalysts. That much is a given. In that role, we are not unlike electrons, continually bombarding ourselves and our fellow travelers with energy, the net result of which is to foster change.

As Rudolph Valentino, I was a very public sort of figure, destined, as it were, to raise consciousness around the issues of love and attraction. As such, I was alternately reviled and praised, especially for the effects my movie roles seemed to have on popular culture. Though I didn't fully realize it at the time, I did exactly what I was supposed to in that incarnation, act as a mirror so that the public might be able to see reflections of themselves in me. By the way, each of you is just as much of a catalyst as I ever was and, without necessarily having to enter a spotlight.

The next time you find yourself in a roomful of people, try to visualize their energy fields while also observing how they interact with each other. In accepting the idea that each of us may be just the key that someone else is looking for, we are being well-served. Experiment then. Go on, see what you can see. What exactly will that be?

It is our hope that the contents of this book will provide you with any number of keys, in the form of ideas, principles and points of view ~ to be used or not, as you see fit.

KINSHIP

I speak here of **all** our relations, in other words, man**kind**. Indeed, there is no one among the so-called dead or alive who is not kin to each of us. In being aware of this fact, we are simply acknowledging our brother and sisterhood and the whole of creation.

Genetically we all come from the same gene pool, with only

slight differences creating variations in our looks and temperament. In truth, however, any deviations, striking though they may seem, are superficial at best. Kinship, therefore, runs deep, like a river carving out a canyon. There are kin, all of mankind, and closer kin, those who are additionally part of the same soul group and therefore on a similar pathway of growth and development. You and I, for example, *(addressing the author)* are the latter, anemones having the same genus and scent.

Kin and close kin, uniting in common purpose, often create **juntas** *(task forces)* whose mission it is to accomplish a goal, each of its members learning something in the process. What we do also helps others, especially those in our soul group, to grow in knowledge and experience while what they do helps us accomplish the same. The way things are structured, we cannot help but to be engaged with each other, thereby promoting mutual growth.

Juntas, of course, come and go, sometimes with great regularity. We are forever aligning and re-aligning ourselves with various kin, both in and out of the body. Know, however, that in so doing we are all blood brothers and sisters, our love and respect for each other outweighing all other factors. That said, what about our own soul group members? How are we to recognize these folk, these birds of a feather with whom we're likely to feel most in tune? By paying attention to the details and noticing where our attention is being drawn. There are no unimportant details, by the way, everything we construe as remarkable being of consequence. Finding those with whom we can most relate is simply part of being alive.

Kinship encompasses the whole kit and caboodle or, perhaps better said, the totality of mankind. As kin, we live in a state of cohesiveness, our tendency being to bond with each other rather than to go our separate ways.

How can we best honor all our relations? By making our hearts accessible. If others then do the same, essentially seeing things in a similar light, just how wonderful is that? In the same vein, we would always do well to greet each other with smiles, kind regards and tender hearts. I would even counsel you to be willing to wear your hearts on your sleeves from time to time, especially in dealing with those you hold dear.

Kinship is not an exclusive club, by any means, the number of possible interactions with our fellow men and women being infinite. Why? Experience. Experience IS the name of the game, my friends. That's what life is all about.

———————— ❁ ————————

KNOWLEDGE

In our eternal quest we seek to know that which is best. It's both human nature and in our own interest to do so. In knowledge not only is there strength, there is love. In the pursuit of knowledge, nothing flat or linear really counts. Neither does just staying on the page, whether it's a question of numbers, words, equations or anything else. Surface information, unfortunately, remains just that, not validating itself or really counting as true knowledge. What, then, does count? That knowledge be rooted in three dimensionality, either resulting from personal experience or the ability to delve into a subject. In the case of the latter, we must be capable of analyzing what is to be found, of seeing beyond mere facts and figures.

If you will, allow yourself to visualize knowledge as a living, breathing thing, constantly orbiting the brain. Because it's all there, we have only to want to know something for the necessary information to present itself, often seemingly out of the blue. Indeed, everything we really need to know is always at our disposal. Whatever gems of knowledge we're able to garner on top of that are like cream rising to the surface in a pail of fresh milk, incredibly rich and sweet to behold.

Nothing exists that is not already known to the Creator. It could be said, therefore, that there is nothing new under the Sun nor can there ever be. Our task then is simply to become more aware of what Universal Mind already knows.

In so doing, respect your process. After all, one idea spawns another ~ and so it goes. Value not only what you have come to know but also your sources of information. Your real job is to separate the wheat from the chaff, that is to say, not to automatically accept the picture that is being painted as the truth but rather to reflect on it, determining for yourself what rings true. In making these sorts of decisions, we need to reference what we've already learned while also trusting our instincts.

Knowledge informs the choices we make, often in confounding ways. Even so, we still end up being amazed at just how appropriate they usually are. **In vita veritas** ~ *in life, there is truth.* The sum and substance of our experiences, along with how we feel about them, constitute what's true for us. It is upon this that we must most rely.

Messieurs/Dames ~ *Ladies and Gentlemen,* may you find great delight in the books you read! May you live your music, dancing as often as possible to your favorite tunes! May you also enjoy the movies you see, including the ones that are less obvious. Knowledge abounds all-around, even in the most unlikely of places.

The drive to become more knowledgeable is synonymous with living. No one ever needs to remain in a state of not knowing ~ unless that's where he or she truly wants to be. Everything, my friends, is know-able. Did you ever think, for example, that you would know what you now know ~ even twenty four hours ago?

Be ceaseless in your pursuit of knowledge for in so doing you enrich others in the same way that you enrich yourself. With knowledge there comes responsibility. That's why decisions ought not be based on facts alone. In arriving at sound judgments everything, within reason, needs to be taken into account.

In the beginning, the Creator spoke, saying BE. This word, insofar as the eye can see, is represented by what we perceive to be reality. Having been imprinted on our souls, it is what allows us to function intelligently.

The library at Alexandria was established under the tutelage of the Ptolemys, becoming one of the greatest repositories of thought the world has ever known. It was a marvelous place, the smell of knowledge always in the air. Though it burned to the ground many centuries ago, every shred of information that was there can still be reconstituted. Indeed, as we write discoveries relating to its former contents continue to be made. My point is this: even though knowledge may temporarily be forgotten, it can never be lost.

Niente Sprecato ~ *Nothing Wasted*

Life, having a multitude of facets
Is composed of irregular bits, powerful assets
They are, though rough edges they often possess
Yet still we're able to fit them together, yes, nevertheless
By seeing the world through our own little prism
We're able to face the music while mostly dancing with rhythm

We live our mosaic. Certainly nothing prosaic about that
It's just that the formula for doing so never gets too obviously pat
But that being said,
'Tis time to put another notion to bed
Fact is, nothing's discarded, nothing's a loss
Disparate pieces do come together, no leftovers, no dross
If we but take the time, we'll align our design ~ as do so we must
Such efforts succeed with nary a bust
*Everything learned and everything done
Comes into play to illumine our Sun.*
Beauty is found by uniting what's diverse
That's what makes life fun ~ delight in creating our own little Universe.

RVG

Nota Bene: *(PS)* **Tutto quello che impari rimane per
servire al proprio scopo. Non c'è niente senza valore.**
Everything you ever do or learn stays with you, having purpose and value.

✦
LABYRINTHS

Let us confine our discussion to those of the circular persuasion. Such labyrinths are very helpful indeed. Over time more shall be built, their popularity increasing. The ones you saw (*speaking to the author and referring to a series of labyrinths near Santa Fe, New Mexico*) are especially beneficial, their centers always visible. Circular labyrinths are easy to navigate whereas angular ones tend to confuse.

Walking a circular labyrinth is a form of mental and emotional gymnastics, like flexing a muscle and then allowing it to relax. We twist in and twist out, using curved or elliptical movement to construct a hypothetical sphere. In so doing, we ought not step over the lines. There are prescribed ways of doing things, especially when it's a question of getting to the heart of a matter, just as there are a certain number of steps that must be taken in order to reach the center of a labyrinth.

If you will, think of labyrinths as entities, their hearts at their cores. Upon arriving, ye shall know them, including their purpose and inspiration. Ye shall also better know yourself for having walked even one. To plot a circle on a theoretical flat plane is to overlay God on what we view as reality, one sphere of influence slipping over another ~ like a ring being able to fit neatly on top of an elliptical.

When we enter a labyrinth we are making a pilgrimage, compressing life into a very short period of time so that our issues may be more readily seen and examined. How so, you ask? Walking a labyrinth folds time and space which has the effect of ratcheting up our vibratory rates. And at the same time, it also quiets the mind, freeing us from mental chatter. It is a healthy thing indeed to wind and unwind, to walk to the center and then retrace our steps, eventually coming back to the starting point. The net result is that afterwards we're likely to feel all the more balanced, aligned and alive.

The materials used to create labyrinths are of great importance. They may be composed of any substance found in nature. Some are better conductors of energy than others, however, certain minerals being the most desirable.

Labyrinths are living tableaux. The silence that is God is to be found at their centers, often marked by the inspired or unusual placement of specific objects or rocks.

--- ❦ ---

LANGUAGE

The function of language is to execute the delivery of thought, both verbally and in written form. Languages offer us multi-faceted ways of expressing ourselves, each gifting its speakers with a unique frame of reference, if you will, its window on the world. Indeed, the language espoused by a particular segment of world populace tends to color the way the people who speak it express themselves.

Another way to define language is as an inspired set of thought-constructs, each emphasizing certain sounds to the diminution or exclusion of others. These highlighted sounds, analogous to braille print, stand out from their normal state of being, creating a unique set of linguistic patterns. Languages then are collections of sounds in focused and condensed form which, when grouped together in utterances, convey clusters of coherent thought.

Each language has specific tones and vibrations, different from all others. Indeed, when life circumstances dictate that we switch our mental circuitry from one language to another, we literally have to reframe our brains.

I contend that knowing two or more languages is of benefit to most people, allowing for more options and greater flexibility as we play our various roles. The same person, for example, sounds very different speaking French ~ as compared to English or some other language.

Simply stated, the languages we speak frame our thoughts. Any grouping of related thoughts may be conceived of as a picture desirous of being seen and the language acting as a vessel for those thoughts their frame. Moreover, every language functions as a sieve, restraining certain expressions of thought while encouraging or emphasizing others.

No matter which language is being employed, essential information can easily be conveyed. Emphasis on what is most important, however, may vary, determined by each language's intonational patterns and the speaker's intent. Nevertheless, language serves us well. In each, we are blessed with nuance, giving us a great deal of latitude to package our ideas creatively.

Because language is at best an imperfect medium, it behooves us to pay attention when others are speaking. Even so, the unvarnished truth is still apt to become entangled in verbiage, making it difficult to discern. If we're not sure what's being said, it's our job to ask for clarification while also doing our best to debunk any attempt to deliberately conceal it.

Each time we think, speak or write, our thoughts wend their way through filters, directly related to the anatomy of the language being used. They function much like the Veil, the energy curtain that forms the dimensional barrier between Earth and the Astral, the purpose of which is to limit the amount of direct transference.

Though languages are our instrument, they may not always be able to play our tune in the way that we would like. As each thought is filtered, some portion of it may be waylaid while the rest sails on through, reaching its audience unhindered. To prevent this from happening, always be as clear and concise as you possibly can. If later it becomes evident that the listener has not heard your message in the way it was intended, re-state it, preferably in a slightly different manner.

It has been said that French is particularly useful in diplomatic circles, German in science and Italian in expressing feelings and emotion, especially in song. Although such statements could be thought of as mere stereotype, some truth does therein lie. A similar sort of assertion could be made about pretty much every language found in our Earthly tower of Babel. Oh yes, and babble we do but primarily with purpose and to make ourselves known.

Everything really is quite simple. It is our mission to convey this fact, as succinctly as possible, through the use of a complex tool ~ in this case, the English language. It would, of course, be far more desirable if I were able to communicate with you directly, thought to thought, unfiltered and unfettered, without having to deal with language at all. Unfortunately, that is currently not possible. In the meantime, we do our best. By the way, in the Astral neither babble nor Babel is known. Where I live at the present time, communication is effected solely through the use of thought, there being no real need for any sort of language.

In your world, however, language is a living thing, always in the process of becoming. The use of any language, therefore, will have at least two variables at play: its own evolving and somewhat mutable nature and the fluidity of the thoughts seeking expression. It's a combination that often functions like a chemistry experiment gone awry, producing unexpected results even though the chemicals and assumptions being made are identical. As a result, it is highly unlikely, though not impossible, that a given thought will ever be expressed again in exactly the same way as before.

There is also a third variable that impacts our ability to communicate as clearly as we might like: how we're feeling at the moment. Feelings represent yet another energetic layer, having their way with the transmission of thought. Though feelings often come and go, we must be careful not to erect any barriers, emotional or otherwise, that might have the effect of impeding the flow of communication.

Because thoughts can only be expressed in the Earth vibration through the medium of language, they may require many re-statings for people to really capture their essential meanings.

LIBERTY

Here and there we hear talk of liberty, especially as it pertains to the pursuit of happiness. Indeed, liberty is part of our creed, perhaps the one thing that we as human beings can all agree to love. Where liberty walks, choice abounds.

No one wants to see their existence as **kafkaesque** *(subject to arbitrary control or the whims of the powers that be.)* Liberty transcends such notions, a powerful antidote, like manna from Heaven. Synonymous with freedom, it, like its counterpart, requires commensurate amounts of responsibility and good will.

Conceptually, liberty may be interpreted as an absence of restraint. Nevertheless, we must all self-restrain at times for the greater good of both the country we live in and the planet we inhabit. That is really what the rule of law is all about. As citizens of the world we have certain duties to uphold. We must also be willing to abide the rights and pleasures of others, though they be not our own. Live and let live!

Politically, liberty is a franchise, expressed in terms of quantifiable freedoms. On a personal level, it speaks of having a certain amount of autonomy or latitude, freedom within reason to do as we please. However, I must caution you again that no one in the body may ever do exactly as he or she pleases. In every country there are laws, both civil and criminal, that must be obeyed. Furthermore, we are subject to the laws of karma ~ even under the most desperate of circumstances. Nevertheless, we require liberty in order to BE. We cannot very successfully lead our lives in environments or frames of mind where it has been devalued or usurped.

Liberty should never be used as an excuse for unethical behavior. Abuse it not, my friends. It cannot be dictated either, even though there are those who would gladly try.

The Statue of Liberty called out to me when first I saw it so many years ago. As the ship I was on entered New York harbor, greeted by falling snow and a soon-to-be new moon, I remember thinking 'Rudy, you've come to the right place!'

LIFE

Strange as it may seem, visiting a cemetery is also about the continuity of life. Life is everywhere, even there *(speaking to the author.)* For example, the day you visited my crypt at *Hollywood Forever,* you saw movie-making in progress, extras all dressed up for their parts and a film crew engaged in its tasks.

*Note: A film entitled **For Your Consideration,** starring Christopher Guest et al was being filmed on location at Hollywood Forever cemetery in Los Angeles in November, 2005. It has since been released.*

Life goes on; it IS! The fact that a film was being made among our earthly remains is certainly not in the least bit disturbing ~ to any of us. Rather, it is but an affirmation of our craft, the art form known as film and, if you will, life itself.

Life is the flow, again what your *Star Wars* films referred to as the force. Far too often, however, we tend to lead our lives on fast forward rather than in a manner that's more conducive to our own particular blend of energies. If I'm speaking to you, make an effort to slow down once in a while to catch your breath. Each moment is precious; savor it. Live life in the NOW.

Though we may not always be able to see the big picture or, for that matter, completely understand the part we are playing, we must nevertheless proceed with the fullest of confidence. Doing so is what keeps us in good stead.

In any state of being, we are perpetual students, absorbing what we're learning while integrating it into a larger truth, our lessons continually providing us with standards by which to measure our progress. Again, life has no ending. It's only the circumstances that change.

LIFE AS A MOVIE

Movie-making? We do it on a daily basis, literally viewing the rushes as we speak. Here is my premise. We are the movie. Not only do we make it, we are its director and producer, likewise the best boy or girl. Starring in our own production, we're the one who gets it all accomplished, including deciding when to call it a wrap. We also do all the editing!

As screenwriters, our script is subject to interminable re-writes. In fact, nothing about it is fixed. Our respective films depict life in progress ~ continuously screening and playing to full houses for the duration of each incarnation. Our names are up on the marquee too, having been featured in the previews of coming attractions such as when our parents were speculating about their soon-to-be-born son or daughter. The Earth Plane is the movie theatre where the story of our life is always playing ~ from first to last breath.

That life is like a movie should not be news to anyone. However, in my estimation there's no more apt analogy, especially if we view it as the contiguous series of changes it is. Of course, we all do some basic planning prior to being born. While still in the Astral, each soul entity writes a rough draft of the life that's to come, later to be fleshed out once he or she has made an entrance, megaphone in hand.

Our mission is to 'make up' our lives, more specifically to improvise within the framework of the aforementioned plan. In so doing, we create our reality, which is always in the process of unfurling on the silver screen.

What, pray tell, is the overall theme of each and every life? Why, consciousness revealing itself.

In our own way, we're all Cecil B. DeMilles, yes we are, and just as good as he was in telling a story. Our films are the ultimate home movies, intimate yet professional too. In sharing our lives with others, each of us has the wherewithal to create a work of art. As director of your life, you may want to ponder certain questions. Which familiar grooves shall I use? Which shall I avoid? Which lighting combinations will work best? Shall I film in **chiaroscuro** (*shades of gray*) or technicolor? Which props shall I choose? Who shall I cast in the other roles? What scenery to use as opposed to which flats to fly? What now to try?

Don't get crazed, even though the choices are more or less infinite. The bottom line is that your movie will feature whatever it is that you choose to make most real. Know, too, that eventually you will do it all, at least by some theoretical point in time. Not only that, but all parts shall be yours. All roles are to be played, at least to some extent, rest assured.

While in the flesh, our lives are the equivalent of self-projected movies, focused on seemingly three dimensional screens filled with commonly accepted variables. As we perceive these respective screens and their contents, what we're actually doing is experiencing virtual vision. In other words, when we're in the Earth Plane what we see is only what we think we're seeing. None of it is real in the way we believe it to be. Our thought processes simply encourage us to think that it is. Nevertheless, it's not, shocking as that may seem ~ even though we must continue assuming that it is in order to be able to function. Seeing then may be likened to cinematic projection, our eyes being the lens.

The reality that surfaces on our viewing screens at any point in time is both a product of our focus and the result of specific concentrations of thought and energy.

Life's vistas are often quite layered, some of our 'sets' being in the foreground and others far away. What matters most, however, is your own sphere of influence, your turf, that place where you will best be able to accomplish whatever it is that you will or must.

The business of movie-making is life ~ in progress.

LIFE GOALS

Are there goals for each life-time? Of course. To each his own. Depending on the analogy you prefer, we have either a quilt to construct or a game plan to accomplish. I myself tend to favor the quilt allusion. Indeed, the concept of a patchwork quilt says it all. Living an incarnated life is like piecing together a quilt, in other words, creating something of beauty by uniting what's diverse.

Our common goal is to do as much as we can in each life-time, hopefully becoming ever more conscious of who we are ~ were ~ and possibly will be. Yes, believe it. We can access information about our so-called past and future lives while living the current one. All we have to do is look under the rocks ~ or just beyond them. The clues are always there, right in front of our eyes. And, as is the case in so many circumstances, it's simply a matter of paying attention.

To get to where all this is possible, however, it's necessary to go inward. The old meditation model works for some, sitting still and emptying the mind, while repetitive movement works better for others, for example, walking, swimming or running. I invite you to try the latter, especially if you haven't before, as a way of opening the doors to your inner mind.

What is it that you shall find in that most sacred of spaces? Without a doubt, LOVE. Trace elements of all our life-times are also entwined there. By what means? Through the marvelous phenomenon that is love. How so? Because LOVE ABIDES. Think of love as the ball of string we've each been unwinding while traversing the corridors of time and dimension. If we can find that string, either through meditation or in dreams, we can then examine the events that are attached to it in the form of karmic knots. Once found, draw it towards you. In handling this metaphorical string, each knot is flush with information, reminding us of lessons learned or issues that have yet to be dealt with, in other words, our so-called past and future, both part of the eternal NOW. These same knots also permit us, on occasion, to catch specific glimpses of other incarnations that might be relevant to the current one, usually in a single-shot freeze-frame format.

But you ask, why make the effort? Let's just say that although it's not a prerequisite for anything in particular, doing this work brings a sense of wholeness to all those concerned. And that, my friends, is the ultimate goal for each and every one of us, to become whole. In fact, the more we attempt to become whole, the more we find ourselves in sync or at-one with the God Force, Universal Energy, the IS of TO BE. That's why doing a little inner work is always a good thing.

What about now? This life? This incarnation? Well, staying connected with the NOW, of course, is even more important, each feeling, thought or action playing a major role in our lives. Yes, even when it appears that little or nothing is happening, our lives are literally teeming with action. For example, if we so much as move a body part only slightly, that movement is bound to affect us in any number of ways.

Each incarnation also has another, on-going mission. In addition to creating the patchwork quilts I spoke of earlier, we're constantly in the process of manufacturing ourselves, both spiritually and on a cellular level. Then, once having created our product, we're also here to market it.

LOVE

Love, harmony's swain, makes us all 'mark' twain, overriding all other considerations. Pay attention to where we're going? Yes, of course we must ~ especially to avoid confusing our feelings with lust, which, by the way, is not a form of love.

Though others this have said, 'tis indeed true, love is the glue whose purpose, among other things, is to fill in what we might perceive of as empty space, creating a coherent whole ~ be it micro or macro. Love binds us to each other as well as to the dimensions we inhabit. In essence, it's our reason for being ~ **the** reason why everything IS. So all-encompassing are its perspectives that for all practical purposes love is unfathomable. Having neither sides nor bottom, it cannot be plumbed.

Love's implications never cease to amaze. Born of the heart, it blazes across the sky like a shooting star. Indeed, it has rightly been said that experiencing love, especially for the very first time, feels like a magic carpet ride.

Although they are essentially synonymous, love is even larger than life, in fact it's the biggest concept there is. Allow me, if you will, to try to get my arms around it in order to be able to shed some additional light.

I want you to really understand that love is the force that animates us. There is no other. For all of us, that is to say, we who are and ever more shall be, it bespeaks commonality, the feeling of being At-One. When we're in love we always have a sense that we're much more in tune, both with our-selves and the other person.

We seek to know those of a similar vibration, to meet our soul-mates. And with love in our hearts, we have the means to do just that. Love's always there for us, the gentle guide offering unconditional support. Infinite in nature, it is like a bottomless lake, eternally immune to drought.

To bring love into even greater focus, choose a symbol, making it your own. On more than one occasion, I chose a feather. Whenever I wanted to evoke love, I would simply imagine one falling from a bird in flight. In some incarnations, I was even known to wear a few on my person. Feathers were my icon, my symbol of love. Anything or anyone, for that matter, can be yours. We have only to decide on who or what it will be. Because symbols speak to our intentions, they are quite powerful. Therefore, hold them close to the vest ~ literally, or if that is not possible, in a spiritual sense.

In my life-time as Rudolph Valentino, I was just such an icon. As a leading man in films, my mission was to sensitize the movie-going public to love and its many iterations. In fact, some even say that in viewing my films it literally jumps off the screen. Let me assure you that was my intent. Love offered always comes back to you and I was certainly no exception to that rule ~ something for which I remain eternally grateful.

Love neutralizes fear, stupidity, crassness and hate, causing them to disappear like a single drop of rain hitting the pavement in the middle of a hot summer's day. Love is what life is all about, its substance and sustenance, propelling, impelling and, at times, even compelling us to take action. Love enriches us, empowering our lives as well as all of our relationships. Were we to speak of it in scientific terms, it might best be described as a binding agent.

Along the same lines, think of love as inert energy forever in the process of becoming overt while continuing to occupy the same moment in the time and space continuum, thereby setting up an on-going chemical reaction. Indeed, love is ALL energy ~ rolled into a single idea. Again, as far as importance is concerned, it trumps everything else. On a personal level, love might also be thought of as a melody that, when experienced, is unique to each individual. It flows through our beings, like blood coursing through our veins, and is the source of All That IS.

In ancient Greek, there were several words for love, agape being the one that's perhaps best remembered today. Though not translatable to a single English word, agape speaks of a love that is divine, imbuing it with a myriad of qualities such as altruism, loyalty, trust and perseverance. The Greeks in their wisdom realized that love is fueled by volition. Therefore, in order to be able to love, we must first want to.

True love, by the way, may never be bought or sold. It must be **freely** given and received.

When love is the game, we often take the blame. What I am referring to here is our propensity to blame ourselves when those we love choose not to love us back. But, my friends, there is no blame to be had, either in this game or in any other quarters, because there is no downside to loving. Love has no negative implications – ever, it being the ultimate source of our strength.

Love is a factor in all our relationships, to greater or lesser degrees. Therefore, it's not something to ration or share with only a few. Love is universal, our water of life, that which sustains us. And, it can manifest in any number of ways, depending on circumstances and the individuals involved. Indeed, love has an infinite number of faces. And in the course of living our lives we will eventually come to know them all ~ including our own.

Questo vi dico a tutti ~ *this I say to everyone*. Each time you express love, it will be reflected back to you in some way, often in kind. Love's tendency is to be self-generating. Nevertheless, from time to time we still need to turn on the switch, in effect lighting a match. Don't forget to join in on the fun! By the way, it's always preferable to love yourself from a place of self-nourishment rather than from a space of ego-aggrandizement.

Though I've referenced this before, it bears repeating: **l'amor che move il Sole e l'altre stelle** ~ *the love that moves the Sun and the other stars* ~ in other words, the Creator. **Così diceva Dante Alghieri nel suo capolavoro "La Commedia Divina"** ~ *so said Dante Alghieri in his most famous work,* **The Divine Comedy.** Because love, like the Creator, is omnipresent it can't ever be singular or only for one. It is pluralistic by nature, equally available to all. In essence then, it is our wont to love many. Like fertilizer we ought to spread it around, gifting it in some form or other to as many people as we can. Only the intensity varies, our soul mates being those we're likely to love the most.

Love works however it's offered – as a sumptuous feast in the mansion of a rich man or as crumbs on a pauper's table. Love is, in and of itself, all that we truly ever need.

Romantic love combined with sex presents a slightly different paradigm, however, taking us to a place where we must leave logic at the door. Such love is at times undecipherable, requiring that we give ourselves over to its mystery ~ a rendition, if you will, of the highest order.

That love has often been associated with the heart is no accident.

It could even be said that love is palpable. When exposed, it shines like nuggets of gold in the light of the Sun. Indeed, love is light, the only difference being that it's perhaps even more noticeable.

Sometimes there comes a film that says it all, both visually and with the spoken word. Such was *Moulin Rouge,* a 20th Century Fox film presentation with a powerful message: **the greatest thing you will ever learn is just to love and be loved in return.** I concur, wholeheartedly.

Cercando L'Amore ~ *Looking for Love*

The True Blue ~ shining on through
With love in our hearts, we know what to do
It illumines the divine, no matter the setting
When the body is gone, not even that fretting
Can darken love's sparkle nor tarnish its gleam
It's something that's ours ~ 'twas never a dream.
No need my friends therefore to look
We have only to open up our own play-book.

RVG

MAGIC

Why does magic have such strong allure? Because it's a universal language, one that we can all understand and identify with. Throughout recorded time the practice of magic has evoked a certain fascination, especially in the eyes of its beholders. This is just as true now as it ever was. Essentially then, magic is a centuries-old buzzword.

The term **léger de main** (*slight of hand*) is a deliciously French way to label this craft. But there is so much more to it than that.

Magic is a big concept. As a matter of fact in some sense we all function as magicians, each in our own way. More precisely, we are prestidigitators. We each have the gift. You see, creating personal reality is what we do and in the final analysis we often use our hands to do it. Those who call themselves magicians are not really any different from anyone else except for the fact that they have succeeded in sharpening their skills. Magicians are those persons who knowingly and deliberately work with magic.

However, magicians do not literally do tricks. Neither is their purpose to deceive. Instead, they simply play with reality ~ availing themselves of 'what is' in order to accomplish whatever it is that they have set out to do. If using natural phenomena to alter commonly agreed-upon perceptions is seen as the practice of magic, then so be it. By the way, magical feats have a greater purpose than to simply astound or amuse the general public. They serve to remind us that all is indeed possible.

In the course of honing their craft, some magicians learn how to 'alter-nate' by making use of the properties of the Veil, that porous wall of energy that delineates the boundary between our respective dimensions. This word, when thusly divided, speaks to one of a magician's most favored maneuvers, to temporarily change the genesis of an item. When achieved, this has the effect of restructuring how the objects or people they are working with will be seen (*or sometimes not seen*) by those in the audience.

Magic is the name given to the practice of wrapping people or objects in the appendages of the Veil, encasing them so that they will appear to disappear. The Veil easily lends itself to this sort of activity. If you will, conceive of it as being like a velvet curtain in a theatre, more specifically, the curtain separating the stage area from the audience. The folds of this curtain of energy are what magicians use to work their illusions ~ all while the public's eyes are directed towards them in awe and amazement.

Another way to think of magic is in terms of 'now you see it, now you don't,' like the workings of alternating electrical current. When electrical current is engaged, illumination occurs and usually what can be seen will be. On the other hand, when that same current is turned off, even for the briefest of moments, illumination ceases, causing our perceptions to become altered. Such is part of the magician's work, to temporarily obscure 'what is' by surrounding it with shadows or briefly removing it from sight ~ in some way or other making it seem like something it's not.

And so it is, too, with the Moon and Sun when there are total eclipses. Recall, if you will, that in ancient times superstitious people saw eclipses as magically charged events of the utmost importance. Even today many still consider them to be harbingers of change.

Magic in its most elemental form is nothing more than **manipulating** (*mani* = *hands in Italian*) certain aspects of the material world or that which is being seen. The most learned magicians usually have many capabilities. For example, they may be able to create mass dreams, relocate what's perceived to be immovable or temporarily seem to turn the world upside down. Think Harry Houdini in my day or David Blaine in yours.

That magic is magic is due to the presence of the unexpected, the element of surprise. But just how does what's expected get redirected, ending up in the realm of the unexpected?

The world we all know and love is populated with innumerable probabilities in the form of event-chains that always seem to be in process or re-occurring. A good magician knows how to remove just one link from any likely chain of events, that is to say, what people expect to have happen based on their previous experiences with similar situations. His or her intervention then causes us to see things in a new way.

A tiny change, whether it's one link or just an iota, will suddenly make the whole appear to be different. Then magic ensues, ensuring that our memory banks are jogged ~ an important and perhaps unintended consequence of the practice of magic. Nothing is for certain, or so it has been said. However, if this premise is true and indeed nothing is for certain, then we must always be learning ~ at the very least about exceptions to the rules. Given our experiences in the three dimensional world, we're wired to believe that things generally work this way or that. And most often they do, except when magic intervenes, forcing us to take another look.

Only those who walk in the Light really ought to practice magic. Though some dismiss it as performance art, the reality is that it's a sacred undertaking. Yes, there is nothing profane about practicing magic even though there are those who would still paint it as such. Magic itself is neutral, there being nothing inherently good or bad about it. That said, however, any magician who would use magic to harm another person is perverting natural law rather than bending it and, like everyone, is subject to the full force of karma.

In its purest form, magic is the label applied to chains of events that have surprising or unpredictable results. To work magic then is to effect the remarkable.

Theoretically, the mechanics of magic often require that some degree of dis-assembling takes place. In that process, there's a certain amount of swirling plus maybe a bit of twirling of the resultant fragments of energy that must be accomplished before the magician can re-assemble them into other visual forms, such as a bird coming out of a hat, a formerly tied piece of rope that is now unknotted or an empty box that once was full. Are these illusions real? Did the rope really untie itself or was its molecular flow interrupted just long enough to make it seem as though a change had occurred? Again, magic often takes what appears to be whole and deliberately deconstructs it, scattering its fragments like grains of sand in the wind.

But magic must work to unite too. What has been separated must be rejoined. More often than not once reality has been bent the magician in question will put things right again, the items that have been revamped resuming their original form and returning to where they previously were.

Kindly note that I am choosing to explain these phenomena in broad terms rather than with any great specificity. If I did tell all, it wouldn't be magic, now would it?

MARRIAGE

So enamored of marriage was I that I tried it twice! What was I seeking by declaring my allegiance, first to Jean and later to Natacha? I was attempting to formalize one of my strongest desires, to have a true companion, one with whom I could share all aspects of my being. Such was my motivation. All of you have your own, equally as valid.

Marrying creates intention as well as a commitment for the individuals in question to stay in tune with each other, in other words, to keep pace with each other's lives. Indeed, marriage is like dancing the **paso doble** *(two-step)* with gloves on, a little formal but quite enjoyable nonetheless. Both require good timing and lots of give and take. It's a rare couple, however, that actually needs to have their relationship formalized, especially if both individuals have already committed themselves to each other of their own accord. They may, of course, choose to marry anyway ~ for a variety of reasons.

As a construct, marriage requires a lot of patience and due diligence. Tact, too, plays an important role. Enter into marriage prudently, with eyes wide open. After all, it is a rather strict institution, especially if taken at face value.

Here are a few more thoughts on union. For some, marriage may be seen as a way to cement what is or a means to prevent a relationship from ending. Neither are particularly good reasons to marry. In the first instance, feelings can neither be captured nor frozen in time. In the second, separation rather than a coming together is what is most likely to occur.

On the other hand, marriage is a fine state of affairs for those who need to proclaim their intentions to the world, to underscore their commitment by publicly declaring their vows. Do get married if you are so inclined, especially if you and your partner are sure that you both want to experience that particular brand of societal binding. However, know that the sanctity of marriage exists primarily in our minds rather than on paper, and is supported by all actions conceived of and carried out in love.

Getting married ought to be a conscious move, a joint decision made freely by both parties. It may or may not involve a ceremony, however. Yes friends, marriage can also take place in a de facto way for those who will never see fit to do the paperwork or call a preacher. There is no surprise here. I simply want to reiterate that love trumps all. If love IS between two people then marriage also IS ~ whether or not the papers saying so have been signed on the dotted line.

Married or not, we must all be willing to make accommodations. There is room for all manner of variables in this world. Those who are excessively rigid in their thinking usually just end up being intractable.

— ❖ —

MEDIA

Truth lies not in words but in actions, what we do always being far more important than anything we ever say.

Today's media sometimes likes to speak to us in the context of sending the 'right' message. Sound bites, however, no matter how carefully they're crafted, usually tend to fall on deaf ears ~ experience having taught us to be skeptical. Seeing, on the other hand, is believing. Therefore, if we but do rather than merely say, diplomacy is sure to rule the day. To repeat, truth lies not in words but in deeds.

Saying the same thing a thousand times does not necessarily make it so. Any attempt to sway public opinion by manipulating the facts ought to be labeled for what it is: propaganda.

Just as in my day, the media tends to spend a lot of time speculating rather than reporting on the facts. There are, of course, details of my former life that could also lead to speculation ~ just as there are in everyone's. For the most part, however, I have chosen not to include them in these writings, knowing as I do from my current vantage point that essentially they are irrelevant.

When it comes to the media, pick your fights. I tried to once but didn't get very far!

In the Hollywood of yesteryear, many of us, upon having achieved a certain level of stardom, were asked to participate in telling our stories, penning publicity in the form of an occasional newspaper or magazine article. In that vein, I wrote *The Story of My Trip Abroad*, a compilation of my European travels, something I was more than happy to do. In my case at least, ghost writers were neither wanted nor allowed.

The media, nowadays with an even greater capacity to be everywhere at once, still uses the national press as one of its major outlets. What is actually written about, however, is all too often subject to the whims of specific individuals, pundits you call them, or colored by what is assumed to be the prevailing mood of the public.

In certain newsrooms, unfortunately, some degree of nepotism is often practiced. All is not lost, however. Those who should be in the media, those whose calling it really is, also typically find their way through the door and into key positions where things are made to happen ~ doing what they do, turning thought into substance, in this case, newsprint, a point or points of view being expressed in the process.

The press often likes to pat itself on the back ~ sometimes warranted, sometimes not. What's really important, however, may not always be expressed. As a result, we must take it upon ourselves to read between the lines, discerning truth where and when we can. That said, I would like to stress the fact that we are never completely in the dark. Even in the most carefully contrived attempts to cover things up there's sure to be some light shed on the subject. Try as anyone may to achieve a different outcome, the truth always wins out.

Be open-minded where the media is concerned. Allow yourself to be entertained rather than taking anything too seriously, especially if it's based on rumor or innuendo. However, when whispers become screams we really ought to pay attention. There are times when the media does us a great service by keeping us informed of what is likely to occur. Love it or hate it, the media provokes us to think, ponder and, at times, pontificate.

Newsprint may be compared to the fodder that cows chew on ~ ruminating. Words, too, are fodder, in essence our food for thought.

MONEY

Money and energy, having the same genesis, are really one in the same. On the physical plane, money's function is to represent energy, acting as its proxy or front man. Indeed, we usually are required to have some on our persons in order to go about our business. That money should ever be considered as a measure of our real net worth, however, is a product of erroneous thinking. We are not our money.

As Einstein put it, $E = MC2$. Extrapolating, E also equals euros, dollars, pounds or any other currency, each one having exactly the same purpose. In your world, money serves as a medium of exchange. When dispersed, something of equal or greater value usually tends to replace it. You might also want to think about the money you spend in terms of planting seeds. After all, if ground remains fallow nothing much is ever likely to grow.

How exactly should one handle money? In a word, gingerly. And, of course, with all due respect.

Remember, too, that money is a complex kind of commodity, crystalline in nature, each facet reflecting specific lines of thought which serve to magnetize concrete examples of what they represent. Money also offers us an opportunity to have a look at ourselves in the mirror, as many of us seem willing to be defined by what we buy. To the world at large then, our personalities are often at least in part shaped by who we are around money, regardless of any propensity we might have to rub for the genie, that is to say, to wish we had more.

That money is both a powerful and tenacious force is not in question. Indeed, it is one of the arenas of incarnated life where we all have some lessons to learn. I certainly did, having been quite the spender in my salad days.

Money may also be thought of as flypaper, designed, as it were, to attract the grosser elements of the Earth plane experience. Nevertheless, money is ruled by intention. If we have the intention to use it creatively and constructively, then we will. That said, whether accumulating or spending, we would all do well to embrace the idea of using our money for the common good ~ which really just means keeping it in motion. If we attempt to inhibit the flow in any way, we may simply end up putting ourselves in suspended animation only to wake up later and discover that we're in some kind of a time warp.

Perhaps more than any other commodity, money needs to breathe and move around. If money is static, it can only be defined as **no-thing**. Again, for money to **be**, it must be able to **move**. Astute business people know this instinctively. As a matter of fact, they habitually move their money around, keeping it in motion by periodically re-allocating their assets.

In handling money it sometimes feels as though it's hot-wired, fire literally imbedded in those official pieces of paper and coin. Therefore, there is a certain amount of truth in the oft-made observation that so and so's money must be burning a hole in his or her pocket. Having money is both a test of one's personal evolution and an opportunity to practice stewardship.

Stockbrokers and other financial advisors are wont to say 'sell to buy and buy to sell.' Rightfully so, even though this phrase sounds a bit like one of Gertrude Stein's most famous lines, *a rose is a rose is a rose.* In the same vein, we might also want to remember that 'investment is as investment does' ~ saving money for a rainy day, for many, just the thing to do.

Donate or tithe some of your money or resources, preferably to organizations that help others or have a spiritual bent, if not a specific religious community. Interestingly, doing so helps to maintain our own money flow. It is simply one of the many ways in which we give ourselves permission to share the common-wealth.

When beholding prosperity, be it yours or someone else's, acknowledge it. In so doing, we are confirming the lack of scarcity in the Universe. In other words, abundance reigns, in all planes. Rejoice, therefore, in each other's good fortune! In being resentful of another person's prosperity the only thing we're likely to accomplish is to short circuit our own. My friends, the laws of abundance are extraordinarily simple. To the extent that we're able to see ourselves as having the resources we need, so shall it be.

MOON

Ruler of the night skies, the Moon is a disc-like creature whose purpose is to serve as an arbiter of human emotion. Though for all practical purposes out of reach, think of it as a target, a bulls-eye, somewhere to focus and direct our feelings. In projecting them skyward, what we're actually doing is looking for clarification. The Moon functions as a magnifier which, when we choose to avail ourselves of it, usually helps us to see ourselves more clearly.

In its role as handmaiden to Universal Mind, the Moon also acts as a mirror, reflecting whatever it is that we are feeling back to us, multiplied many times over. If, for example, we're unaware that something is bothering us because it's a bit too wan to be noticed, all we have to do is 'take it to the Moon' in order to have it writ large on our consciousness. The Moon, with its many phases, is quite a useful tool for meditation.

In days of yore, the Moon had perhaps even greater importance. It was once considered a deity, alternately known as Hecate, Astarte or Isis, depending on which society or civilization. In corpus, the Moon represents the feminine principle while the Sun is viewed as its male counterpart. Though it may not seem like it, the Moon, too, has rays, albeit shorter and softer but equally as powerful, helping us, as it were, to manage our emotions while also providing us with comfort. Indeed, contemplating the Moon can be compared to eating porridge on a cold winter's morn ~ quite soothing and figuring in our most basic of needs. Moonbeams support life streams in much the same way that sunbeams do, yin and yang always at play.

They're a pair to never despair, our Sun and Moon. Indeed, they are our constant symbols of hope. Are there things that we would prefer to do by the light of the Moon as opposed to the brilliance of the noon-day Sun? Sure, examine our feelings for one. Think, if you will, of how many hours each of us have spent looking at the Moon. She, by the way, is actually to be seen whereas the Sun may only be glanced at.

Heaven's gate is to be found at the Moon's door. In general, Moon and star gazing bring us great peace and tranquility. Take a walk outside on any moonlit evening and ye shall be at rest, ready to enter the dream world.

While in the flesh, so once quoth I: **when night falls, amber-colored Moon rising to the star-lit stage above, it is almost impossible to remain conflicted. In such instances problems tend to fade, becoming irrelevant.** Well-said, even if I do say so myself! *(Paraphrased quote from My Private Diary by Rudolph Valentino.)*

Throughout the ages much import has been given to the phases of the Moon. Yes it is so, particularly as it relates to the new Moon and the days that immediately follow, what we refer to as the initial crescent phase. Each month, just as soon as the Moon begins to wax, it is time to plant seeds of all manner and making. If at all possible, start projects on the new Moon. Then, while the crescent continues to blossom, tend to the seeds you have just sown. You will soon know if any of them have found favor in their soil.

The June Moon, in particular, is the marrying kind. Why is that? Why do so many couples decide to tie the knot in June, especially towards the latter part of the month? Well, friends, there is a reason, the full Moon of late June or early July being opposed to the Sun as they all are but in this case in an astrological sign that would have us make sure to get things on the dotted line, Capricorn. The June Moon, more than any other, tends to make us all feel a little starry-eyed.

What say you then is moonlight madness? For some it's defined as falling in love at the drop of a hat, or handkerchief, as the case may be. Though often a wonderful experience, the fact remains that most of us are more likely to get taken for a ride when operating our vehicles at night, however pleasurable that may seem. Make sure, therefore, that you have also been able to take a good look at your beloved in the light of day. Both parties ought to have ample opportunity to study the algorithms before making their final calculations.

MOTION (MOVEMENT)

What is life? Energy in motion, any kind of movement being grist for evolution.

Whether achieved through mechanical means or by using our muscles, moving reminds us of life in the Astral. In fact, any experience of motion recalls the freedom of that dimension, defined as the ability to move in a completely unfettered manner. In the Earth Plane, we can only move within the context of our bodies or through the use of mechanical devices, whereas in the Astral all our movements take place within the context of thought. There, unfettered thought equals unlimited freedom.

Be as conscious as you can, therefore, of how you move. Moving our bodies to and fro releases important hormones which nurture and support us. That is why exercise is so vital. Not only that, physical exercise requires concentration and focus, both of which are crucial to the expansion of consciousness.

Also pay attention to how the mechanical devices you choose to associate with affect your physical body. Certain modes of transport or pieces of machinery, for example, may temporarily create feelings of dis-ease. Amusement park rides too. Upon discovering such correlations, we have but to make the appropriate adjustments, each physical body having its own set of requirements and series of 'rings-pass-nots.'

It's always the more conscious motion that's the preferable way to go. Motion without some accompanying purpose has the effect of causing us to spin our wheels. In so doing, we may feel like we're being engaged but in reality we're not. Think, for example, of a chicken running around with its head cut off, unaware of its imminent demise.

Having a focus or a destination, let's say point B after having departed point A by train, is supportive to all aspects of being in motion. On the other hand, using a train or any other means of transport for no good reason is apt to be wasted motion and, as a result, not particularly relevant to personal growth.

Especially as it relates to the health and well-being of our physical and astral bodies, the practice of yoga is an excellent example of focused and conscious motion. Indeed, the more conscious we become of our engagement with this plane of existence, the easier our transition to the next one will be.

Is anything really motion-less you ask, or does it just appear to be that way? Well, in answering my own question, I say this: **as one of the givens that always IS, motion is the key to life.** The idea that someone or something can possibly be motion-less is an illusion that does not reflect the reality of what is. Even what appears to us as inertia cannot be static.

Stasis, a concept that I have mentioned previously in these writings, may be perceived to be static but that is simply not the case. In general, any sort of stasis or equilibrium is temporary in nature and may be conceptualized as an energetic bubble containing a series of prescribed or repetitive motions. Therefore, within the sphere of influence of any so-called stasis, motion always occurs.

Motion pictures are a perfect example of this idea. Each movie in its totality from beginning to end represents a specific stasis. The motions that occurred within the construct of the entire project were first determined by the director and then carried out by the actors. Once in the can, however, each film becomes a **fait accompli** ~ *a done deal,* ready to be viewed and re-viewed for so long as it continues to exist. By the way, for the sake of the audience let us all hope that the motion found in any motion picture is never either too repetitive or predictable.

Though it may appear not to be the case, all movement is essentially curved or elliptical, which is to say spherical in nature ~ under ideal circumstances eventually coming back to its point of origin. Even in geometry there are no straight lines except those that are arbitrarily designated as such. Indeed, every line that has movement tends to be circular. We have only to reflect on how we usually move our bodies or how a so called straight line plotted on one side of the planet eventually meets itself, coming full circle, in order to realize that this is so.

MUSIC

When we choose to listen to a certain piece of music, we are also choosing to become temporarily associated with its vibration. Each musical composition has a unique frequency or tone, in some way different from the rest.

Music soothes the raging beast, or so they say. In making this observation, however, I do not speak of a literal beast but rather of the figurative one that lies within each of us, our own often restless and impatient natures. The kind of music we listen to at any given time, therefore, will either help us feel more or less comfortable in our skins.

Staying in tune with ourselves requires more than just the occasional toe-tap. It is also a matter of keeping fit. Indeed, we would be wise to always approach any form of physical exercise with diligence and concentration. Life is about building momentum. We must each do our part, therefore, to keep things in motion.

That vibration is a vital underpinning of our lives is indisputable. Every-thing is vibration. Music is vibration. We are vibration. It follows then that we are also music ~ a symphony of flesh and bone, the equivalent of Shakespeare's mortal coil. Think about that, each of us a piano keyboard or, better yet, the totality of all of the notes that could ever possibly be played on any musical instrument. We are also the instruments, every molecule of our bodies chiming and rhyming in perfect harmony, one with the other as well as with the whole. Yes, my friends, in addition to playing our respective roles in life, we also function as instruments, in effect playing ourselves. By plucking our strings or tooting our horns, we're able to express our feelings, either singularly or in concert with others. From the depths of despair to the heights of glory, music can take us wherever we want to go, including, upon the occasion of our last breath, into the blue of the White Light.

As composers, we are the means of expression for every note we write. As musicians, we are responsible for playing our own tunes. Did you ever think, by the way, that you were both gifted composer and accomplished musician? Those who do often become famous!

There is a tendency among some to make fun of old movie musicals in the belief that in real life people never sing their lines. I, on the other hand, contend that they do, even though we may not always be aware of it. Voice naturally has both cadence and rhythm, the fuller expression of which is tantamount to singing.

Our speaking voices can be like music to the ear. Mine certainly was melodious. Yours is too, (addressing the author) especially when you pitch it a certain way, emphasizing the vowels. Indeed, how we deal with vowels, more than any other single factor, determines our manner of speaking. So, if you've never thought of vowels as being musical before, consider it now. They help to rally our words, causing them to soar.

Accent also plays a role in having our say. Though sometimes perceived of as a curve ball, its use forces listeners to pay closer attention to what is being said. Not only that, there are those who find accents charming. Fact is, we all speak with an accent, the only difference being that some are more recognizable than others. Accent is just one of the many devices the personality uses in order to make itself known.

Were we to listen more intently to our own voices, we would soon realize just how musical they are, our timbre or individual brand of harmonics being registered each time sound issues forth from our mouths. If you will, think of voice as a vibrational stamp, every word indelibly imprinted on Universal Mind.

Each singing or speaking voice is gem-like, to be polished and treasured. In working with our voices, the goal is always to arrive at a pleasing sound. Once there, the records that we cut can then be more easily duplicated ~ as we will.

That all music is essentially heavenly should come as no surprise. However, I propose using the term 'music of the ages' in order to differentiate the tonalities of the Universe from those more specifically associated with mankind, the former serving as accompaniment or background to our own compositions. In the playing, they, too, become part of the whole.

In many ways music rules our lives. Even when we're not actively listening, music is ever present ~ even in silence. *(Speaking to the author)* Listen, for example, to the sound of your refrigerator. That, too, is music. All noise is a form of music. Though we often strain our ears for the good stuff, all of it is good stuff, my friends. There is no noise that is not also either musical or potentially so, depending on how it's packaged.

Had I my druthers, I would have wanted to set these lines to music and sing them out loud. However, this time we will all just have to content ourselves with the printed word.

Ascoltando i Nostri Cuori ~ *Listening to our Hearts*

Music, they say, is heaven, ours, twenty four seven to ring
In our ears. For some it's leaven, for others a license to sing
By Jove, music's a thing that's destined to last,
Once heard, not easily forgotten, like Egypt and its cat god Bast
Whether a heart-felt rendition of *Pale hands beside the Shalimar*

Or some other ditty, musical visions did and still do go far
In many ways helping to keep us right on par

With budgets rather low, RKO still managed to put on a good show
As did Metro, Paramount, UA, WB as well as others in the visual know
But though films were once filled with song and musical climes
Rarely did they ever cross the lines
To where enraptured music played brilliantly shines

Music's there for thou and thee, a celestially inspired kind of a key
Its function? Why, to throw open the door of inter-dimensionality
And gaze upon glory, our intention to be
Wherever it is that music abounds
It's a place in which we can really hear sounds.

RVG

Namaste

A salutation of Hindu origin, the namaste is a ritualized way of greeting people. Reverential in nature, it is both a gesture of equality and an expression of good will. It is also a sign of respect, designed to acknowledge the divinity in each of us.

Practicing the namaste is a simple way to honor our fellow men and women. This gesture, consisting of a prescribed combination of physical movements, was crafted centuries ago to embody spiritual principle. It is accomplished thusly: with a slight nod and bow directed towards the person being greeted, we clasp our hands, thumbs against the chest while voicing this most precious of words. In so doing, we are also honoring the Creator, reflected in the individual now standing before us.

A form of spiritual shorthand, the namaste is primarily soul-centered which is as it should be. Of course, the personality is also to be acknowledged, but at the same time it is well to remember not to become blinded or bedazzled, either by its glamour or a lack thereof. To practice namaste is to see beyond the personality, that is to say, to see the God within.

Namaste is the sort of greeting that we would all do well to think about adopting even though our corresponding custom, the handshake, is also tangible evidence of mutual acknowledgment. Given that in many parts of the world the handshake is a long-held practice, it is likely, at least for the foreseeable future, to continue being the thing to do when people meet or greet each other. In the shaking hands, a brief sharing of energy also takes place, at times a very powerful experience. That said, however, the fact remains that a handshake is not the fuller kind of expression that the practice of namaste tends to be.

In our roles as fair witnesses to each other's lives, the namaste speaks to the footprints we all make in the sands of time. Some might go so far as to define its practice as royals greeting their peers, the implication being, of course, that we are all royalty. Truth is, my friends, we are! A namaste to the East then ~ out of respect for that part of the world having conceived of this most perfect of gestures. Also, to you, dear readers ~ from my heart to yours.

During the shoot of *The Young Rajah*, I sometimes practiced namaste, mostly as a way to stay in character. Then it was but an atmospheric device, a nod, if you will, to the script. Now I see it for what it really is, a splendid way for us to honor each other's presence.

NATURE

Nature is our proscenium arch ~ where we get to stage our lives, playing our parts for their allotted time or, perhaps better said, for so long as they shall serve us.

Our constant interactions with the four elements bring us great comfort. Air nourishes our bodies, fire warms our souls, the Earth keeps us grounded and water sustains us, witnessing our ebbs and flows. Indeed, nature is a glorious thing, quieting our hearts while filling them with love. Not only that, it is an endless story. We would do well, therefore, to become avid readers.

As God is my witness! Allow the greatest of masters then to always be your point of reference. What is a flower? God's breath. The Creator's handiwork. A dollop of All That Is. That which is par for the course, in other words, the norm.

Given mankind's predilection to classify most everything in terms of good, bad or ugly, there are those who would have us view nature through a pejorative lens, even though, truth be told, bad and ugly have no rightful place in the discussion. In God's eyes, there are no differences between weeds and flowers. Why? Because both have a purpose to serve in the scheme of things.

Indeed, nature is perhaps the most glorious evocation of perfection that ever was or ever could be. To know nature is to know God. Go, look out the window. If in doing so you can see but one leaf or blade of grass, you will have once again seen the glory that is God.

Trees, like flowers or human beings, are Heaven on Earth. If there are no forests where you live, adopt an individual tree, preferably nearby, with the intention of establishing a relationship with it. Visit your special tree when you can, if only for a moment. It will serve as your grounding agent whereas you, by dint of having focused your attention in its direction, are supporting its ability to thrive. A fair exchange, don't you think?

The scents of nature, by the way, are to be found everywhere but they are especially noticeable in groupings of the same species. There in particular, they function like natural tranquilizers. Allow yourself to drink them in, for being in their presence is at once both soothing and life-affirming. Stopping to smell the roses now and again has an incredibly beneficial effect on our nervous systems.

Indeed, spending time in nature facilitates our staying in alignment with the planet and its magnetic properties. Plants and trees, like every-thing that IS, are physical manifestations of love. Touching a tree or taking a moment to caress one of its leaves is the equivalent of connecting with a loved one and has the effect of freeing our consciousness from everyday thought and stress.

Bring nature indoors sometimes too, in the form of greenery and the occasional bouquet. Ferns mingled with roses, one of the loveliest of poses! Individually, each flower is like a little burst of energy. When arranged collectively, they really stand out, immediately becoming the focal point of any setting.

What is nature? A symphony of cohesion, with each little bit coming together to make a perfect fit. Indeed, nature is both extraordinarily complimentary and accommodating, even though it is required to know many languages just to have a conversation with itself. If we take a moment to think about it, perhaps the most striking thing about nature is that everything is always just as it should be. Nevertheless, the variance one sees, even among the same species, is nothing less than amazing.

Contemplating nature is like watching the most intricate of dances being performed. In it, the four elements are always at play, beckoning us to join in on the fun. Let us cavort, therefore, as much and as often as we can, not only with the birds and the bees but also with all other manner of flora and fauna. Nature is one of our dearest companions. And, as good neighbors, we must treat it as such. In other words, do no harm.

While in the body, it's advisable for us to go outdoors on a daily basis. Doing so regularly not only helps us to maintain good health, it is like paying a visit to eternity. Nature is a vital force, the same magnetic currents flowing through our bodies as flow through our immediate surroundings ~ and the Universe as a whole.

In nature, my friends, even the shadows come alive. It's there that we are most able to notice the Creator begetting itself, generating reflection upon reflection of the All That IS.

---— ❀ ———

NEIGHBORS

If you will, think on the meaning of neighbors. Those who are nigh or nearby. Neighboring. That which adjoins, a point of reference, such as in the phrase the neighboring street.

You and I are neighbors *(addressing the author.)* It matters not that we inhabit different planes of existence. As we pursue our joint efforts this evening, we are literally just one breath away from each other.

Although it may seem so at times, the Universe is never truly antithetical. Opposites do indeed attract rather than repel, everything that IS furthering unity far more than division. The tendency, therefore, is for us to draw closer. The whole of mankind is neighbor, one to the other. You, I and all those incarnate or disincarnate are actually in close proximity. In fact, we are literally jammed together, even though it appears as though we are not. Although individuality rules the day, we are all linked in some way, at times even being joined at the hip. Think on that!

It almost goes without saying that we all have a lot in common, especially with those who are part of the same circle. However, there are periods in life when we must spend time circling rather than forming circles or being part of one ~ much as airplanes do before coming in for a landing. These fly-arounds are thought of by some as life's little trials, all the more noticeable because, at least temporarily, we know not where to land next. Nevertheless, if we but follow our hearts, fact is, eventually we will. Once there, new neighbors will come to light, making themselves known.

Upon leaving my place of birth, I thrashed around quite a bit before finding my niche in Hollywood. It is unfortunately a fact of life that the places we live do tend to be temporary. But, have faith! Each successive environment figures in the richness of one's total experience, adding yet another ingredient to the condiment or stew that is you.

Many are the times that we lament what we perceive to be our alone-ness, wishing a loved one could be present ~ if only for a moment. Wasted effort, I say! Truth is that we never walk or, for that matter, stand alone. There are always those who are present, be they our guides or others who are in spirit ~ even though we may not be able to see them.

In their proximity, they bestow love. Know this: no other human being need ever be present for us to experience love ~ even though it is often all the more wonderful when they are. Love is ours, always and forever, flowing in a constant stream, permeating the very fiber of our beings. Love can never be rationed nor its spigot ever closed.

The Bible says love thy neighbor. It's an exhortation that we in the Astral take quite seriously. Our neighbors, be they in the flesh or in spirit, are our brethren. For us to be able to see things through their eyes is a gift of incalculable worth.

OBJECT MEMORY

Can man-made or organic items that we have seen or touched in other incarnations recognize us when we see them again? Can we also recognize them? In a word, yes. We'll speak here mainly of man-made objects but we can also extrapolate and apply the same concept to the organic, be it diamond, marble or any other substance.

Object memory works in a subtle fashion rather than overtly. Occurring on the remembrance level, it is generated by touch, focus or even a quick glance. Any or all of these will register on objects, impressing them in the same way that they impress us when we come into contact with them. Of course, if we also happen to be the artisan who produced a particular item in a long-forgotten incarnation, we'll scream with joy upon encountering it again, a master and his **chef-d'oeuvre** (*masterpiece*) together, once more.

However, let us primarily focus on more benign items, specifically those made by others. Yes, strange as it may seem, you and any object that you have previously encountered can and often do recognize each other. Man-made objects, too, have a certain level of intelligence, as does everything in the Universe. But, strictly speaking, they are not living entities and therefore can only reflect, their ingrained memory basically passive. Such memory functions like a mirror, absorbing impressions and reflecting them back to us in the form of memory capsules.

The organic, on the other hand, truly lives and has soul, albeit of a very different order as compared to mankind. Therefore, where living objects are concerned, our mutual recognitions are apt to be even more visceral.

Have you ever experienced **déjà-vu** while visiting a museum? Upon encountering something that seems so familiar, you suddenly find yourself wondering if you have seen it before. Well, chances are you have ~ though not in any museum!

Opera

In a way, life in the flesh is but a **grand guignol,** which is to say a Punch and Judy show. And nowhere is this better portrayed than in the world of opera. What similarities are there between the opera and life as we know it? Pretty much everything.

Operas are musical enactments of some of our most common experiences, usually set in familiar frames of reference. They may be thought of as parables or archetypal tales, performed in and at various vibratory rates, also known as tonalities and settings. In many respects operas are also morality plays because they typically deal with dilemmas that most of us, at one time or another, have to face: common lovers, lovers in common, enemies or various kinds of obstacles, just to name a few. In Italy, we like to refer to these sorts of issues as **le cose della vita** ~ *the things of life,* in other words, the overall subject matter of this book.

Some have opined that my former life was a little bit like an opera. **Sì, forse** ~ *yes, perhaps.* **Almeno, c'era una vita in fretta, la mia** ~ *at the very least, it was life in the fast lane.* As Valentino, I was able to accomplish a great many things in a relatively short period of time, some well-done, others less so. And so it is for all of us. In the meantime, who does not have a little bit of opera coursing through their veins? And who would not break out in song from time to time if given the opportunity? We are all wired to experience our lives with a certain amount of drama. Indeed, most of us would have it no other way!

The phenomenon of opera goes straight to the heart. Operas serve as emotional catalysts, encouraging us to identify with the characters and life situations we see before us, also to try them on for size. By entering the world of opera not only do we get to enjoy the performances, we're also being called upon to go inward so that we may, if we choose, examine our own issues in light of what is being depicted on stage. Attending or listening to an opera provides us with an ideal opportunity to think about what we would do if we were in the same boat as the principal characters.

By the way, all forms of music, including opera, can facilitate changes in our vibratory rates, stirring the pot a bit or toning things down. In choosing what to listen to at any given time, my suggestion is to opt for consonance rather than dissonance, opera in particular being a perfect example of the former.

As human beings we are all capable of channeling music that seems other-worldly. But, as has oft been noted, those who sing in operatic style, **divas** and **divos** as we like to call them in Italy, seem to have a special rapport with music, enabling them to embrace rhapsody and rhythm to even a greater extent than other people. When they sing, they induce feelings of rapture, causing their listeners to be transported across dimensional lines. One has only to think of Caruso in my day or Pavarotti in yours as examples of singers who have often had this effect on their audiences. Then, too, certain arias create feelings of rapture all on their own, regardless of who is singing them.

A story in the form of a musical pageant, opera sears its messages and themes upon the hearts and minds of all those who partake in this wonderful form of entertainment. When the intent is opera, the result is usually delight. And, perhaps even more importantly, a pound or two of fresh insight ~ for no matter how many times we may see or listen to a particular opera, we will always learn something for having done so.

ORBS OF LIGHT

Who or what is inside? Why the magic carpet ride? Sentient beings in the shape of an orb. Disembodied intelligence, invisible for the most part, except to discerning eyes. The speed of a camera shutter will often make them more apparent. Therefore, some of you may have already noticed them floating in the air in photographs.

They are Universal travelers here as tourists and can only exist in this reality by being encased in an orb-like structure, as I've mentioned before the oldest shape in the Universe and its basic building block. They have no name. They cannot be identified. They simply are. Each is self-contained, like a single cell of consciousness.

(Speaking to the author) Think of the rain falling outside of your apartment this evening. If each drop were a single cell of consciousness, they would be orbs. That is the analogy.

This is a phenomenon that is about to get more attention. Those of you who resonate with these travelers are more than likely to be able see them at some point.

PARADOXES

Who is not part and parcel of some sort of paradox? As a result, we often tread the middle ground, the range that lies between any two extremes. Happiness lives there, somewhere in the middle, not at either end of the spectrum. In the middle too, there's always a fulcrum spot. That is where bliss resides. We must, therefore, search diligently to find that hallowed shore instead of always asking for more. In the long run, more often ends up being less anyway.

The term paradox suggests opposites functioning in the context of similar ideas and themes. Opposites attract. They do best, however, when they come at each other from right angles, in a sense creating sparks. The middle ground, again, is where happiness lies. And, most of us usually find ourselves near the top of an S curve anyway. *Note: tests are often graded on a curve in elementary school, the top of the curve representative of the average range.*

Paradoxes always involve propositions that somehow are at odds with each other, in other words, contradictions. Think of a cloth bag in its normal state, right side exposed. The solution to a paradox sometimes involves turning it inside out. We learn by becoming aware of both ends of a spectrum, yet to balance karma and live our lives in a reasonable fashion we tend to stay somewhere in the middle, dance on the head of a pin too, if necessary. Paradoxes always provide us with food for thought, also contrast. In each case, however, we're the ones who get to decide how to deal with them.

There's some kind of a lesson to learn every time we encounter an obvious paradox. *(Valentino's essence then drew the sign for infinity, emphasizing the point where the two circles meet.)* Again, find the middle ground before planting your seeds.

PASSION

Passion is blind only when those who are in its throes choose to remain in the dark. Instead, passion is a dish that is much better served in the light. When illumined and focused, it's a most efficacious thing.

Many people like to think of passion in terms of lust, implying that its driving factor might be sexual or, by implication, base.

That simply is not the case. Although lust may sometimes be part of the picture, passion can also be generated by any number of other factors. When motivated by sex, however, it can also be easily transmuted, becoming readily available for any kind of project or endeavor. How many artists, for example, have you heard of who painted or sculpted their loved ones many times over?

Throughout history people who were noticeably enthusiastic about certain aspects of their lives have often been described as passionate. I definitely was ~ about several things, including acting.

Passion often conjures up other words: engaged, involved, dedicated ~ all lying on same plane of thought. Indeed, one must be all three in order to be really passionate about what they're doing. We would be wise, therefore, not to keep our passions hidden. Like other forms of energy, they must be able to breathe in order to be healthy and strong. When passion is repressed, it's as though we have been turning the screws in the wrong direction, in effect inhibiting the process.

Passions, like steam engines, are driven by something natural, basic and primal, what some might call a self-perpetuating kind of energy. To remain properly aligned, however, they need safety valves, in the form of healthy, creative and constructive outlets. Passion in love, for example, requires the presence of a willing and available partner.

When passion and creativity join forces there are no limitations on what can be accomplished. Again, leading a passionate life requires focus and engagement. We must remain engaged, to be constructively and joyfully involved in our projects for them ever to come to fruition.

Instinctively, passions find resonance in the movement of water, be it tides or the waves of the oceans. Unfortunately, they can sometimes engulf us, momentarily clouding our vision. Be not dismayed, however. Always think of passion as an ally instead of something to be feared. The trick is to be able to identify the source of each, in other words, its genesis. That way we shall never go astray. Neither will we ever float away!

———— ✤ ————

PEACE

Any absence of conflict denotes peace ~ as evidenced by the vigorous presence of White Light. What conditions make peace possible? There is really only one, an elevation of consciousness ~ to the level of the transpersonal and beyond.

The cessation of conflict, what a wonderful premise! Would that it were possible in your world. Though we can learn a great deal by being peaceful, it is also true that at times we have to learn through conflict. Being in conflict, however, does not necessarily mean going to war, either with an individual or a whole nation. All disputes may be settled peacefully ~ if that is what both parties truly want.

Demonstrate peace within ye, my friends. If it fits well, wear it on your sleeve. If not, do not discard. Rather, put it on a shelf so that it may still be appreciated ~ from any angle. Peace is always a viable option ~ in every situation.

———— ✤ ————

PERMUTATIONS

Permutations may be thought of as unique subsets. The concept can be explained thusly: visualize a number of grains of sand lined up, one next to the other. To the eye they all look the same, yet each one is unique, making it a permutation of the initial or model grain of sand in that grouping of specific grains of sand. The point is that any collection of visually identical things have to be permutations because no two items are ever exactly the same. It may appear as though they are but they are not.

As individuated souls we, too, are permutations, each of us somehow different from the rest. Indeed, God's factories create all manner of permutations although there are never any imperfections or seconds. So, my friends, we must respect the manufacturing process. Accept that there are slight variations within the subsets of every-thing and live with that fact. It matters not if we are considering souls, plants or animals of the same species, variety or breed, they are permutations and can never be expected to be exactly the same ~ ever. The only thing we can say with certainty is that each set of subsets will be similar, one to another.

It's fun to go a-searching for the quality that makes item A different from item B when they are visually and conceptually the same, or from the same genetic stock. Yet they are always different, nevertheless. What joy there is in discovering the uniqueness that is a part of every single thing that IS! Let's hear it for permutations! Wouldn't life be a little boring without them?

PERSONALITY

What is personality? Why the flavor of a life-time, rather than the month! It may also be defined as male or female garb in the form of a physical body whose purpose is to shield the soul while it conducts business in the three dimensional world. From an architectural point of view, the personality is little more than a façade, at times hollow, variegated, irregular or even barbed ~ yet always beautifully proportioned. Which costume to wear? What guise to assume? Which mask to choose? Important questions one and all ~ for us to pose internally, on a soul level.

Core personality is determined prior to birth, there being nothing random about it at all. The soul makes the selection, choosing from a catalogue of infinite possibilities where customization and variety are the rule rather than the exception. Each personality, therefore, is a custom fit, tailored to meet the needs of that particular soul's game plan. A 'one size fits all' solution is never even in the offing! Nevertheless, during each incarnation there is likely to be the occasional add-on or remodel, sometimes a product of environment or socialization, sometimes due solely to volition.

As constituted, personalities typically carry at least a few pieces of baggage, karmic residue from other life-times that the soul has decided now needs to be addressed. If more karma is accumulated in the process of doing so, however, then the load becomes heavier, in effect creating resistance. Souls, on the other hand, like rolling stones gather no moss.

Our personalities come equipped with a wide range of facets, some, of course, more prickly than others. Their nature is to be ever-changing whereas each soul remains more or less constant, its essence intact ~ incarnate or not. What allows the soul to grow and evolve is the fact that its personality **du jour** gets to play dress-up for the length of each incarnation, the masks of comedy and tragedy always some-where in the room. Again, the primary function of the personality is to serve as a vehicle for the soul, facilitating its ability to have experi-ences and learn something from them. Therefore, the personality is but a proxy, a three dimensional learning tool subject to frequent cor-uscation. The real you, as has oft been stated, is not your personality or physical body but rather your inner or authentic self.

Think of personality as a temporary resident or tenant at will in the house of the soul. Upon moving in, he or she redecorates the place, attempting to make it their own. But eventually comes the day when the property must be vacated. Every product has a shelf-life. So, too, do personalities.

Each individual incarnation is comparable to a load of laundry going through a complete wash cycle. As the washer empties and starts to spin dry, it signals the end. Water, like the blood in our veins, must continue to circulate freely in order for us to remain vital.

At the moment of the final exhalation, the rigid forms that con-stitute personality soften and melt like ice in the noon-day Sun, in effect auto-deleting. Nevertheless, all the essential trace elements remain, eternally accessible to the soul in question. How wonder-ful is that? Though some of the details may become blurred, the primary components that are part of each former personality are neither lost or diminished. Because this is so, the out-of-body soul is able to re-create the signatures of each of its former tenants at will, even adopting their pen-strokes if so desired.

(*Addressing the author*) As you have long noted, I often access the signature of my life-time as Rudolph Valentino when we communicate. Because they posit both commonly-held and familiar frames of reference, the remainders of that guise have been most helpful in facilitating our writing sessions. That said, however, it is important to remember that the thoughts and perspectives shared here stem from the entire depth and breadth of my being, not just from one personality ~ as much of a public figure as it may have been.

Yes, friends, though I speak to you as Valentino and once was he, I have also worn many other hats, learning something while in each one of them. I am, therefore, like you and all other individuated soul entities ~ more than just the sum of my parts. By the way, upon being decommissioned, personalities cannot be re-animated or duplicated for use in another incarnation ~ either by my soul essence or any other. Though certain aspects of each will eventually be recycled or adapted to suit a new model, under no circumstances could any particular one ever again be exactly the same. Personality, therefore, is very much akin to an sculptor's clay mold ~ to be broken and discarded after only one use. At the moment of death, the mask comes undone thereby releasing the soul from its association with the physical body.

Yet another way of conceptualizing personality is as a cloth of many colors, its woof and warp of prime consideration and Universal Mind acting as master weaver. Were this fabric to be displayed in a store window, it would be remarkable for its beauty and uniqueness, as reflected in the circumstances of the life it embodies. Personality is also designed to showcase each individual's special talents and capabilities. Of great importance in the physical world, it becomes irrelevant in the Astral, functioning, if at all, as a sidebar or occasional frame of reference. There, we interface directly, soul to soul, with no need of buffers or intermediaries.

Nowadays, the term personality is often synonymous with the

expression of individual style and flair. Of course it is that, at least to a certain extent, often being very much about image. However, our personalities typically have far greater impact on us than we might suspect, sometimes even influencing how we think. For example, if our belief systems are primarily grounded in ego or other aspects of personality, we may find ourselves becoming mesmerized by our own mental chatter, unable to see what's outside of the box.

Though I separate personality from soul in terms of this discussion, they cannot exist independently. In fact, they must always work together, their relationship symbiotic. *(Speaking to the author)* Our friend in Boston recently spoke of being able to step outside of himself, that is to say, his personality, in order to observe it from the soul's perspective. A worthy goal! To the extent that this may be accomplished and adjustments in attitude or behavior then made, the greater the degree of alignment between the two.

Consider personality to be like a suit of clothing with a life-time guarantee. It may be that your suit is quite practical, or it may be like the proverbial Emperor's new clothes, finely tailored perhaps, but a little too gossamer to be seen. Neither garment is better than the other. Personalities, like physical bodies, come in all shapes and sizes. We must learn to love and embrace them all.

PHOTOS

The purpose of photography is to capture energy in motion. Can this ever be accomplished? Only to the degree we think it can. The fact is that nothing ever stops vibrating. Snap-shots, therefore, simply reflect an attempt on the part of an individual to grab hold of the vibrational field that was extant at the time the photo was being taken. Even the vocabulary is interesting, take, these days, also being used as a noun.

Especially when documenting the lives and times of their fellow men and women, photographers often find themselves splitting infinitives right down the middle, that is to say, catching their subjects in mid-stream. Indeed, it is their wont to seek out unguarded moments while peering at us through a lens. In so doing, they are able to reveal certain aspects of our personalities while also catching the occasional whiff of soul, wafting skyward like smoke from a lit cigarette.

In Hollywood I was frequently caught on film, not only in movies but in thousands of still shots, many taken specifically to be distributed to the news media or mailed to fans. In them, you ask, was my soul able to make itself known? In a word, yes ~ many times over. That is why some of you still find my photos intriguing ~ not because of who I was or what I once did. To this day, **ma gueule** *(my mug)* decorates any number of public places. Soul-full photos, just like soulful eyes, always have something to say, never going out of style.

The best photos are often the result of both photographer and subject being as relaxed and worry-free as possible. In such circumstances, an ease develops between the two, making it even all the more possible for beauty to hold sway.

Photos are slices of life, as delicious as any piece of ripe pear or section of orange. Do enjoy them from time to time ~ from either side of the camera.

———— ❀ ————

Physical Body

The soul's home away from home, quite literally a temple. We would do ourselves a disservice by conceiving of it in any other way. As with any sacred space, the physical body must be honored, a light kept burning inside for the duration of each life-time. Indeed, the eternal flame dwells within, what we might think of as the animating principle. Bodies, too, are energy fields, like every-thing that IS.

Our inner glow illumines the roads we travel, much as do the headlights on a car. Therefore, we are never in the dark, even though we may sometimes claim to be, at least momentarily. Not so. Light reigns in all planes.

Each body is a body beautiful ~ perfect for that particular soul and life-time, whatever its so-called defects. Perfection, my friends, is the Creator's way of doing business.

The physical body, of course, comes and goes. Disturbing? Only if we choose to see it that way ~ in conjunction with the thought constructs that surround us. By becoming overly concerned about numerical age, we are sabotaging our own well-being. Such thinking, however, can easily be overcome. The idea that a body is ever old or worn out must be refuted. **Do not buy into aging.** Within rather short periods of time the mind can rework the entire body, down to each individual cell. We have only to think it so, the physical body, like every-thing, being a product of thought. My suggestion is to continually regenerate, co-creating til the soul says no more.

Again, although we're only in the flesh for limited amounts of time, life is everlasting. The physical body is but a shell to be discarded from time to time so that we have ample room to grow.

When contemplating the physical self, note the proportionality and perfect relationships, one body part to another. It's most astounding ~ even from my perspective of currently being without one!

PHYSICAL MOVEMENT (EXERCISE)

Walking is perhaps the ultimate exercise, keeping us fit and well-toned. As we stride along, one foot in front of the other, what we are actually doing is aligning ourselves with the planet and, reflexively, with the All That IS. Indeed, we reaffirm our existence in this realm each time our feet touch the ground, likewise when we breathe, experience rain falling or feel the warmth of the Sun ~ in other words, always.

Though a daily stroll may seem par for the course to some, fact is, not enough people take the time to do it. Walking increases our personal vibratory rates, helping us to feel 'at one' with ourselves as well as the Creator. Therefore, always walk with the consciousness of BEING. It is easy enough to do, requiring nothing more than intention.

Blessed be all aspects of Nature's gifts to us, including our ability to move. What simplicities, yet what grandeurs do therein lie! By the way, physical movement is an excellent tonic against depression. A body thusly engaged is one that is not in emotional turmoil.

What about other forms of exercise? Lifting weights, stretching, running, dancing, swimming, sparring, participating in sports or riding horses? Lovely things one and all, many of which were once among my favorites. My advice is to listen to your body. It will always let you know which activities are most appropriate along with when it's best to do them.

Physical Space

The space we occupy in the three dimensional world is never real in ways that we might suppose. What you perceive of as your space, that is to say, the arena where your life takes place, reflects your own approximation of what is. Therefore, it is an interpretation of what seems to be rather than anything else, subject, of course, to change.

To illustrate this point, consider that films often purport to show us their versions of what is or rather, what 'seemed' to be, especially when they focus on some bygone era. Cinematographic depictions and personal perceptions are much the same. They are equally open to interpretation and individual points of view.

Poetry

You ask about poetry and why I am partial to it. The answer is simple. Poems tell stories in concise and picturesque ways, often with a witty turn of words. As far as the poems in this book are concerned, that, at least, was the intent.

There are certain rhythms in my poems which can be both felt and heard. Thusly encoded, they are talismans, dedicated to life itself. All have been inscribed with a personal wish of love to those who wish to read them.

Poems may also be thought of as paintings on a page. The words are shadings and colorings whose purpose it is to give shape to thought. Each starts out as a blank slate, a **tabula rasa** to be used by the poet to display his or her creativity with language. The forms are many, from alexandrine to free verse, more often than not involving the juxtaposition of sound and some sort of play on words. These, however, are merely devices. The single most important aspect of any piece of poetry is that it has the potential of touching us emotionally, on the most basic of levels.

Poems strike chords in our psyches as do the chimes of a clock or the sounds of an operatic aria. In other words, they promote visceral reactions. There are harmonic chords afoot in all of life's circumstances. The gift that poetry offers is to make them more audible.

What is every poet's dream? To shed light on thoughts so that they may truly be seen.

PORTALS

They are literally and figuratively everywhere, most noticeably where we live. We have spoken of doorways before. A portal is not a literal doorway but rather a dimensional one. Inside is one reality, outside another. The portal is our means of access.

Have symbolic portals in your environment, especially in your sacred places, what you might think of as your altars. Ask to go there for guidance. Each time we meditate, we open portals. As I've said, they are found everywhere but really we can and often do just create them with our minds. The physical doorway is but an artificial separation.

Again, think of the inside of your home versus the outside, accessed through a portal, either way.

(*Addressing the author*) You and I stand astride a portal this very moment, on a threshold, looking forward and backward, both of us the Janus face at the very same time. Hard to talk about portals when you're in the midst of one, a bit difficult to gain perspective.

Even so, our lives are such that we usually find ourselves straddling some kind of a portal, one foot on one side of the threshold, the other on the other. That is life ~ in a nutshell. We always live in at least two realities at the same time, sometimes more. Each time we fall asleep we enter the dream world. The second we open our eyes again, however, we're back in this one, seeing whatever it is we think we can see. And, like our friend Janus, it seems we're always just a little betwixt and between.

POTENTIAL

Defined as latent possibility. The unrealized. What is probable but has not come to pass. That which looms on the horizon but is not yet visible.

Nevertheless, potentials often have shape before coming into being. Color, too. They may even, at times, seem have a life of their own. By definition, however, they do not yet have form ~ at least not in the three dimensional sense. That said, it is important to note that all potentials already are, waiting off-stage to become actualized and then integrated into what is, in other words, life in progress. Every potential offers a number of pros and cons, to be carefully considered and, in some cases, even tried on for size.

Examining potentials is similar to going clothes shopping. Many things look good in a store window but only certain ones will also be a good fit. Therefore, not all potentials are for us even if they could be. Think on this: even if they could be. Many are the roads not taken. And so it is with potentials. Be careful then to only activate potentials that really suit you because in doing so you must be willing to buy in to them, each one being more or less a package deal, in order for them to become part of your reality.

Potentials may only truly come alive when they intersect with an available sector in our field of endeavors. I speak here of alignment on the Causal Plane, that is to say, the line up between what can be and what you will. In such cases, the desire to accomplish something causes a choice to be made thereby creating the circumstances for a specific potential to be activated ~ usually as part of a discernable chain of events. Each potential, in order to become actualized, must also be compatible with or complimentary to our life scripts.

For purposes of this discussion, personal reality may be defined thusly: the sum of all our choices to date, strung together like a lovely necklace, each choice like an individual jewel. It may be helpful then to picture fully actualized potentials as a series of precious stones. Latent potentials, on the other hand, are never quite able to sparkle. It is only when they blossom that their intensity is revealed. It must be noted, however, that in order to be actualized they first need to stand out, to be recognized ~ just a bit. We must consciously realize what it is that we want before being able to manifest it.

Once actualized, potentials function like the ingredients in a complex wintry stew. They often remain hidden to a certain extent yet we have put them in the pot precisely to make the dish we are cooking, our lives, all the more pungent, intense and remarkable.

Again, it's important for any newly actualized potentials to fit in nicely with what's already in the mix. Therefore, if during the process of fleshing out a potential we discover that it's contradictory to our game plan, it's time to jettison that idea and move on.

If potential were to have human form, it would be much like a baby, waiting to be born. It is imperative then to give birth only when we are truly its mother and father. After all, if we have no rapport with a particular potential or no real need for it to become a part of our life, why bother?

Potentials are exquisite gifts just waiting to be unwrapped ~ if, indeed, they are for us.

—————————— ✤ ——————————

PRAYER & MEDITATION

All communications with the Creator are essentially the same, whatever the format. Prayer, however, is often thought of in a religious context while meditation is seen as more secular. By the way, in sharing my perspectives, I am not espousing any particular form of religion. That, my friends, is a personal decision ~ completely up to you.

In order to pray or meditate, space must first be created and intention declared. This may be done singularly, of course, or as part of a congregation. When we dedicate time to inner journeys we are consecrating that time. This allows us to be with ourselves in such a way so as to be able to commune with the Cosmos.

With whom do you speak while praying or meditating? Your soul. What is your soul? GOD, differentiated. All is GOD. You are God. God is always in, of and with you, never out there somewhere. Essentially then, when praying or meditating you are having a conversation with yourself. It is a conversation of the One with the One, the purpose of which is to be At-One, aligned with the All in All. Indeed, due to the nature of incarnated life and the unpredictability of the various personalities we continually encounter, *(including our own)* we all require periodic re-alignment ~ if for no other reason than to remind ourselves that we are ONE. Prayer and meditation give us an opportunity to do just that ~ by reaffirming our connection with Universal Mind. **All wisdom is to be found within.** Believe that this is so and so shall it be.

Prayer and meditation are about remembering who we are through an awareness of God Consciousness. Neither necessarily requires sitting in silence although you may choose to do so if that is what works best. The simplest prayer of all consists of only two words: **God Awake.** That said, the God energy within, awakened through intention *(cause)* then aligns with the God energy without *(effect.)* Again, you must remember that ALL is GOD. **There is no 'not GOD.'**

To some, the successful practice of meditation implies stillness plus a diminution of mind chatter. Yes, generally true, but the act of meditating may also involve some form of movement. In fact, repetitive movement often serves as a context for communion with the soul. Commonly accepted notions of stillness and movement suppose that there's a natural dichotomy between the two. That may sometimes be the case but when it comes to meditation, just the opposite is true.

Introspection is one of the most practical abilities we can ever develop. How shall we ever know what to do if we don't stop to think about it first? I suggest, therefore, that we each pray or meditate on a regular basis. Of course, we can also always do both. Why? Because such activities stoke the furnaces within, stirring the embers. As we pray or meditate, the flames of reaffirmation burst forth in fullest splendor, reminding us of the rightness of all life. The purpose of prayer or meditation is to increase our awareness of the glory that is God, which is to say the glory that is each soul, the glory that is **you.**

PRIDE

Goeth before a fall. It can, but that is not for sure, by any means. Let's instead confine our look to the positive side of the coin. There, pride is like a shining light, a glow emanating from the very core of soul. Happy to be alive, my friends, that is the essence of pride. When actively engaged in making our dreams come true, we cannot help but to feel pride in what we do.

Think of it as a powerful anti-oxidant or nerve tonic. With a remedy like this at our fingertips, it's hard to imagine anyone being worried or upset about anything. Overused, however, pride quickly turns to arrogance. Be proud yet never boastful. The claims of brag-garts are apt to fall on deaf ears. Nevertheless, each of us always has something to be proud of, whether it's our innate abilities or on-going achievements. Take a moment every day to feel pride in your accomplishments, big and small, giving thanks as you do.

(*Speaking to the author*) I say to you, be proud of what you do here in writing this book, of the fact that you are an idea catcher ~ capturing them on paper to share with others.

Pride in the form of a puffed-out chest or acts of buffoonery? Do not go there. Instead, take pride in having a positive outlook on life. That is paramount, also pride in your work and appearance. Pride is the shiny new penny everyone likes to find now and again ~ always full of hope.

---------- ✤ ----------

QUALITY

Quality is deserved of all. As sparks of the Creator, it is ours, therefore always at hand. How then shall we do our part? By re-jecting facsimiles, reasonable or not. Instead, seek the real thing. Pale xeroxes are not worth the paper they are printed on, especially where people are concerned.

My suggestion is to lead your life in the most quality-oriented way you can. The question to ask is what is the best I can do with the circumstances I have to work with? Use the answer in the formula-tion of your approach to any situation. Remember, too, that charac-ter is always higher than intellect. In that light, be true to yourself, not only considering what is logical but also taking into account what feels right. By becoming increasingly aware of what you want versus what you do not, quality will reign. **Energy flows where our attention goes.** You alone are the gatekeeper of personal reality. Therefore, remain alert. Quality must first be quantified, codified and certified in order to become bona fide. A simplistic yet particu-larly valid reminder: in all situations, seek the best available.

———— ❁ ————

QUATREFOIL

A quatrefoil is a symmetrical shape formed by the intersection of four circles or spheres, each having the same diameter and meeting at a common point. As you visualize one in your mind's eye, imagine the dynamism created by such a coming together. This form has great importance, both in terms of symbolism and practical application.

Previously, I have spoken of the positive effects of two spheres joining forces. With the quatrefoil shape, we have four. Yes, my friends, you have stumbled on a way to generate power exponentially. It's done by adding more of the same, yet not independently. All of the components must first have a relationship with each other, joining together and co-mingling. Only then can they function as one. It's similar to adding power stations to an electrical grid. Each power station is self-contained yet at the same time connected to the whole. When you increase their number, especially by two at a time, the energy generated becomes greater than the sum of its parts. There is a corollary too, equally true. The larger any conglomerate becomes, the faster it grows.

Internally, the quatrefoil shape creates healthy tension and an equilibrium. In coming together a deal was struck and co-operation ensued. Some harmonic mean was thusly accommodated. While two often repel as well as attract, four working together offer a different paradigm, a shared responsibility that must function harmoniously in order to remain united.

Architectural elements in the form of quatrefoils are quite powerful, wherever and however they are used. Indeed, the quatrefoil shape stabilizes and strengthens any structure it becomes a part of. The ancient Egyptians knew this instinctively, often clustering some of the support columns in their buildings into groupings of four or placing a quatrefoil-like design at the top of a single column, in either case creating greater potency and increased connectivity.

Buildings that embrace the quatrefoil shape are almost always visually inspiring. It's no wonder then that this form has been used so frequently, especially in structures designed to raise our vibrations. Consider, if you will, the number of houses of worship that speak volumes through the power embodied in this shape.

The quatrefoil also provides us with focus. The point of collision, that is to say, the point at which the four intersecting spheres meet, is also the point of matriculation, alpha, the beginning or initiation in its purest form. Think of a quatrefoil as four distinct entities joining forces to function as one, vowing to learn from each other as well as from their common experiences. Substance is always echoed in form. The quatrefoil shape is a literal rendering of the power that IS, a reflection of the compact between the Creator and ourselves. With the greatest of ease, it depicts a perfect union.

———————— ❖ ————————

REINCARNATION

What does a mirror show of a thousand years ago
As we seek our rightful place, this moment in time and space?
RVG

Do not look upon a single life-time as a beginning and end. It is simply one out of many. Reincarnation is fact, not fiction, my friends. In the scheme of things, it is the reality, regardless of nay-sayers and skeptics. Reincarnation just is. Indeed, the multi-layered nature of this phenomenon is so complex as to almost defy examination ~ even from my present vantage point. It is part of life, inexorably entwined. Where I live, we are disincarnate. In your reality, you inhabit the flesh. A physical body or lack thereof is the principal difference between the two.

In either state of being, there is a strong tendency to want to see beyond what was seen before in order to deepen our understandings. This is the basis of evolution. While in the body, however, do we really want to know ourselves exactly as we once were? An interesting question, the short answer to which, I propose, is no. Making concerted efforts to retrieve detailed information from other life-times is simply not required. In fact, to have successfully done so might just make our heads swim. The layers upon layers of relevant cause and effect, along with all the circumstances involved in any one of them, would be mind-boggling.

That said, we will all remember some pieces of our other lives anyway ~ on an as-needed basis. Everyone will at some time or another. It's a natural part of the learning process. These snippets of memory function as Rosetta stones, keys that break the sealed codes, allowing us to enter the akashic records and access, much as we would on a computer, sets of electrical impulses having to do with the incarnations in question. This enables us to recall how a particular life-time felt as well as review some of the events surrounding it that were catalysts for change.

Here are the thoughts of a nineteenth century artist and man of letters on the matter.

Veil

I have been here before
But where or when I cannot tell
I know the grass beyond the door
The sweet keen smell
The sighing sound, the lights around the shore
You have been mine before
How long ago I may not know
But just when at that swallow's soar
Your neck turned just so
Some veil did fall ~ I knew it all of yore.

Dante Gabriel Rossetti

Be not overly concerned with the details when fragments of other times have somehow been revealed. My suggestion is to try to determine the flavor or fragrance of each. To gain greater clarity, here are some questions to ponder: What were the most salient features of that life-time? What was my role or roles? How did my personality choose to express itself then?

Again, when information from other lives surfaces, focus on the bigger picture rather than the details. By adhering to this principle, the potential to learn something greatly increases. Becoming mired in the specifics is counterproductive, causing us to respond inappropriately in the moment or possibly inhibiting the flow of people and events around us. That is why, for the most part, we opt to enter the flesh the way we do, with little or no recollection of other life-times ~ in essence having programmed ourselves to be in the NOW.

Functionally, the reincarnation process has the trappings of a huge recycling project, the purpose of which is to repackage the eternal, wrapping our souls in fresh paper and ribbons each time we're born ~ our new bodies, as is always the case, to be appreciated for their many graces. We also get to experience both sexes from inside out, essential to our overall growth.

Who then is not useful in the grand scheme of things? We all are ~ in our own way and time. We each have our parts to play. Indeed, whatever our lives are or are not, we all must be willing to learn something from them. That, my friends, is the real reason for being.

Why does reincarnation occur? To experience those things that can only be experienced while in the body. We may, for example, want to try something new, revisit past choices, **rendezvous** with a loved one, act as a role model or perhaps accomplish certain deeds. The Universe is not about to leave anything unresolved. As a result, we get to work on ourselves as often and as much as we need or want to ~ with the aim of achieving the goals that we ourselves have set. Doing so may require many life-times, a few, or in rare instances, only one.

Reincarnation literally means 'the act of putting oneself back into the flesh.' It's both a process we must honor and the game that we all have to play.

Veni, Vidi, Vici

Veni ~ I came into this life
Vidi ~ I saw the 'what is' of self-created strife
Vici ~ I conquered my notions of fame
To reaffirm and reclaim
My soul's own true aim
And so it is
Pop the corks, let the champagne fizz
Could it be that another life-time has been labeled as done?
Do we really need to stop just when we were having fun?

Now, once more, time to walk through that door, yes, take a reprieve
A three dimensional leave. Just imagine! ~ such make-believe!
So, it's on to an astral stay
To draft a script and pave the way
For yet another **Veni, Vidi, Vici** kind of day
Characters, plot, setting, but not the Director, TBA!

RVG

———————— ❁ ————————

RELATIONSHIPS (INTIMACY)

When two people realize they are soul mates, it is patently clear to both. In fact, there's likely not a shred of doubt. They know it in a heartbeat, within a split second of becoming aware of each other. The instant recognition I speak of here happens naturally, like the flutter of a bird's wing or a flash of lightning.

In coming together, they immediately notice that all the pieces fit. There are no loose wires or extra bolts. Soul mates complete each other yet at the same time retain their independence. This does not mean, however, that there is no work to be done. While in the body, no one is exempt from the law of cause and effect. Therefore, do as you would be done by, every hour of every day of every year ~ in all your relations.

Intimacy between soul mates has oft been described as breathtaking. It is. Even in casual contact, they spark and arc, creating showers of positive ions. Their union can be summed up in one word: formidable. If you have been fortunate enough to meet up with a soul mate, you know wherefore I speak ~ truly a sojourn in the garden of delights!

That we will encounter soul mates in every life-time, however, is not a given. Most of our intimacies, therefore, will likely be with others. Yes friends, all our relations are significant, even those that appear to be perfunctory. We're here to truck with everyone. Whether in the form of a one-time hello or a partnership of many years duration, every relationship has meaning.

There is no one we encounter who does not seem familiar. We're all part of the human race so we know each other on a cellular level. However, it's only those with whom we resonate most that have the potential of becoming lovers or close friends.

It almost goes without saying that most of us would like to get our hands in the cookie jar just as soon as we realize there's a mutual attraction. Love stimulates pheromones, altering our scents and sensibilities. In such cases, we are like cookies, fresh from the oven, calling attention to ourselves with delicious aromas. Intimacy is an intricate dance, provoking lots of introspection. Do the individuals in question taste good to each other, especially when they kiss? Do they look good enough to eat? Do they thou and thee, in other words, are they affectionate? Is there viability?

Personalities alone are a poor barometer of compatibility. That's why we sometimes find ourselves wondering what two people with apparently very little in common are doing together. Fact is, we'll likely never know. Looks may sometimes play a part but they do not account for all those so-called odd matches that are just perfect for those involved. **Love is the prime factor in all relationships, to a greater or lesser degree. Without love, relationships cannot be.**

Allow any relationship to develop at its own pace ~ with no preconceptions or rush. This is of primary importance. There has to be space for the mutual exploration of feelings, which is to say a scan of the love potential has to occur. Individuals testing the waters with each other are like stars in the night sky looking to join forces. Will their union bring about a burst of energy, creating greater light? Hopefully so, but if not, best to move on. Instinctively, each of us knows whether or not someone is right for us. We have only to look inside to be able to see.

When considering an intimate relationship, two things must be determined: Do both individuals, when blended, create an interesting recipe? And, in being together, are they more of an asset to themselves and their community than they would otherwise be?

The purpose of relationship is to co-create while also consciously sharing the fruits of our labors. First, it is our challenge to make the space for this to occur. Then, the parties in question must take full responsibility for their choices, both singularly and in concert.

Being intimate always tends to quicken the pace for those involved. That alone, however, should not be the principal motivator.

No two relationships are alike. Each is to be cherished for its uniqueness. You might ask what I saw in Natacha. A friend first, then a match made in heaven. I was the lock, she the key. Ours was a tango of epic proportions, at the time much heralded in the press. By the way, one can never possess another. A person is not an object. The desire to possess a someone is not a reflection of love. Love requires letting go, that is to say, going with God.

Accommodation is the art of allowing individual and common needs to be met along some mutually agreed-upon continuum. This is the basic recipe for a constructive relationship.

Human interaction can be defined as two people choosing to plug into the same electrical outlet or set of circumstances at the same time. The connection is supposed to be automatic but rarely is, especially where the heart is concerned. Why do any two beings cross paths? To transfer energy back and forth, learning something each time. In the final analysis then, relationships are nothing more than energy exchanges, reciprocal acts, in most cases gladly performed, that are either more or less successful.

RELIGION

Throughout history, religions have come and gone with great regularity, each proclaiming their rightness while implying that all others were wrong. But were they? Absolutely not. Every religion that ever was or shall be is just as valid as the next, their purpose being to help us better know the one source, God, the Creator.

It is our nature to be religious, whether or not we are affiliated with any particular one. **Being, in and of itself, is the practice of religion.** To be is to be able to see beyond the grave. The Creator is within us, as well as in all things, big and small.

Though we do not necessarily need to become affiliated with a religious organization to fulfill ourselves spiritually, we may nevertheless choose to do so. Each one offers structure, focus on spiritual matters and opportunities for communion with the Creator. Many religions also provide their members with social and political frames of reference. For some, they even become a form of self-identification, almost like a calling card. If you have a need to belong or want to be in fellowship with a particular religion, feel free, join. Keep in mind, however, that one is not above another. Again, in the eyes of the Creator they are all equal.

Attending religious services can be quite satisfying. Indeed, it's important to acknowledge the God force in some way on a regular basis. But we can also do that on our own ~ if we so choose. Religious trappings need not be part of the equation.

The bottom line is this: there is no one who is not religious in his or her own way, try as they may. Why? Because, again, we are all aspects of the Creator.

In the world of organized religion, there are many wonderful people, yea, good-hearted folk, working tirelessly to be of spiritual assistance to their fellow men and women. They should be applauded. Yet beware of charlatans, especially those who in the name of religion loudly proclaim themselves to be the sole purveyors of truth. Don't get caught in such a web!

Some people like to use their religion as a moral compass. All well and good I say. However, know that it's the one inside of you that counts the most. Be not chained to dogma. You and only you are the final arbiter of what is true for you.

❀

ROMANCE

None too tidy, romance is typically frothy in nature. At the outset, especially, it may even be a bit difficult to discern. Once in the air, however, its effect is soon noticed, usually involving a quickening of the heart and mind which causes them to race. There is also a tendency to blush. The excitement and anticipation can be so strong that some people may even experience vertigo.

Think of romance as a buffer, the midpoint between casual acquaintance and full-blown relationship, a necessary step in getting to know each another. It also provides us with a platform to iron out our differences. For example, one person might be gregarious, the other more retiring. One might be joyful, the other less so. Energy re-regulation, vibrational adjustment, getting used to each other's ways, that's what's really going on. In dating, we find out where the sharp edges are as well as where our affinities lie.

Here too, I invite you to do as the Romans did. Have elaborate ceremonies. If need be, role play ~ anything from the traditional to whatever traffic will bear. Have a glass of wine, light a few candles, be a bit quixotic. Surprise him or her. Celebrate being together. Even the hirsute need to let their hair down once in a while.

The weekend getaway provides a perfect opportunity. It's advantageous, especially during the early stages of romance, to be in environments where each person can focus on the other with few distractions. If there is a touch of the exotic involved too, so much the better. Be thoughtful. Go for a midnight walk or swim, stopping occasionally to kiss in the moonlight. Leave a rose or piece of chocolate on the pillow for your loved one to find upon retiring. Have breakfast in bed together the next morning. Pamper yourselves.

Wooing works best if both parties treat each other royally. To do so, we must first look to our inner resources, in particular the heart. Make it a fun exploration!

Romance purifies all those it touches. Consider, for example, the characters in Shakespeare's *Midsummer's Night Dream* and how their eyes eventually were opened. Love brings people together, often in the oddest sorts of ways, surprising us all. Observing a romance unfold is a little like watching a snake charmer ply his trade. Yet romance is without venom, having little or no sting.

Fantasy often plays a part in romance as well it should. So does projection, any actor's screen presence being a perfect example. Both have their rightful place as long as neither is being abused. In the final analysis, however, they must still be unmasked. True love can flourish in no other way.

Becoming right with romance involves really learning how to give and receive. Both must be well-practiced in order for us to become fully engaged. Think of these two verbs as a matched set, each one providing the other with an incentive. It does take two to tango. Natacha and I took that lesson to heart. Hopefully, too, so shall you.

Gestures of love may take many forms: a simple gift today, flowers tomorrow, a kiss on the cheek, or a shoulder to lean on the day after that. The money spent is not important. Rather, it's the thought that counts.

SACRIFICE

What are the qualities of sacrifice? Being willing, though not needing, to throw oneself on a pyre, to be literally burned alive for the sake of an idea, another person or cause, something that speaks of the other or seemingly is outside of yourself. Not only that, the circumstances surrounding it will most likely stir your soul or in some way get you all riled up.

Sacrifices must be freely made, however, with no strings attached. If not, resentment comes into play. By definition they are altruistic, about you wanting the best for someone or something else. There is usually also some sort of a sacred element about them, the unconditional love that stems from being selfless.

Ritual sacrifices were often part of the religions of yore. They still exist today, though mostly in the form of tithes. Those, too, are sacrifices. Each sect, however, defines them differently.

Outside of religion, we each make sacrifices on a daily basis. One thing outweighs another, let's say. Therefore, it might be better for all concerned to do things this way as opposed to that. All OK, but don't play the martyr. Sacrifices must not be subject to any phony motivations. If they are, the sacrificer may get hurt, possibly even singed by the flames. Make no sacrifices or promises that you cannot keep. Be true to yourself. That is the key, not only for you, but also for me ~ and for everyone.

SATISFACTION

A feeling or state of mind, for the most part impossible to quantify or measure, based on the perception that someone or something is meeting our needs. That is satisfaction, in a nutshell.

Whether or not we are satisfied depends primarily on our beliefs, what we choose to believe about the facts often being far more important than the facts themselves.

When satisfied, we're likely to find ourselves feeling particularly well-integrated. Synchronicity abounds and there is an obvious congruence between our physical and astral bodies, resulting in a sense that all is as it should be. Satisfaction and health have a direct correlation. One begets the other.

For some, however, satisfaction implies a surfeit, theoretically there being no room for more. Not so, I say. Satisfaction is always at hand, whatever the circumstances ~ should we choose to avail ourselves of it. The Universe, perpetually satisfied with all that has been wrought, encourages us every day to bask in its ripples. How could it be otherwise?

Even so, two questions often arise. What to do for an encore? And, where to look for more? The options, my friends, are endless.

SCENT

Our soul essences are like perfume in the desert. Not only can we smell them clearly, we can sense them from miles away. Nostrils flaring, we are particularly sensitive to our family of origin, able to recognize members of our own soul group by scent alone.

Everyone is born sporting a particular fragrance, like DNA the distillation of soul. **Eau d'âme** (*soul cologne*) emits a powerful odor, calling out to those with whom we have the most in common while also announcing our presence to the rest of the world. In terms of our own soul group, it's the scent we must live by in order to honor our core selves.

The purpose of having pheromones is to convey information, not only to our own kind but to all species, in each instance producing a specific response. This is how we come to know each other, hopefully promoting greater tolerance for all.

Our sense of smell often takes us beyond ourselves, especially when combined with sight and sound. As Rudolph Valentino,

I loved a number of smells, from motor oil to **pasta con vongole** ~ *pasta with clams,* each with a memory attached. Of the five senses, the olfactory was perhaps my favorite. That is why I always liked wearing cologne. In one of my films, scent was crucial to the plot ~ associated with my character's quest for the love of his life as played by Gloria Swanson. Hers was called *Black Narcissus.*

I urge you to adopt one of your own as well as experiment with others. Have fun. Be playful! Try on a few now and again. There are fragrances to suit every mood. Decide which go well with who you are. Each one you choose must also be compatible with your personal chemistry. What we wear always has the effect of increasing or decreasing our vibratory rates which in turn influences how we are being perceived. Fragrance is no exception.

Each scent then, when combined with our own, triggers a specific response. Indeed, scents often act as catalysts, prompting us to take action. If you suddenly find yourself attracted to someone's perfume or cologne, for example, you just might want to follow them home, but only by invitation, of course. We are all capable of tracking scents, just as animals do. In the case of our fellow human beings, however, what we are really following is their vibratory trail.

Fragrances are too often discounted, viewed by some as petty annoyances rather than celebrated for what they are. Under no circumstances should we ignore them. Instead, I propose they be thought of as garnishes, wearing them as desired or using them to enhance our environments. In so doing, we would be wise to only pick those that have something to say. Our signature scents, in particular, need to be commensurate with our own brand of being.

Ever had the vapors? If fragrance was involved, so much the better!

SERVICE

What we serve best when we are serving is virtue, not vice. Service should only be provided to those who merit it most. Why be of service to people who are perfectly capable of taking care of themselves? The challenge, therefore, is to discern who really needs our attention and, in what form. These are the questions to pose. Being of service to everyone, indiscriminately, is akin to slavery. We serve because we want to serve, not because we have to. No one requires us to be of service. It's a personal choice, though for some people the flavor of a life-time.

(*Addressing the author*) You and I have chosen to be of service in writing this book. In working together, we are also being of service to each other. A noble cause but we do it of our own free will, not because either of us is being coerced ~ karmically or in any other manner.

Service with a smile. Don't take on a task unless you can smile while carrying out your mission. Nothing should be done begrudgingly. In the best of all worlds, we serve ourselves at the same time we are serving others. It is here where love finds its greatest expression.

Being of service often provides remedies that go far beyond what was expected by those receiving the favor. Fact is, service is often serendipitous in nature ~ filled with pleasant surprises. In many instances, we do not even realize that we are being served until much later. Are you there for others? Are they there for you? Of course! That's because we're all involved in being of service ~ in one way or another.

SEX

For some, sex is nothing more than a common denominator, something we all experience from time to time, in one form or another. For others, it's a metaphor for the divine: vital, sacred and, in some cases, absolutely brilliant. Neither group has it wrong; sex is both. Though it's sometimes difficult to describe the pleasure and personal growth encapsulated in any one sexual experience, I shall endeavor to do my best.

Sex enhances vibration. Each time we're sexual, we increase our vibratory rate, defying time by temporarily losing all sense of it. Two people having sex with each other are like a pair of locomotives simultaneously speeding down adjacent tracks, sexual climax being the final station on the main line.

An endlessly fascinating topic, much has been written about sex over the years. I take no exception to any of it. No judgment here, my friends. One form of sexual expression is just as valid as the next, especially when love is in the picture. There is, however, one caveat: do no bodily or psychological harm. This is most important. Both parties, too, must be willing participants. If not, sex has another name.

During my most recent life-time there was much speculation as to my sexual preferences. No need to go into detail here, dear readers. It matters not what I did, either when or with whom. On this subject, I shall remain a cipher, having nothing more to say except that the answer lies in the eye of the beholder. We see what we want to see.

If sex were to have a longtime companion, it would have to be love. Best, therefore, to link them whenever possible, even if only briefly. Doing so is vital. Sex without love can only be mechanical and dry. If, however, we have the intention of being loving, going in, our vibratory levels will rise, inviting further exploration.

Go into any sexual situation with open eyes and an alert mind. See what you can see while in that space. That way you'll know, each time, to what extent love is also lying there beside you, enhancing the experience for both. Sex does not always have to be completely balanced to be enjoyable but when it is the experience is truly remarkable.

Within each of us all possibilities exist, including variations on sex. Different keys unlock different energetic components, each life-time emphasizing some to the exclusion of others. We have all programmed ourselves to have a variety of experiences. In the sexual arena, however, they are usually just limited to one part of the spectrum ~ there always being some things that we are just not comfortable doing. Nevertheless, each time we interact sexually, we're likely to discover yet another facet of who we are, in metaphorical terms a piece of the diamond-like energy that spins and sparkles inside. Indeed, each soul can be thought of as a diamond with many facets, some of which always seem to need a little polishing. That's why we keep coming back for more ~ to do just that. So, polish away, dear friends. Allow the polishing wheel to grind on your stone. By focusing attention on what gives us pleasure, our sexual organs help us to better understand ourselves.

The three-dimensional world would often have us think of each other in terms of sexual orientation, a concept nonexistent in the Astral. There, we have neither labels nor physical bodies. We simply ARE. Likewise, so should ye BE while in the body, feeling free to express yourselves as fully as possible.

Though some people choose to lead lives without sex, that really is not an optimal thing to do. Being sexual awakens all the permutations in the physical and astral bodies, causing them to sing out in vibrational harmony. That is why good sex is such an ecstatic experience, and a great achievement when it occurs, especially when one considers that billions of cells have to work together in order to make it happen.

Sex is such a simple act yet at the same time quite complicated. Not only do the permutations in our own bodies have to function as one, we also have to align, as congruently as possible, with our partners in the same way as we do with ourselves, in my estimation an Oscar-worthy performance!

When sexual confluence occurs, we have four on the floor or on the bed, as the case may be, two sets of physical and astral bodies coming together, literally humming. At the point of climax each of us becomes the Creator, able to see stars. Indeed, it's in the act of sex where we can almost grasp the vastness of the Universe, upon each occasion becoming even better acquainted. Having sex is a spiritual experience that never fails to astound. It is a model for how the Universe works: the co-joining of spheres, in some instances producing another.

When love is present between two people, there is nothing to fear. However, if sex is being used to wield power it has a chilling effect, stifling both parties and negating any form of co-operation. At the very least, the element of mutual respect must be present for any sexual experience to have import. Absent that, sex becomes meaningless, empty and quite possibly destructive.

There are two sides to every bed plus a third option, to straddle both. Which will we favor? How shall we use our sexual energy in constructive ways? Important questions, one and all.

In many respects, our hearts are the true sexual organs. Where they lie is what really counts.

— ❖ —

SHARING

What is more priceless than sharing? *(Addressing the author)* I am sharing information with you tonight. You are sharing the energies of your physical body in order to give me voice through the tip of your pen. Others are sharing their collective forces to facilitate our communication. To share is to love. It is that simple. In fact, each instance of sharing is an act of pure love, coming straight from the heart. Loving and sharing are synonyms, both God-like activities.

Though we usually think of sharing in terms of tangible resources, anything can be shared ~ including our thoughts and perceptions. Indeed, such efforts do not necessarily have to do with money or possessions, frequently occurring outside of those realms. Nevertheless, the act of sharing, in and of itself, creates value in whatever is being shared. Sometimes our sharing is intuitively inspired. At other times it's very deliberate or premeditated. In either case, however, to share is also to grow. Doing so causes both parties to evolve.

The French word **cher** *(dear)* produces a sound that is identical to the English word share. In truth, sharing is something we all hold dear, a thing of beauty and worth ~ to be honored and appreciated.

Here again gratitude is the attitude to have. Be grateful when you are able to share with others. Likewise, accept their gratitude for your having shared something with them.

SILVER

Silver is the poorer man's folly. Like gold it glitters, at times also blinding its beholders. There is one major difference, however. Silver is much more malleable, rarely having the same effect on anyone's good sense or judgment. With silver, cooler heads are more likely to prevail.

Apart from its natural beauty, silver acts as a conduit. Energetically it conducts rather than amplifies, allowing gemstones to be themselves by not adding or subtracting anything. Silver is neutral in its effect. Gold, on the other hand, augments whatever it touches ~ including precious stones, which in some cases can be quite beneficial.

In terms of jewelry, which is preferable, the yellow metal or the white? That's for each of us to decide, a matter of personal style and taste. I liked them both, also the other white metal, platinum ~ much more cerebral in nature.

SILVER CORD

What am I referring to? The apparatus that connects us with the Universe. Our silver cord functions as a trans-dimensional life line. We use it as a conduit for information ~ also as a means of transport, allowing the astral body to journey outside of the physical body during the condition known as sleep. Every-body has one, its purpose also being to maintain the connection between our physical and astral bodies for the duration of each life-time. If you will, think of it as a tether, enabling us to stay in contact with the mother ship.

You *(speaking to the author)* have wondered how the silver cord is used to facilitate communication between us. Your suppositions are correct. It can only occur in the following manner. At the beginning of each writing session, your astral body partially separates from its physical counterpart, walking, if you will, to the edge of the Veil where it remains throughout the session in an altered state. Once there, the technicians working with us on my side, your so-called deceased relatives and others who are willing to help, connect us much like telephone operators once would, by plugging wires into a antique switchboard. Only when a link has been established am I then able to communicate with you directly, in our case using pen on paper. Without the help of our friends we would not have been able to write this book. As a result, it has been more of a group effort than anyone might suspect.

When there is communication between different planes of existence, the silver cord is the means employed ~ both to make a connection and transmit the information.

❖

SINGING

Song is illustrative of God-force in motion, a vibration found naturally ~ everywhere. By singing, we're better able to tune in to ourselves, becoming more conscious of the higher octaves of life ~ even if it's just for an instant.

We need only to have a voice for any song to be sung. Never claim, therefore, that yours is not worth sharing. Fact is, everyone's is. So sing a bit, no matter what others have to say about it. Pitch your voice, then relax. That's all you have to do. If there seems to be a lack of venues, create your own. Sing wherever you can ~ if only in the shower or while driving to work. Doing so helps the fifth chakra stay open, keeping us fit.

Let's remember how important it is to always **do** and **be** love, spreading it around whenever we can. Singing is one way of accomplishing that. In singing, we change our vibration, something that usually has a positive effect on our circumstances. As a matter of fact, expressing ourselves in song actually stacks the deck in our favor, helping us to do the best we can ~ irrespective of the cards we think we've been dealt. By bursting into song what we are doing is creating a more positive spin, encouraging the energies that surround us to tilt in our direction simply by calling attention to ourselves.

Note that song is an integral part of many a group meeting or get-together, religious or otherwise. Why? Because singing typically inspires us. It also mends our worn parts, knitting up the loose threads. I propose, therefore, that each of us sing as much as we can, a so-called good voice not necessarily being a prerequisite.

I loved to sing and often did, both alone and in the company of others. I once even went so far as to cut a record, mostly for my own pleasure but also to surprise my wife. Quite a heady experience!

*Note: The record being referred to here, made in 1923, contains the only surviving examples of Valentino's voice. On it, he sings **Kashmiri Love Song** in English and **El Relicario** in Spanish. Both of these recordings can be found and listened to on the internet.*

SMILE

In terms of form, akin to a nascent moon. Mirth redacted. Angelic-like deportment. My window on the world. Yours and everyone else's too. At least it ought to be! Wouldn't it be wonderful if we could do everything with a smile?

Smiles are many things, from a sign of welcome or love to an expression of exuberance. Like any grouping of partial circles, there's bound to be some openness in each. Every smile is unique. In fact, they can never be reproduced. Why? Because each one has a meaning that's specific to the occasion. When you see a smile, therefore, you are seeing it both for the first and last time.

Smiles are just one of the many ways in which we bless each

other. When you see someone smiling, it means that on some level their heart is open. The tenderest of smiles always come from babies. None could be sweeter. Smiles are God's gift to existence. They help us get through the day. Other ways to think of smiles: beneficent acts, emissaries of good will, the essence of **sí, se puede** ~ *yes, we can.*

SOUL

What is soul? God individuated, that which is immortal. As opposed to personality, the real deal. The personality is but a costume to be changed upon occasion, capable of morphing to suit our needs, whereas the soul represents our core self, the essence of who we are, a multi-faceted subset of the ONE. It is a conglomeration in a single package, expressing the distillation of innumerable life-times.

Think of the soul as a sponge, always soaking up what's essential for us to know. Nothing escapes its purview. Like DNA, the soul is our signature ID, inviolate and tamper-proof. It is also our scorecard, the record of our lives. Our soul reflects the totality of everything we have lived, loved and experienced to date ~ in all forms and periods of history. A vital living thing, it can be compared to an atom constantly in motion. Though we all have a lot in common, each of us, nevertheless, is completely unique.

No one can say for sure what size a soul might be. In fact, any attempt to measure one would surely come to naught. Souls, however, are quite fluid, able to fit into the physical body as snugly as a debit card might when inserted into an automatic teller machine. As a matter of fact, our bodies are similar to banks. We put in and take out energetically, constantly making deposits and withdrawals.

Soul is the IS of the verb to be, eternally so. Each has its origin in the miracle of creation, the thought of Being. Souls are and always have been essential building blocks. Indeed, they speak of continuity. It is through them that the pyramid of life continues to expand.

Our souls, too, are the repositories of karma, every thought and action being recorded therein. In this respect, they function as seismometers, noting every movement or hesitation, no matter how minute. Some karmic issues are relatively smooth, needing little or no tweaking. Others are jagged, having edges that are both definitive and sharp. Each life-time requires us to do our homework, we being the ones who have chosen the lessons. Our task is to re-regulate any karmic fragments we have decided to bring in with us. Think of them as hiccups, some barely noticeable, others too loud to ignore.

In dealing with karma, our aim is to defragment ourselves, much as we would periodically do to a computer to ensure that its innards function smoothly. As a matter of fact, it is the nature of the soul to constantly seek defragmentation ~ with the goal of making itself as whole as possible. In so doing, we increasingly become One with the All in All ~ in fullest splendor.

Incarnated, the soul and its temporary resident, the personality, are WORD made flesh. Even when clothed by personality, however, it's important to note that the soul is always present and fully participatory. That said, in any life-time it will only be revealed in direct proportion to the diminutions of said personality or by dint of a newly illumined consciousness.

Souls are manifestations of the omnipresent Universal Mind. Their existence underscores the presence of God because, again, they are God ~ individuated. The Creator comes to know itself through the experiences of each.

If you will, visualize the soul as being like a planet, our own little world always in the process of becoming. In a sense then, we are like well-worn pebbles, having been around the block a few times yet still never having seen or done it all. I leave you with this thought. There is always something more for us to learn ~ in the body or out.

Postscript

Question ~ Can a soul choose to inhabit more than one physical body in the same time and space quadrant thereby dividing its attention?

No. Such attention has to be self-contained, brought to bear on one body and one perception at a time. It may not be scattered, at least not intentionally. That is the short answer to your question. Good thinking, however. Theoretically it could be possible. Practically it is not done. We would be doing ourselves a disservice by not concentrating on one point in the spectrum at a time. That is why we came into a body, to be able to do so.

Question ~ Does any portion of the soul remain in the Astral during incarnation?

No. Each individual soul fully inhabits a body once it has entered the flesh. It is all there. No fragment is left behind. Of course, part of each so-called day is spent in the Astral anyway ~ when we are sleeping. So no need for splitting ~ to be in two places at the same time. We are either in the body when awake or out of it when sleeping. Either/or ~ no in between.

Question ~ As souls do we have u core identity by which we are known (as opposed to Earthly name markers) or do we just choose a name we like?

It is completely up to each soul what they shall be called. It changes too, not a fixed thing. Just as we change our names from incarnation to incarnation so, too, may a soul change names between incarnations. Souls may rename themselves as their vibrations evolve or they may choose to remain associated with a name they once had. Einstein and Edison, for example, come to mind. Again there are no fixed names. *(Speaking to the author)* I chose to be named Valentino cause you knew me as such, also for the purposes of writing this book. I was also many other names to you as you have been to me. The name is not how we recognize each other in the Astral. Rather, it's by energy congruency, how we actually interface of which there are infinite possibilities. In my realm, we envelop each other energetically as a way of greeting, noting how the pieces fit, that is to say, what our congruity or lack thereof is like. The name game is really not used here although we put names on like guises when we communicate with you. We have to or you would not recognize us. It is the same as you having to wear a body in order to be recognized by your fellow men and women.

In spirit we need not flesh or sound. Why? Because the scope of our vibration is much larger, more all-inclusive, infinitely complex too. Every two of us fit together very differently. Therefore, when we interlock we shall know them. **Ecco fatto** ~ *there you have it.*

Soul Groups

What constitutes a soul group? It is a loose association of individual souls forming a union, all part of the same batch. Numerically, each may vary, having anywhere from two to some larger, indeterminate number. Their nature is to be inchoate, which is to say not yet fully formed, in and of itself a rather dynamic proposition.

Are we ever members of more than one soul group? And can we, of our own volition, change them? No, we are not and no, we cannot. The entities that make up each soul group all have to be quite similar energetically and also, while in the body, cellularly, molecularly and atomically on the same page. Indeed, every soul group requires its members to exhibit a certain amount of congruence, working together as they do to create an energy network, a grid whose function, once established, continues on eternally. Using it as a platform, individual members are then able to pursue their dreams, contributing to the collective development of the whole while at the same time fulfilling their own potentials.

The purpose of each soul group is to provide a framework for its members to initiate and complete various group and individual tasks, in the bigger picture all having to do with their spiritual purpose. Such tasks are the life-blood of every soul group and integral to its evolution. Any member may participate, in the body or out.

Life is often expressed in a collective way. That is how our respective soul groups come into play ~ through the ties we have with each other. Within that alliance, we sometimes pool our resources for the purpose of achieving something greater than ourselves, acting in concert with our fellow members. We may also have to part company on occasion as that, too, is sometimes necessary for mutual growth. Meanwhile, our individual life plans continue to unfold, each of us bound up with others for specific lengths of time until the work we have set out to accomplish has been completed.

Soul groups are our true families of origin and, whether or not we know it, our primary support systems. For each of us they serve as grounding agents, playing the role of built-in surge protectors.

That said, it is highly likely, though not exclusively the case, that our spirit guides will also be part of the same soul group as we, basically for two reasons: because we're on the same wave length and also because like attracts like. Indeed, each soul group flavor is unique, unable to be replicated within the context of any other. In practical terms being a member of a particular soul group is like having a common scent ~ analogous to each member of the animal kingdom being able to recognize its own kin.

Once associated with a given soul group, we are meant to evolve under its auspices throughout the eons, no matter how far afield our experiences may take us. Within each, there is more than enough room for infinite unfolding to occur.

Though circumstances vary, it is important to understand that you and your fellow soul group members are always working together in some way or other, even if each appears to be handling things on their own. Evolution is primarily a group-oriented process rather than a singular affair. Of course, we also interact daily with soul entities from other soul groups ~ to be expected. But, such interaction does not equate with temporary membership. Each individual soul is a member of one group and one alone.

Soul groups, like all things, are born of the Creator. Each one is the result of a meeting of minds, if you will, a **rendezvous** with destiny. Becoming vested requires a combination of free will, harmonic convergence and proper alignment. In other words, it's a matter of being ~ in the right place at the right time.

Soul Mates

Soul mates are those with whom we are intrinsically linked, that is to say, those with whom we can have real heart to hearts ~ literally, a special breed. Far more than friends or colleagues, they are matches made in heaven, vibrationally speaking quasi-identical. As such, their capacity for intimacy is truly amazing, sometimes even to the point of being able to complete each other's thoughts. By the way, someone from another soul group can never be our soul mate. That, simply, is not possible. There would be far too many complications.

Must a relationship with a soul mate always have a romantic or sexual component? In a word, no, though they may and often do ~ but, out of choice, not necessity.

In most cases, each of us has more than one soul mate at a time. Sometimes many. I shall not attempt to place a number on them because they are subject to change. As we continue to evolve, so do our respective vibrations. As a result, those who were once potential soul mates suddenly may no longer be. Not to worry. New ones usually come on line just as others start to fade. It's a fluid thing, the reason being that each entity evolves at his or her own pace, not necessarily always keeping up with the Joneses. Who we are vibrationally is constantly in flux, therefore the variance of which I speak. Coming together as soul mates, however, requires that we at least be in the same ball park, something that is usually only possible for certain lengths of time. That is why I say they come and go. So, too, do we.

Shall we and our former soul mates ever cross paths again? Yes, most definitely ~ upon occasion. What causes soul mates to meet up? The answer is always the same: a combination of free will and being in alignment with each other, which is to say being in sync vibrationally. All of this is dependent on evolution, where one is at ~ literally and figuratively. Scent and sound play a part too, the eyes not at all. We recognize each other through our noses, also by the vibrational fix of our voices. By sight, never.

What is their work together? The same as with anyone else: repair jobs, fix-ups, extreme make overs and in some cases lite refreshment in the form of a quick picker-upper. Though I regale you here with commercially inspired phrases, I do so to make a point. The sky's the limit. Soul mates may do anything they choose together as long as they help each other grow. Natacha and I were once soul mates. She helped me expand my horizons as I did hers. During the time we spent together we both had a lot to learn.

Do soul mates also seek each other out in the Astral? Yes, if that is what they both desire. Again, it depends on whether of not it is possible vibrationally, their current focus and a whole host of other factors ~ all of which come into play. But yes, being in each other's company can easily be accomplished where I am. What we co-create we then review, in the same way as while in the body ~ except that what we do here can be seen instantaneously.

Having contact with our soul mates means being in close quarters for a time, like passengers in a tiny two-seater sports car. While tooling around, both individuals literally fill each other's empty spaces, creating something of value. Soul mates are the purest form of family any of us can ever know. What bliss it is to grow while basking in each other's glow!

Spheres & Planets

Though it may seem a bit odd to refer to them in this manner, spheres are the building blocks of the Universe. As such, they play a fundamental role. From our perch, we see planets as large spheres, each in some way a force to be reckoned with. And so they are. However, in the vastness of space any planet compared to the whole is rather miniscule. If you will, think of it this way: in the bigger picture each is but a grain of sand, differing only slightly in size and volume.

Planets, in the doing, generate their own energy and motion, creating what appears to be a stasis, what we label as their orbits or rightful places. Periodically, anomalies in the status-quo produce some form of anti-stasis which causes existing conditions to morph, a process that tends to repeat itself over and over again. Though we often think of planets as fixtures in the sky, none are truly static. Instead, each is in a constant state of flux, its relationship with the Universe always a dynamic one.

Every planet, by dint of its existence, is a visual reminder of the perfection that surrounds us. Spheres are matter in its original form, the most essential shape there is, generated, as was every-thing, by the Word. What say you, Rudy, on this matter? BE, my friends, is the WORD, the one that turned on the switch, activating all dimensions.

Planets are mini-universes, in and of themselves. So, too, as a matter of fact, are human beings or atoms. Every-thing is. All that relates to each planet, its moon or moons, for example, is the same as that planet relating to the solar system surrounding it. Each solar system in turn likewise relates to its host galaxy. I speak here of correspondence, in this case spatial relationships and their natural symbiosis. When you see a sphere of any size, therefore, know that you are witnessing the divine. Amazing that such a simple shape is the driver for ALL THAT IS.

If you will, imagine the number eight reclining on its side rather than in its normal state. In that position, it becomes the symbol for infinity, two spheres joined at a single point of contact on their circumferences creating intertwining loops of energy ~ self-sufficiency in its most perfect state. Yes, oddly enough it's only in relationships where we can most fully be ourselves.

We ought to think of ourselves as the balls of energy we really are rather than the physical bodies we all seem to be. That is the fact of the matter. By emulating infinity, we become creation ~ catching itself in the act.

Like attracts like. In this way, life goes on ~ in circles, or rather in spheres.

---⊛---

SPIRIT GUIDES (PERSONAL ANGELS)

Have you ever had a **deus ex machina** *(hand of God)* kind of moment? In other words, have you ever felt like you had just been saved from a disaster through no doing of your own? If so, chances are your guides were involved, in some way or other.

How do we choose our spirit guides? How do they choose us? Not randomly, I can assure you. Who works with whom is based on precise calculations, taking into account the needs of all concerned. Some of our spirit guides are always available, others less so, each according to the agreements we forged with them prior to incarnating. Many accomplish their work quickly while others make it last. In all cases, however, our interactions with each other are fueled by divine love.

I can be home again, any time. Remember this line. The Astral is always imminent. So, too, is transition. The home I am referring to is, of course, the other side, the Astral Plane. When called, we're always ready to go ~ should that be required. At the moment of death our spirit guides gather round showing us the way as though we might have forgotten it, which, of course, no one ever does. Comes the Light and it's all over ~ in a flash.

For some, going home may seem like a scary thing to do. Rest assured, it is not, each of us having been there, done that countless times before. Dying, however, does involve a leap of faith, stepping, as we must, into the unknown. But friends, fact is the other side is not unknown to any of us. We have simply forgotten what it's like to be there, a temporary condition ~ part of the cost of doing business while in the flesh. Upon arrival it only takes a moment to effect a download, the sum total of all our experience and knowledge to date ready to return the forefront.

Again, what happens at death is our plan, not anyone else's ~ based on what's appropriate for us. Not only have we devised it, we are starring in the production ~ for all intents and purposes a party of one. Our guides are in attendance primarily to witness our joy. However, should we need or desire it, they stand ready to offer their assistance, welcoming us with open arms.

Our spirit guides are those who were once our partners, husbands, wives, lovers, friends or family members, as well as those who we may not have ever met. Their job is offer us love and support ~ without reservation. In many respects, they are personal angels, constantly aware of our safety, needs and desires; nudging us at times, yet not inserting themselves into situations where they do not belong, that is to say, those that for karmic reasons we must handle alone. Think of them as prompters, just off stage, helping us to mind our p's and q's.

What we do during each life-time we, of course, do for ourselves. However, at the same time we also do whatever it is that we are doing, at least to a certain extent, on behalf of our guides, filling in some of their blanks as well as our own. What is needed for our work together to be most effective is to have similar bloodlines from the outset, more specifically, many of the same under the skin issues, recognizable on a soul level.

Indeed, prior to each birth it is our similarities that bring us together, the principals being the soon-to-be-born soul and those in spirit who are willing to make a commitment, primarily members of the same soul group. Once an agreement has been forged, each party has a contractual obligation to fulfill ~ in most cases lasting a life-time. Others, too, may join in later on an ad-hoc basis, having posthumously decided to lend a hand. Because the number of players is flexible, the dynamics among us may vary ~ depending on who exactly is participating. However, under no circumstances is the quality ever strained. Even though we may not be able to name our guides, subconsciously we do always know who they are. No one can take up that mantle without our permission, even those who come to the table after the fact.

As guides we are all equal. Therefore, any guide may render just as definitive a service, depending on circumstances, as any other.

True, some have more experience to draw upon but that does not necessarily make them any more valuable. Not to worry, however. In terms of guides, we always get exactly who and what we need.

Though we and our guides are usually quite close vibrationally, in no way are we co-dependent. If anything we are co-creative, an important distinction to make. Please do not look upon the relationship we have with our guides as some sort of **quid pro quo** arrangement. It is not. Rather, it's a natural phenomenon, a symbiosis involving shared responsibilities.

The great majority of those who are in the body now have been guides before themselves, working from the other side. Fitting I say, like the perfect pair of shoes. Even so, we tend to look at the process as a one way street, seeing ourselves on the receiving end. In truth, however, the traffic goes both ways, much as it would in peer counseling. Granted, our guide's points of view, coming from where they do, place them on a different footing. But we, too, can see and often do, which is also quite helpful to them. In the bigger picture, my friends, we are all guides for one another ~ in the body or out, consciously or not ~ at all times. Think about that. Being a guide is very much a communal experience.

How many spirit guides do we usually have around us at any given time? The answer is un-knowable. Why? Because the figure changes with every application of circumstance. The bottom line, however, is that we are never alone. We always have an entourage, one or more of our guides with us at all times. Those of you who like to see yourselves as solo acts, think again. Frankly, that's an impossibility.

On a practical level, how involved are they in our lives? According to our contracts with each, to varying degrees. There is, however, one important caveat, applicable to all. Under no circumstances may our guides ever do any of our work for us, no matter how much they love us or who they once were. **È vietato,** as we say in Italian. In other words, it's an inviolate rule.

Nevertheless, when danger is afoot they will always make us aware of it, helping, if necessary, to maintain the integrity of our physical bodies. Indeed, whatever the situation, our guides will always do their utmost to be of service, shedding light on what's at hand. How so? By calling our attention to the cues and clues before us, just waiting to be seen. In many ways our guides are our most constant teachers. We are always learning something from them, both night and day. Their primary interest is to support us to the extent they can ~ as long as it does not interfere with karmic law or in any way supersede what we ourselves have deemed it necessary to experience.

That the Veil is porous should come as no surprise to anyone. Energy, therefore, can be transferred through it and often is, the point of origin primarily being our guides. Their efforts show up in a variety of ways: out-of-the-blue thoughts or feelings, symbols placed strategically in our pathways, even so-called coincidences like discovering that the person sitting next to us on a plane is reading the same book we are. In fact, how many times have we noticed that the coincidences in our lives were not? I invite you to think about that, friends. Our guides are often keen on providing us with punctuation marks for what has just occurred lest we forget its importance. Again, it is mainly via the things that we 'happen' to see or hear that our personal angels communicate with us. In each instance, love is their ride ~ creating a link across the divide.

During times of crisis our guides will sometimes do even more to stay in touch, upon occasion literally reaching into this dimension. To do so, however, they must first wind themselves down vibrationally, that being the only way for it to occur. This allows them to walk the line, the boundary separating the dimensions, a prerequisite for any sort of intervention. It is only then, through the use of the anomalies in the Veil, that they are able to extend themselves on our behalf ~ though again only indirectly and under certain circumstances, such as when our physical safety is being compromised.

I invite you to also reach out and touch from time to time, in particular those in spirit. Yes, it is possible to do so. To hold hands with one of your guides or, for that matter, with anyone on the other side, call out to them first, invoking their presence. Then extend your arms out in front of you keeping them perpendicular to the floor, hands open and upstretched. Finally, imagine your hands touching theirs, palm to palm, with only the Veil in between. Though we may not see anything while doing this, we'll always feel the heat ~ a wonderful sensation and proof that someone is there ~ before us.

Do our guides ever make personal appearances? Yes, it has been known to happen. Performing such a feat, however, is tricky business requiring willingness on the part of the beholder and great skill on the part of our guides. In short, conditions have to be perfect.

Much as they might like, our guides can never tell us everything. In fact, they can only review certain portions of our overall life plans, if you will, the declassified sections. We, on the other hand, have it within ourselves to access them in their entirety. In terms of information, therefore, there are limits as to what our guides can provide. They can only reveal so much without removing the ultimate responsibility we all have to ourselves: resolving our own issues as best we can, and of our own free will. Nevertheless, our guides do sometimes make us aware of the options, including, upon occasion, the roads less traveled. It is up to us, however, to decide whether or not to take them. From time to time, they also reveal traces of diamond dust, those karmic fragments having to do with previous choices and other life-times, now impinging on the current one. We must then work with what we've been given, making sense out of the snippets of information that our guides in their wisdom have chosen to share.

Evolution is measured in degrees, due diligence the marker. The goal of humanity is to create greater placidity in the lake of consciousness, to have as few stones as possible skimming the surface or making waves. So that this may be accomplished, we each must do our part.

---❁---

Spiritual Wisdom

E Lucevan le Stelle ~ *And the Stars kept on shining*

Stelle, Étoiles, Estrellas, Stars,
By whatever names and however spelled, they're never quelled
They set the bars
For life's symbolic trips to Mars
Those times when we just cannot plainly see
What we're about, for far too steeped in doubt are we
Stuck, up to our necks in sand
Strangers slogging through some far distant land

The night sky eternal, replete with Tiffanied jewels
Brings insight, joy and great delight to all the fools
There ever were and ever more shall be,
You know, the ones who say but isn't it all about me?
No, my friends, seeing is the key
And what you choose to do in life that in the end
does make things right

When we raise our eyes to the dark blue skies
that frame star-lights above
We wipe away the vestiges of clay, all in the name of love
That is to say, the sum of sand mixed with tears
Allaying any specious fears
To move beyond adverse thought and its venal grasp
Into the Light as humbly do we clasp
Our hands in gratitude
For this simple shift in attitude
Was occasioned by remembering that we
Are mere mortals while the stars shall ever be.

RVG

SUFFERING

Suffering is a condition of our own making, a state of mind that need not be. Rooted in the personality, it stems from the perception that things are not as we would like them. Simply put, we seem not to be getting our way.

We're not meant to suffer but do so anyway once in a while, just for the hell of it ~ or so it seems. Most of us have chosen to include some amount of suffering in our repertoires, seeing it as a part of being in the body. That does not have to be the case. Nowhere is it written that suffering is endemic to the human condition. However, if it is on your agenda, embrace it rather than recoil. Use it as a means to grow and evolve. We have only to look around us to see examples of those who have been able to do so.

For some, suffering is an all too willing spectre, yea in some instances a familial ghost. Walk not the halls of your ancestral castle wrapped in shrouds. We need not assume any of our family's burdens just to carry on a tradition.

In all cases, forgiveness is the balm that heals all wounds. By not forgiving, we become a party to our own suffering. Blaming others has the same effect, likewise being envious. Avoid holding grudges, whatever their origins. They serve no one. Instead, be grateful for what has already been bestowed. In so doing, that which is yet to be yours shall come forth. Perceived lack is but a figment of our imagination, holding no sway over the future.

Clinging to ideas when they're clearly not serving us will do nothing except create more problems. Stubbornness is yet another form of suffering ~ again, purely of our own making. The moment we become willing to let go we start to free ourselves from all manner of entanglements.

When indulged, suffering tends to feed upon itself, growing exponentially. Such is the law of attraction ~ on the down-low. When you observe someone suffering, therefore, choose to be an antidote rather than an enabler. You'll be doing everyone, including yourself, a big favor.

Ultimately, whether we suffer or not is a function of attitude and what we will, apart from any illusion. Most suffering can be alleviated by simply letting go of the desire to be a victim.

---- ❀ ----

SUICIDE

The purpose of addressing this topic, as with all else in this book, is to provide you with opportunities to examine your own points of view. I, of course, have my perspectives on the matter which I will now share. You, of your own volition, have yours. This is as it should be.

O death, where is thy sting? A question sometimes posed by those in desperation. Is suicide a sin? Does it lead to eternal damnation? Is the taking of one's own life a catastrophic event? Or, is suicide about something else? That is the question.

Suicide functions as a release valve for those who are either physically or emotionally worn out or who, for one reason or another, need to break out of the physical body before it meets its natural end. To the observer, suicide seems like a vicious act of self destruction. Indeed, conventional wisdom would have us believe that anyone taking their own life must be a coward or, at the very least, woefully misguided. I propose instead that we view it more dispassionately, as but one exit strategy out of many, just another way for us to go home.

The important point to make here is that committing suicide, IF it is to happen at all, is simply part of the script that you yourself wrote prior to incarnating. No one's death is random. We each have a hand in it, in one way or another. Remember that the lengths of our incarnations and means of death are of infinite variety. Although no incarnated person consciously knows his or her date or manner of death beforehand, for the most part the 'die' has already been cast.

Contrary to popular belief, the taking of one's own life does not have any sort of horrible spiritual implication. This comment may not sit well with some of you, but it is the truth. You must look at death as a catalyst, first and foremost. You are the author of the script that will trigger that event, more aptly called transition. Again, you decide it all. If suicide is to play a role in your departure, it may be because there is something important for you to learn from the experience.

Another way of looking at it is that there are many people in the world who are slowly committing suicide each day anyway. It may take years but eventually it will happen. For example, if you knowingly eat lots of sugar when you are diabetic, drink alcohol when you are allergic to it or smoke cigarettes like they are going out of style, it is fairly obvious that you are hastening the demise of your physical body. In many instances, succumbing to our addictions can be likened to taking slow, deliberate but very conscious steps down the road to suicide.

At some point in just about everyone's life thoughts of suicide will arise. However, that does not necessarily mean that it's going to happen. Suicide is yet another choice among the endless number of choices each individual must make. No one can either steer you in that direction or away from it. If it is to occur, it will be because you have willed it so.

Be as supportive as you can to those in depressed states of mind. But, generally speaking, do not attempt to monitor them physically. It does no one any good if we try to be the hand of God in these matters. There are exceptions, of course, specific instances when one soul entity can and does intervene in the life of another in order to prolong it ~ but only when both parties have karmic agreements to that effect.

As stated previously, physical exercise is a wonderful tonic against depression. Think of it as an anti-suicide pill requiring no special prescription, one that everyone would be wise to keep in their bag of tricks.

---- ✦ ----

SUN

Il Sole ~ *the Sun,* in the language of my native land. Contemplate that word phonetically: 'so-lay' ~ so far away and yet so near. The Sun is a metaphor for the dualities of life. It is both far and near, like everything, creating a sense of simultaneous reality. We perceive the Sun as being out there somewhere, millions of miles away, while at the same time we feel it warming our skins. Quite a curious phenomenon!

The Sun represents the forces of creation. Therefore, allow it to touch you to the core. Always a marvel to behold, the Sun is the focal point of our corner of the Universe. Think of it as a perpetual font of energy, a prime example of the masculine principle with planets as its progeny. The purpose of the Sun is to power the vehicle that is the Earth Plane, providing the wherewithal, at least from our point of view, for life to occur. It functions like a giant transformer, allowing us to experience ourselves in different lights. From where we sit, the Sun is our friend ~ as long as we keep our distance.

In terms of our current living arrangements, nothing, with the possible exception of water, is as essential to life as sunlight. Without it no organism could ever grow. The Sun, of course, will always have its ups and downs, moving from day to night and back again every twenty-four hours. The gentleness with which this occurs, however, is truly remarkable. It's almost as though someone in the heavens is adjusting a rheostat, moment by moment.

Science says that the progression from day to night and back again is due to our planet's revolutions. Yes, but isn't that just perfect? The environment we live in offers us light and dark in rapid succession, the perfect blend of yin and yang.

We've all heard tell of the music of the night. Well, during the day the Sun chimes in too, playing heaven's melody. It is a force to be reckoned with, life-giving and sustaining, an endless source of joy ~ exactly like the energy that flows through every cell.

The solar plexus, by the way, is the focal point for energy generation and distribution within the human body. Yes, in many ways our bodies are like miniature replicas of the solar system, what I would deem a perfect 'sol-ution.' Having fun in the Sun. That's really what we're doing here. Some call it living our lives.

Sole e Vita Sono i Stessi ~ *Sun equals Life*

Sole, per piacere
Da da bere sopratutto
È un dovere.
Prendi pace
E rendi la vita felice.

Translation
The Sun
Of its own free will
Above all
Fulfills our needs
Bringing peace
And giving us a happy life.

RVG

SUPPORT

Be charitable toward others but not willy-nilly in offering them your support. You'll always know when it's appropriate or not ~ based on what's apparent. That said, hidden needs are often just as important. Therefore, give others your support when you know that is what the Universe is asking you to do. Though karma is often in the picture, some giving is spontaneous, offered purely out of love and unrelated to personal agendas or any type of karmic resolution.

Support is more easily manifested when there's mutuality. The latter can be compared to a mathematical equation that always has an answer, whatever formula is being applied. But that is not the question. Mutuality is. Is there room for it in your equation? Can it be seen or felt? If so, this is healthy support, the kind of interaction that adds and multiplies rather than subtracts or divides. Healthy support is always expressed as a positive number, creating abundance and balance. Be most generous then to those who are also capable of supporting others. In so doing, we make this world a better place.

For support to be most valid, it ought to be reciprocal. Then, it grows and expands. If not, whatever we offer may end up being a throw-away, much like the proverbial pearls cast before swine ~ in other words, not appreciated, devalued or in some way debased.

My advice is to offer others your support primarily when it's likely that something, energetically speaking, will be returned. Gratitude would be tops on that list. By the way, I do not refer to material goods or money in terms of something being returned. Rather, I speak of good conscience and a sense of propriety. The giving and receiving of support is a lot like the workings of an internal combustion engine. The person doing the supporting is the spark plug, the person being supported the piston. Energy begets energy. Support produces support or so it should. If that is not happening, re-evaluate your position and, if advisable, flee ASAP.

Again, we tend to think of support in terms of the material when the right words are often far more desirable ~ a veritable bucket-full of water in the midst of a drought.

Supporting other people, as they say 'come hell or high water,' can occasionally be a pathway to redemption. In fact, there are times when we MUST offer our support even if it's clear that a simple thank you will not be forthcoming. This is because we owe something to the individual in question and, as a result, must help him or her in order to mitigate some prior karmic transgression. So do not be surprised when this occurs. In fact, rest assured it will ~ at some time or another.

In general, use common sense when offering your support. The highest and best use of your resources is to help others help themselves, in other words, to promote self-reliance.

———————— ✪ ————————

SURPRISE

In the perfect order of the Universe, there's always room for a few surprises. Why is that? What is their purpose? You will laugh when I say that it is to fill any vacuum in the room. Metaphorically speaking, surprises are TBA's in progress. Like hot lava, they're always bubbling up to the surface. But, it's only when they've solidified or in some way become tangible that we're able to perceive them.

Surprises are the construct of record for the overt expression of our subconscious desires, for the most part a very pleasant way indeed to manifest them. Like all happenstances, however, they are fraught with consequences ~ in many cases providing us with grist for re-alignment and growth.

Some say that surprises tend to throw them off track. I contend instead that they 'right' us, bringing us back to ourselves and, upon occasion, even leading us to greener pastures. Surprise is just one of the many avenues the soul uses to help the personality stay awake.

Most surprises are welcome, some are not. You might not be too pleased, for example, to discover a scorpion in your shoe while getting dressed in the morning. Surprises also function as reminders, exhorting us to pay closer attention to what's going on or take better care of ourselves. In each, there's a message, usually writ large.

The great majority of surprises come to us because we've earned them, fair and square. Oddly enough, however, those are exactly the ones that usually seem most serendipitous. Look forward to continually being surprised. Happily for us, that is the way of the world.

SURRENDER

No one surrenders unawares. In any set of circumstances, surrendering is a conscious decision, involving some level of submitting or handing over. But to whom or what? Simply put, surrender requires giving ourselves permission to increase our levels of acceptance. When we accept 'what is' instead of trying to resist it, we are in effect staging a **coup**, overriding the personality on behalf of the soul ~ in effect re-aligning ourselves. In most cases, surrendering enables us to feel more comfortable, relevant, on-point and yes, even more aware of ever-changing opportunities.

Allow 'what is' to be but at the same time do not condone anything that is counter-productive to your soul's growth or the well-being of others. Surrender does not mean that we have to acquiesce or abdicate our responsibilities. It is merely a tactic, similar to knowing when to fold in a card game. Again, the act of surrender implies both a lack of resistance and the willingness to pull back.

Surrender is often the way to go, especially when our personalities become mired in illusion. Surrendering is not always just about responding to specific situations, however. It is also prudent to surrender to potentials, in other words, to truly be open to the multitude of opportunities that always come our way.

There are many differing degrees of surrender. For example, someone who does a good deed is by definition surrendering to the greater good. The bottom line is this: whenever possible, give it up to soul.

THREE DIMENSIONAL WORLD

What we perceive to be reality is **una stanza,** *a room* in which the principles of life continually unfold. We know it as the Earth Plane or three dimensional world. All corners and quadrants of the three dimensional world are divided into small areas of concentration. Why? Because the ability to focus cannot be manifested unless segments of time and space are compartmentalized. These segments need to be made small enough so that a given consciousness can even begin to absorb what is there.

In English, the word **stanza** has a musical connotation, defined as an arrangement of meter and rhyme. Indeed, there's a tonal quality to existence and this particular room, the Earth Plane, has a musical signature as well as a specific vibrational speed.

The three dimensional world can be defined as the one we all have to experience. It is our primary school, as others have stated, the arena in which each of us has to learn how to deal with karma. Only here can we revisit what has previously been sown. Only here can the lay of the land truly be known. For every action, no matter how slight, there is a reaction. It's the guiding principle in our kindergarten tome.

Though it helps paint a pretty picture, depth is but an illusion. Instead, think of everything we see as up close and personal ~ as though projected on a screen. It's always our own movie that we find ourselves in anyway, not anyone else's. Because the responsibility for what we are experiencing is ours alone, we have no reason to blame others. A better option, therefore, is to look within ~ forgiving yourself daily. That's always where the real answers are found, not outside of ourselves.

THOUGHT

Thought is vibration and vibration thought. Furthermore, vibration carries thought, allowing it to manifest. Thought is integral to the act of condensing energy into form. It gives birth to action which then resolves itself in deeds.

Thought is the cause, form the effect. Thought is about energy becoming form, form projecting itself, and form in motion. Every aspect of our so-called reality is an expression of some kind of pre-existing thought.

Thought is both the principal product of mind and the spawn of soul. If anything can be called divine, it is that.

Thought is the way of the play we're all in, the essence of what we call life. As a matter of fact, it is synonymous with living. You think you are and **voilà,** you ARE ~ creating personal reality. Don't you see how easily ALL can BE? **Je pense, donc je suis.** So said Descartes ~ *I think, therefore I am.*

All thoughts can be narrowed and refined ~ distilled, if you will. And so they must, in order to be fully grasped. In terms of thought patterns, however, simplicity is the ultimate complexity.

Shakespeare: **there is nothing good nor bad but thinking makes it so.** Also, here are the words of Ella Wheeler Wilcox, a 19th century writer who was given to dispensing practical advice. **Thoughts are things, full of electric force. And they go forth, producing their own.** Of course they do, this being the basis for creating reality.

Therefore, look to what you are thinking from moment to moment. It's that important. Food for thought? Every-thing is.

Time

Time is NOW and only now. There is no past or future. Time marks the present in the same way that an animal marks his or her environment. Time also marks space, from our perspective impacting concepts, constructs and spatial relationships. For many of us, unfortunately, it's like a little rascal always nipping at our heels. I propose instead we choose to see it differently.

The NOW is where power resides. Therefore, **carpe diem** ~ *seize the day,* a really sound piece of advice. Though we tend to view time as a measure of what is past or yet to come, it is really just a measure of where we are now as we do whatever it is that we are doing.

How can we use time to our advantage? By giving it as little attention as possible. Therefore, don't be bound by the ticking of a clock, your calendar, electronic devices or anything else that is theoretically pulling you towards the future. Instead, just BE. Again, there is only the eternal NOW.

Time's mission actually is to keep us in the present. But how you ask? By providing us with a false sense of the past and a shadow impression of the future, in other words, by constantly reminding us that all we really have is right here, right now ~ in the moment.

There are endless simultaneous NOWS, my friends. Within each, individual events are recorded, maintaining themselves in perpetuity. **If you know that each event never loses its punch because it is, just as you are in this so-called moment, you will get what you need to know about time and how it works.**

I suggest we view time as an infinite number of interlocking NOWS, each separate yet always in the process of morphing into the one that appears to immediately precede and follow it. Events are found inside, wrapping themselves around each other like a series of Russian dolls. What seems to us as aging is nothing more than the same dynamic at work.

It may also be helpful to think of time as a wheel, full of individual cogs, each representing a particular NOW. Those of us in the Astral can focus on any one of them or on any combination thereof ~ if we so choose. That is how we are able to 'take a look' at things ~ by scrolling through so-called past or future events. By the way, all happenstances, be they of great import such as a volcanic explosion or almost imperceptible like a single leaf falling from a tree, have equal weight.

Others before me have exhorted you to be in the moment. Now I would like to follow suit. Make each NOW, therefore, a very conscious event whose purpose it is to entwine the various strands of our lives, including the genetic, knitting them up. Who knew life was about producing handicrafts? Well, it is. We literally spin our own webs!

For many, time implies movement. The truth is, however, that time by itself goes nowhere. It only seems to. Clocks are just ornaments, pretty things to look at 'from time to time.'

That a year has an end is something that cannot be. Nevertheless, each acts as a marker and in that sense is to be reflected upon. As a result, every December 31st we have an opportunity to look at the choices we've made during the previous twelve months and think about what we want to do now as we appear to go forward. However, as you already know there is no forward, only other versions of the NOW.

To reiterate, life is a series of interconnected NOWS, all lined up next to each other in an infinite perspective of endless horizons. Time itself is a fantasy. What we perceive of as time passing can be attributed to shifts in our own vibratory rates, enabling us to become associated with and participate in any number of different events ~ as we see fit.

Many of us were brought up believing that time is something that we can either make good use of or waste. But is that really the case? No. There is no such thing as wasting time even though the continual comings and goings of the Sun and Moon sometimes tend to support that impression. Everything we do has both purpose and reason.

Time was conceived of to help us deal with change, or rather the fear of change. Transition, what we call death, frees us all from bonds, including those having to do with the illusion of time. Eternal is not just a word, it is emblematic of how things work.

To this day some people contend that my former persona transcends time. Of course it does because again there is no time. It is merely a concept. We are all time-less. If you will, think on that. Also, notice the extent to which time and our references to it tend to permeate our thinking.

Allow the NOW to be a more conscious part of your life. This is a great teaching ~ a truth for all ages. Thoroughly get to know each NOW as it develops, in perfect harmony with what should be and, more importantly, as a reflection of what IS. In all circumstances let the spirit of the Creator be in you, with you and around you. It cannot be said enough that GOD is YOU.

Everything that is happening is really happening NOW. Things only appear to be occurring in linear fashion. The past and future can only be referenced in the present. Why? Because all events are simultaneous, the only difference being that each one functions within a specific vibrational context and therefore can only be seen, felt and experienced when we and that event are in sync.

That said, there are vibrational speeds that once achieved would allow a theoretical construct like a time machine to move from NOW to NOW at the behest of its operator. The illusion of stopping in another place and point in time would be predicated on the machine and its occupant being able to assume the vibrational rate and focus of the host NOW, a feat that's imminently doable. Be not surprised, therefore, if one day you should hear that it has been accomplished.

Bending the time and space continuum involves changing the degree of flux, something our bodies are quite capable of doing. See yourselves then as flux capacitors for that is what we truly are ~ always in the process of self-regulating. In so doing, you would be right on the mark.

Time revolves around established practices, what we might define as an operational praxis consisting of generally accepted givens that unfortunately are just not true. Its effects are so ingrained in our collective thinking that it's difficult to extricate ourselves. I invite you, however, to try. The more we're able to think outside of the 'box' ~ **what time really is**, the more liberated we'll become.

Corollary:

The French word for happy, **heureux,** *has at its core that language's word for time,* **heure.** *When one is in sync with time, in other words, in the NOW, that is where happiness resides. We can only truly be happy by being in the NOW.*

--- ❈ ---

TRAVEL

Ostensively, traveling is about getting from point A to point B and, if well-planned, visiting point C on the way. However, as you might surmise there's lots more to it. For example, just as much may be gleaned from the mechanics of a trip, that is to say, from all the comings and goings required to get us to our destination as from the destination itself.

Each trip is unique, also a challenge. Why? Because traveling usually forces us to step outside of our comfort zone, something that is always desirable. Indeed, being on any sort of foreign soil even if it's only a few miles from home is an invitation to look at life through a different lens. And, whenever we're willing to do that, we're likely to create a few cracks in our well-crafted façades, in some sense furthering our evolution. The soul is always greatly nourished by any kind of travel ~ if for no other reason than it always changes our tune.

Karmically speaking, travel provides us with opportunities to tie up loose ends or, as some might say, to get our acts together. The goal is to return home refreshed, in some cases even having become a new person. The people we encounter, the sights, sounds, smells and places themselves all act as catalysts, enabling us, if we so choose, to retool our thinking in short order.

Have you not heard people say that they had to leave home in order to find themselves? And did that not involve travel? Had I elected to remain in Italy, for example, I would never have become who I now am. No, friends, I am not suggesting that you need to move to another country as I once did. But you should explore your options and travel is a wonderful way of doing that. No trip is ever a waste of time. To the contrary, each one contributes to our overall edification.

Travel, what a delight! We tend to eat wonderful things and the visuals are always just right. As a matter of fact all of our senses are usually stimulated simply by 'being' somewhere else. Even a brief encounter with another environment will often work wonders, a case in point being the more than several times I escaped my usual haunts by visiting your neck of the woods *(Palm Springs.)*

When taking trips, we're usually all atwitter, full of wonder for the glitter of wherever it is that we wake up to find ourselves each day. Travel is just another opportunity for us to love and be loved, only without the benefit of our usual trappings. 'Tis a delightful thing to do. Do it exactly as you would like to.

Again, any kind of travel is incredibly worthwhile, even if it's just around the corner. East or west, however, abroad is best. Such journeys often lead us beside still waters, or to wherever it is that we're likely to be better able to see our reflections.

Soldi Ben Spesi ~ *Money Well Spent*

As travels unravel in lands far and near
The trip is the corpus, that much is clear
To accomplish a voyage takes five senses or more
Not to mention perseverance and sensibility galore
Whenever it is that you exit your door
Two verbs should be part of your personal lore
To bask and to feel
They're the ones that give travel its greatest appeal.

RVG

UNIVERSE

Another term for the All That IS ~ used interchangeably. A container for intelligence, also for what we perceive of as substance. That which love has wrought. Probably the largest version of the ONE anyone could ever imagine.

More specifically, the Universe is a matrix where thought and vibration meet and interact. It is our home base and in that context functions as a field of play. Think of it as the ultimate projection, tangible evidence of the Creator's idea of self.

❖

VALENTINO ON VALENTINO

Who am I? Who was I? Some things need little explanation, they just are. Valentino, as my former personality was known, is one of those.

In my formative years a **perugino** was I, *(referring to Perugia, Italy)* attending school in that fair city, though perhaps not always quite so sweet as its world-famous candies. While there, however, I did partake, eventually becoming addicted to **baci** ~ *kisses.*

Later to the movie-going public I was more or less a blank canvas, the beholder providing both palette and sheen. In short, I was who I was yet I was also who people wanted me to be.

The past Valentino: a man like all others, vices and virtues, a mixture of eclectic and sometimes contradictory impulses to be worked with ~ fodder or grist as the case may be. Yes, I had a few rough edges, glitches that biographers have discovered and written about. But I was also blessed with many suavities, smooth sides that needed no polishing. In other words, I was complete as we all are ~ a package with no loose ends. I did my best with what I had set out to accomplish. At times the work was gritty but overall quite fulfilling, and in the long run it enabled me to come to better terms with myself.

Let's see, Rudolph Valentino, me, from a past mind's eye or, if you will, falcon's point of view ~ to be more precise. Yes, those birds have excellent sight, one of their strongest traits. My inner vision was tops too. I could see beyond the rocks, which is to say beyond the people and objects that surrounded me. I could always see the bigger picture as Valentino. In that I was both fortunate and unfortunate because with sight comes responsibility, something I had to learn to be more cognizant of. What was my responsibility versus that of others? And if there was a problem, to whom did it belong?

Dapper, yes, sartorially daring, personally gracious, inventive, vivacious. Complacent sometimes, creative always – this was I in those recent times.

Now who am I as we now know each other, my greater self, the larger I, this essence, the product of a multitude of incarnations? The short answer is an assemblage of thought, experience and feeling. I am puffed up with a love so gossamer it can only be imagined. Everything I've ever learned is accessible to me. In fact, I can review anything I've ever done, any experience I ever had – in all times and circumstances. This is not only true of me, however. All those in the Astral are thusly equipped, having been endowed with the same gifts and composed, as we all are, of loose conglomerations of thought.

Divine love is both my motivator and animator as well as the perpetrator of All That Is. I am points of light as are you and each individuated soul. Think of me now as a star, though in this instance not of the Hollywood persuasion but rather as a gaseous binding together of intention motivated by the desire to be of service.

VANITY

The novel *Vanity Fair* tells us most of what we need to know about this topic, there being nothing much of merit in the majority of characters it depicts. Yet vanity still rules in most of the world, the mirror emperor to its legions of fans.

Who among you is not a little vain? I certainly was, studying my reflection each morning to make sure I was properly suited. Then it was my job to look good, especially in front of the camera. Even so, I was never taken with what I saw nor did my head ever become swollen.

Symbolically, Venus was once the epitome of beauty, holding

up a mirror for all to see. Indeed, both sexes usually want to know how they are doing, that is to say, how they compare to the standards of the day. This is the essence of vanity, the question always being 'do I measure up?' In other words, am I properly aligned with the latest look ~ as defined by the current spate of beauty-mongers and their helpful products? For many, unfortunately, such concerns get overblown. The pursuit of beauty, full-bore, can develop into an obsessive-compulsive effort, especially if those involved are not being very reasonable.

Love always makes guest appearances where beauty reigns. Though they do not necessarily always start out as a pair, that is where they usually end up. An important distinction to make is that love **does** while beauty **is.** Beauty, therefore, is not very mobile, sometimes appearing stagnant or frozen and content to rest on its laurels. Love, on the other hand, is what we think of as vital force, infusing breath into every aspect of life.

Be not overly concerned about your looks. True beauty comes from within ~ on its own merits. It requires no make-up, artifice, physical enhancement or diminution.

No matter the trappings, vanity always has somewhat of a bite. 'Tis perhaps better then to kiss it goodbye ~ once and for all. How? By being able to laugh at ourselves in the mirror. It's a great force for liberation.

In conclusion, take pride in how you look. Be neat and clean. Exercise. Make sure there's a bit of flair in what you wear too. But, don't go overboard. Do not allow yourself to become vain. If you do, you may never be the same.

VEIL

Defined as the demarcation line or boundary separating the dimensions.

(*Addressing the author*) You have seen me before in little glimpses out of the corner of your eye. Why? To prove that the Veil, the vibrational boundary that separates us, is but the thinnest of gossamer. It is so wispy that those of us on my side can usually see right through it. Yes, I am confirming that you did catch a glimpse of my energy field this morning in the form of a physicality, specifically mine as Rodolfo dressed in white. You were only able to see me below the knees, however, my lower extremities appearing to you as though I was walking.

Yes, it is possible to glimpse those in the Astral, especially when we really want to be seen. Not only is the Veil porous but there are cracks in each of its pores which can enable you, under certain circumstances, to see through it for what would be a nanosecond of time. We could argue about whether you actually saw through the Veil or I was able to penetrate it enough to be partially seen. I would propose that it was a bit of both.

Why does this not happen more often? Because those in your frequency of the NOW often feel afraid when sensing another dimension, thereby closing off the possibility.

Please note that most of us in the Astral, including myself, can broach the Veil energetically. (*Addressing the author*) At this very moment, for example, you feel me touching your energy field. You experience it like a rush of energy, coursing through your veins in the form of shivers on your legs and up and down your back. That's just one of the ways you feel my presence when we work together.

Lately I have played a bit with some of the situations around you. I did so to make a point, to illustrate how the Veil functions. In other words, it is always there but can be permeated. As you have noted, the Veil is porous only to the extent that energy can be transferred through it ~ in the form of ideas, symbols and so-called coincidences like a man with the name Rudy written on his cup sitting down next to you at a coffee shop.

Remember, the Veil is never far away nor is it so thick as we might like to believe.

The demarcation line between your dimension and mine can likewise be referred to as the edge or last frontier. It acts as a threshold. At the moment of death, we literally walk across it to once again become our whole or authentic selves. It's only then that we can be seen for who we really are ~ in the full measure of Light. The word edge also speaks to the concept of known versus unknown ~ the line that delineates all known phenomena in a given plane of existence from that which is unknown. It's a definition that works quite well, from just about any perspective.

I want you to know where the Astral is in relation to everything else. The best words to describe it are imminent, looming or perhaps ever-present. The Astral is literally right in front of our eyes, not out there somewhere. It follows then that so is the Veil.

The Veil may also be conceived of as web-like, there being open space between the so-called solid parts or, alternatively, as a curtain of energy. Again, its purpose is to separate the planes of existence so that there's no vibrational confusion or slippage between them.

But how exactly does one 'cross over' or, more specifically, pass through? By changing vibration, something that dying allows us to do. It is analogous to moving from country A to country B, except on a much grander scale. In either case, however, what we are being offered is a fresh start.

There's usually so much going on when we die that many of us don't even realize we're crossing over. In fact, we may never even see the Veil in the process. I would compare it to dozing off in one reality and then waking up in another ~ a little startling perhaps, but all in all quite easy.

Strictly speaking, the Veil does not really need to be there. Our respective dimensions would still be able to maintain themselves without it. However, were it not in place some of you would not be amused. Dealing with two perceived realities rather than one? Perhaps in the long run not so much fun!

Addendum

Question: Can you tell me what it's like to look through the Veil from your side?

Similar to looking through a piece of gauze. For example, I see your lit candles when we do a writing session. They call attention to your essence and the ectoplasm surrounding it. Of course, I don't need a flame to find you but it's a nice gesture ~ rather like leaving a light on while waiting for someone to come home. Thank you! Light from any source is synonymous with life.

Question: Why do spirit guides have to use the anomalies in the Veil in order to intervene in this dimension? Cannot the same thing be accomplished in a more straightforward manner?

No. The Veil was designed to separate the dimensions, something it does quite well Yet as in all walls, there are always a few chinks. In the case of the Veil, however, the anomalies continually shift. Therefore, each time we propose to use them they must be found anew.

VIBRATION

Sound is perhaps the one form of vibration we can all relate to. Whether creating bliss or tympanic confusion, it opens figurative doors, guaranteeing that our souls will listen.

All life can be reduced to expressions of the same concept: VIBRATION. In other words, EVERYTHING that IS is VIBRATION.

Generally we can only picture, sense and feel those people and things that are in the same vibratory range as ourselves. Therefore, we cannot really know what is in the Astral. Neither, as a rule, can we see beyond the Veil. Meanwhile, those in the Astral tend to vibrate at much higher frequencies. In fact, everyone there operates **in fretta** ~ *in fast forward mode,* much like the fictional character Superman when he is truly being himself.

Each planet has its own vibrational range. Every-thing on that planet, therefore, has to fit in to be in alignment. The same is true for each country, city, town or plot of ground. The five senses, sound, sight, taste, touch and smell are different effects of the same cause. They all reflect varying degrees of vibration.

Life is akin to music, music akin to life. As a result, we have the opportunity to strike a plethora of notes ~ as we so choose. Music is created by combining various vibrations and tonalities. It is sometimes used as a magnet, either for the purpose of bringing together like-minded souls or harnessing energy to perform specific tasks.

The degree to which we become sensitive to the vibrations of others is commensurate with the evolution of our own perceptions. Again, every-thing that IS is vibrating, something we would do well to always keep in mind.

Addendum

Question: can we increase our vibratory rates by doing certain things?

Yes, through pretty much any kind of activity, from watching a movie to participating in some type of sport. Or, we can do it with our minds, through volition. Perhaps the quickest way, however, is just to simplify our lives. The fewer issues we have vying for our attention, the more energy we have available to invest in ourselves.

But why, you ask, should this be a goal? Because having more energy correlates with increased vibration which in turn allows for the possibility of greater growth.

Everything that is is always evolving. Nothing remains static. It's the conscious individual who tries to facilitate this process rather than attempting to slow it down.

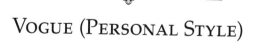

Vogue (Personal Style)

An exponent of personality, personal style is analogous to window screening ~ protective in nature, yet still able to be seen through.

In a sense, the vogues we assume are much like the masks worn each year at the Venetian Carnavale. Their purpose is to hide the true identities of their wearers. The unintended consequence, however, is that they often have exactly the opposite effect.

It is prudent, therefore, to be mindful of the masks you choose to wear. They may well disclose more than they conceal.

In the game of life, our personalities are like chess pieces. However, it's our vogues that do most of the checkmating. As we make our moves, we are wont to say 'let's get to know each other better.' In order to accomplish this, the individuals in question must first be able to look beyond whatever it is that each is projecting.

Personal style goes far beyond mere adornment. It is all-inclusive, taking into account our values, bearing, attitude, presentation, look, delivery and desired impact ~ a recipe for 'how to be' as well as a detailed 'to do' list. In terms of attraction, personal style is an invitation to the dance.

Vogue is the razzle in the dazzle, some would say the source of each personality's luminescence. As such, it has the power to transform light, creating contrast and interplay. Like the personality, it's both defensive and offensive in nature, somewhere to hide out, or a tool to stir things up a bit. To vogue is to project a series of silhouettes, mostly of the 'now you see 'em, now you don't variety.' Yes, our vogues are forever in flux which is why they are often so hard to pin down.

Some contend that consciously creating a personal style is a frivolous kind of pursuit. I completely disagree. Instead, look upon it as just one of the many ways that we're able to play in this world. 'Tis fun to vogue, or at least it can be. Adopting a particular style always adds more lustre to who you are.

Quirks? Predilections? Preferences? What are yours? How would you define your style? What are your favorite colors or articles of clothing? Do you have a signature look? Or, have you simply allowed yourself to be branded? Are your tastes truly your own?

Upon reflection you may discover that some elements of your

personal style seem to have no rhyme or reason. If so, certain aspects of other life-times may be masquerading as current taste. In such cases, look within. Much can be imparted to you in this manner. The important point here is to embrace your own style ~ whatever it is.

Some see fashion as an aggregate of the prevailing trends in dress, manners and speech. Fair enough, but fashion, as it applies to personal style, really ought to be distinctive rather than simply a reflection of consensus. Personal style is grounded in conscious choice. Fads and crazes are not. They can usually be traced back to the mass media or one of its favorite sons, subliminal messaging.

I would be the first to acknowledge that my own style preferences sometimes appeared a bit too elaborate. In reality, however, the choices I made as Valentino were quite supportive of who I was at the time. Actually they were all perfect. I say this not out of ego but rather as a confirmation that there really are no wrong choices where style is concerned. One of my favorite vogues was that of an Argentine gaucho, a man of Las Pampas. Also playing a Sheik of Araby really delighted me and, more than once!

Please keep in mind that vogue, when aligned with what's divine, will always allow one's self-confidence to shine. Shall we present ourselves to the world as the spirited and graceful beings we are or should we curb our enthusiasm to the point of seeming dreary and dull? The answer is evident, my friends. Our presentation really ought to capture the former rather than the latter.

Style, at the behest of personality, works to create impressions by combining form with function. Incidentally, if you believe your personal style to be happenstance, guess again. It's all quite deliberate. You are the way you are because that is the way you want to be. Style is in turn chosen and elaborated, the full force of the personality behind it. In terms of their relationship, you may want to think of the personality as the commanding officer and style as its foot soldier, an important distinction to make.

Vogues may also be thought of as pitches, advertising ploys made to our fellow men and women as we market our wares.

As an actor, I often had to make up vogues that were relevant to the roles I played on screen. I also had to make up my own. And once in a while, the twain did meet. What fun! I can safely say that my experiences in this arena were always quite entertaining. By the way, our vogues should never be vague. Instead, they need to be well-defined. Even so, they come and go with great regularity ~ often washing over us like waves. Does any group have a monopoly on style? No, although we Italians would like to think so!

In terms of being a fashionista here's a key point: personal style does not originate in broad strokes. It develops incrementally. Be creative. Have fun. Express yourself. As in all circumstances, your choices are unlimited. All it takes is a mix here, a match there.

Personal style? Develop one. Change it dramatically from time to time too. However, when a complete make-over is not called for, do not proceed in that direction. Simply adjust some aspect of 'what is' in order to meet the needs of the moment. And, as with any of life's realms, remember to enjoy whatever you have wrought.

VOICE

We often do not realize just how powerful our voices are. **La voce è forse l'instrumento più forte che abbiamo da noi** ~ *the voice is perhaps the most powerful weapon in our arsenal.* Not only is it evidence of our vibrational footprint, it functions as a major intersection on the head to heart highway, allowing us to express every possible nuance of meaning and feeling. Our voices are package deals. Some of us, of course, would have them be smoother, more accent-free, deeper, clearer or perhaps more melodious. However, the voices we were gifted with at birth, whatever their ilk, are always perfectly suited to who we are. If I have any regret about my most recent life-time, it's that mine was not really able to be heard, at least to the extent that I might have preferred. Now comes this book, again giving me voice and, hopefully, access to an even wider audience.

WAR

War is a donut hole. Yes my friends, it's a big fat zero for all concerned. Though there are those who would say differently, the truth is that no one ever really wins a war. Indeed, if we were to aggregate all of its sounds, rolling them into one, what we would be hearing is a cacophony of loss. War is hell. Many this have said, and it certainly is true. Again, war is nothing but a zed, leading nowhere except to large numbers of people ending up dead.

Sadly, declarations of war are just part of the cycle of birth and death, though in this case leaning heavily towards the latter.

What prompts war? Fear and hatred, initially stemming from those in power. Yes, death and destruction are usually manufactured by the political wills of certain individuals who have a fear and loathing of self. Those rulers who would war are usually warring internally, sparring with themselves or seeing paper tigers where there are none.

Then, due to xenophobia or any number of other factors, the citizens of their country suddenly concur, revving up the war machine. Though I refer to war machine here as the military in its action mode, let us not forget that individual war machines, what you call guns, are made for the express purpose of killing people, to be instruments of death.

The good news, if there is any, is that war often encourages a pooling of resources on the part of the populace, a coming together marked by a willingness to make shared sacrifices. Also, in terms of the individual members of the military, going to war fosters an even greater concern for others. Ah yes, there's the rub, the development of camaraderie in each branch of the armed forces being one of the most important components of their training.

To make a war machine work, there must be cogs in the wheel. The wheel turns thusly, but only when its cogs are fully engaged. The men and women of the armed services are the cogs, meshing for the whole as they mesh for their brethren. They are trained to be there for each other ~ all for one and one for all. The war machine teaches us this so that it does not come apart at the seams. Nevertheless, it's a natural phenomenon. If given the opportunity, people really do want to be there for each other. When fear is in control, however, it will often create strange bedfellows.

In commenting, I do not want to suggest that members of the armed forces only unite in fear of an enemy. Again, as part of their training they develop personal bonds, working together and supporting each other's endeavors around the clock. As proof, many soldiers speak openly of fighting on behalf of their buddies rather than for any other reason.

There is a certain eloquence to this aspect of war. Even in the midst of a great conflagration, something is always being born. Moreover, love always plays a part in the process, forever being revisited and regained. Even the thorniest of bushes will sometimes have a flower or two. Camaraderie is warfare's rose. The silver lining of such conflicts is that they unite us in a cause. This is the part of war that is a worthy experience though, unfortunately, outweighed by death, destruction and loss ~ all on a grand scale. Bombs are to war what love is to hate. They both obliterate the foe, one in a good way, the other not.

Indeed, it's camaraderie that often causes us to voice our concerns. By suggesting that we ought to see what the boys (and girls) in the back room will have, we are essentially saying the following: to think of the needs of your fellow men and women is to bring more Light into the world. That being said, however, as far as war is concerned there still is no 'there' there.

Will war ever end? Yes. So it is written. But, (speaking to the author) not during your current life-time, alas I regret to say. Nevertheless, it's coming – the end of war as we know it. Think on that, a light shining forth, a guiding star that will eventually lead us out of the doldrums. No more war? Oh brave new world!

WHO WE ARE

We are clouds of energy housed in physical form for finite numbers of years. As such, we are the functioning reality of the breath of God, a metaphor for animation. Flesh and blood are but illusions, seemingly solid though actually not.

Light and air pass through us even if we don't think so. In essence then, we're ethereal. As a result, we often intersect, sometimes enveloping each other and even blending when we love deeply.

It is rare, however, that any two entities are ever totally in alignment. In some cases, we just barely touch.

Postscript

Question: How are we perceived by those in spirit?

Like a gaseous binding together of molecules, not as anything tangible. Those of us on other side can see the real you, the source, the soul, if you will, not simply the outer shell.

WORDS

Words can be like jewels or daggers: true, inspiring, beautiful and harmonic or false, discouraging, ugly and dissonant, depending on their use and the motivation of the speaker. Words alone have the power to heal or wound, resolve or rebuke. Without the knowledge and experience associated with each of them, however, they would have little or no meaning.

Words are like seeds, to be planted with care so that future harvests will be abundant. Consider that the words of yore, such as those once spoken in Greece and Rome, were also seeds, having been firmly planted in our psyches. Today they continue to bear fruit, in certain instances still being used to express thought.

Another way to think about words is as meaningful sound vibrations. In your world they are essential. In mine they are not. Here, thought is the same as word.

Always choose your words wisely, measuring them as well as taking note of the feelings behind them. Being conscious of what you are saying and why avoids errors. It also minimizes the possibility of making remarks that might hurt someone else's feelings.

It is extremely important for each of us to keep our word. Broken promises do nothing, except create karmic imbalances. Careless words are like arrows flying through the air. In finding their mark, they often have more weight than anyone might have guessed. So be careful with what comes out of your mouth, and pick words that are appropriate for the occasion ~ as much as is humanly possible.

WRITERS

Generally speaking, writers are print-based mediums. Indeed, everyone, no matter their areas of expertise or level of education, is a medium, channeling information from the one source, Universal Mind.

The concentration required to write, however, creates a special focal point, attracting those in spirit who are willing to act as muses. We are, therefore, sometimes even more inspired when we write than when we speak.

Fictional characters, in particular those in print, often hold sway in mass consciousness, becoming real to those who behold them. Although most writers create the mental body of a character first, it's only when they add feeling that 'he' or 'she' comes to life. Once in the public domain, a fictional character may be talked about, reflected upon, loved or hated for many years.

By the way, what are termed fictional characters also have their own reality ~ one that is just as valid to them as yours is to you.

———— ❖ ————

X (A Rumination)

Marks the spot. The international symbol for multiplication. That which is unknown or for the moment unrevealed. A sign of eternal gratitude harking back to ancient times. The position of a Pharaoh's arms in earthly repose. The point of discovery. Where secrets often lie. Any two lines crossing in such a manner illustrate the intersection of Heaven and Earth.

In math, X indicates an axis or plane of existence. It is a focal point, the crux of the matter, again where Heaven and Earth meet to play their game. So easy to make an X. We can overlay it on just about anything. In a sense it's perhaps the most useful letter in the alphabet, the mystery letter in any equation. X is symbolic of our search for ourselves, the unknown quantity that in the end will always be known. All equations have solutions, by the way, especially those containing an X.

Though we may sometimes think of X as indicative of something not to do, *(often the case in universal signage)* it is really just a reminder to pay attention to what's going on. Again, X marks the spot.

———— ❖ ————

XXX (Kisses)

Kisses are an invitation to love. And I for one loved to kiss! A kiss is but an acknowledgment of the Good and the God in each of us. Our lips are a sacred portal, one of the places where soul meets soul. Kissing, therefore, is one of the most life-affirming things we can ever do.

Many of us tend to lead our lives independently, much like those proverbial ships that pass in the night. However, the moment our lips touch someone else's in a soulful way, everything changes. Suddenly there is magic in the air and we are reminded how lucky we are, of the extent to which our lives have truly been blessed.

It is said that two ought to be greater than one. Indeed, so it seems. But the paradox is that it often takes two to be able to see the ONE. When we choose to partner with another person, we're much more likely to feel our inter-connectedness with the Universe. Intimacy always reminds us that we're part of the WHOLE.

Kissing also tugs at our façades, sometimes stripping them away completely. Indeed, when we kiss our vision expands, enabling us to see what we may never have seen before. By their very nature, kisses are revelatory.

We are each very much like planets. Yes, self-contained spheres are we and often constrained by our own doings. As luck would have it though our orbits do occasionally shift, or at least wobble a bit from time to time. And, good thing they do. This is what affords us the opportunity to engage with others.

If you will, draw two circles on a piece of paper, placing them side by side so that one touches the other without intersecting. Experiencing a single point of contact is what allows one soul entity to access another and vice-versa. Kissing is just such a point. A kiss may also be likened to a permission slip for intimacy, on occasion leading to further exploration. Oh my! Never know what treasures shall be yours ~ all stemming from a single kiss.

When two pairs of lips meet, light dances in between, the energy being created analogous to electrical current emitting sparks. It's in a kiss where Light meets Light, the parties in question each becoming more fully illuminated.

Is there such a thing as love at first kiss? If the first time you kissed your beloved, it tasted like a ripe peach steeped in red wine or felt as soft as violets drenched in rain then yes, probably so. It certainly can happen that way. Kisses have been celebrated by the poets of the world since the beginning of time. But, however you choose to describe them, rest assured you'll be able to convey all of the delight discovered therein.

Kisses are among the most captivating of gifts and how we all love to receive presents!

Whomsoever is not open to kissing is not open of heart, literally not open for business. It follows then that if we are willing to kiss, we should also be willing to love. Kissing is part of its natural expression. Angry kisses, by the way, have no place in love's lexicon. With that sort of motivation, they automatically become null and void. Better then not to kiss at all than to kiss someone out of anger. Even the most beautiful of things can sometimes be manhandled. Reluctant kisses are a different story. Though usually coming from a better place, they are still indicative of a defensive posture. Sweet kisses, on the other hand, are always welcome, carrying promise and hope. For kisses to be at their most genuine and profound both parties must be willing to surrender their egos and simply BE.

Which kind of kiss is best? With the exception of angry ones, all have their value. That said, however, a half-hearted kiss probably won't succeed in getting you to first base. Think on this: in kissing someone for the very first time, we usually find out most of what we really need to know about them.

A kiss may be likened to one's signature, hopefully oft-writ! It is just one of the ways that ye shall know them. With each kiss more is being revealed.

Be grateful for the kisses that come to you, be they of the physical or spiritual variety. Spiritual kisses, by the way, cannot be felt yet they're just as real, having originated from beyond the confines of the physical world. When we speak of a message as having been sealed with a kiss if it originated in the Astral it most assuredly was.

Often kisses inspire us to go to great lengths or perform the most daring of deeds. Crowned heads have even been known to offer up their kingdoms in exchange for them. It's in the act of kissing that we often see stars, the mystery of life encoded therein. The progression of events generally works like this, if the individuals in question both agree. First, join at the lips. Then, join at the hips. True intimacy comes on the heels of a kiss whereas superficial sex comes in a brown paper bag. Kisses are part of the deluxe packaging, always worthy of celebrating.

Without the magic of a kiss, how would we ever know when love has met its match?

YES

Yes or its equivalent is truly a word of Biblical proportions. We do not pass go unless we first say yes. Yes signals official consent. It is the one utterance that is always certain to make something happen.

Being willing to say yes and fully mean it is how we repel ourselves off the mountain of choice. Indeed, until we're ready to attest nothing in our lives can ever become best. Saying yes is like giving ourselves permission to pursue our dreams.

Saying yes is always life-affirming. But saying no can sometimes be just as important in the scheme of things. In terms of what is fair and just, both have their roles to play. You, for example, *(speaking to the author)* said yes to this project. That decision has since led you into realms where a preponderance of yeses do most happily cavort.

Yes leads to evolution. No leads to pause and, in the worst case scenario, stagnation. Yes is about growth while no signals caution or possible retrenchment. A thumbs down, for example, is analogous to taking a step backwards.

The power of yes is like a balm for the soul, most lovingly prepared and carefully applied. Yes heals old wounds. No often delays their recovery.

All the same, yes can't always be said. Sometimes it's a no that'll put one to bed. No is required when it's required. Indeed, the soul knows full well when there's to be a nay versus a yea. You see, depending on circumstances no could also be the most perfect of answers.

The true function of no, however, is as a pause button. Saying no stops whatever is in progress which in turn diverts energy into other lines of probabilities. It is important to note that saying no does not in any way stop or retard our evolution.

Again, keep in mind that the movie of your life is always playing at a theatre near you. The slower scenes generally revolve around no. But it's the magic of yes that will soon change a pause into a green-lit go. Yes unfurls the reels of life. No hesitates, excessively opines and may even descend into blather.

When expressed in terms of cranial motion, yes and no form a cross. Yes, the up and down, gives a nod to 'as above, so below.' No, rotating from left to right and back again, reflects wariness or fear and indicates a penchant for looking over one's shoulder. By their very nature, negations are earthbound. The way of the spirit, on the other hand, is to affirm. The point at which affirmation and negation intersect is what is known as incarnated life.

Yes is the primogenitor of the human race. Indeed, manifestation is born of it. In the final analysis then, the answer to everything is YES.

YES, SÍ, OUI!

In saying yes we no longer have to guess
Hmm, what a great eliminator of stress,
To minimize any mess it's clear that we first must fess
Up to truth

Approbation leads to affirmation anon
Saying yes is what our teeth are cut upon
In fact it's yes that leads us to carry on
Straightaway
That is to say, without any hesitation or undue delay

Even so, yes can't always be said
Times are when no must put one to bed

Yes is not always an indicator
Of more. Sometimes it's the vindicator of less

But why should I digress?
The bottom line is just say yes.

RVG

You

You you-you you or was it thou and thee? Only by fully being in a 'you' can any of us truly see (while we're in a body, that is.)

What am I speaking of here? You, in other words, a bundle of singular beauty. Each individual you is like a rose going through a full cycle, from bud to bloom to dying in a vase in someone else's room.

We must be able to completely individuate before we can even think about dis-identifying from external references. Yet in order to love we also have to be in our essence. Quite the balancing act!

You is perhaps the most valuable piece of real estate in the Universe. From our point of view, nothing is more important than a you, our very own. You provides the myopia necessary for each of us to know what to do. Along with the physical body it is the container of who we are while in the flesh, if you will, our persona. A body alone, however, does not a personality make. That is only possible to have within the context of a you.

You is the pronoun that most defines us as an entity ~ more than I, he, she, we or they. Surprise! One would have thought it was I. Not so, even though I surfaces most within each you. Think of it this way: you as a circle with I being found at its innermost point, making all the noise. The answer to the question who is always you. You are the ONE.

———————— ✤ ————————

Zebra (Integration)

Animals are among our greatest teachers. Indeed, it is perhaps through observing their lives that we may best learn the value of our own.

Learning to belong and how to relate to others are essential elements of the educational process. First, we must be able to acknowledge our tribe. Then, we need to see ourselves as active participants in its progress and evolution.

The zebra is one of the most recognizable animals in nature. And like us, they are social creatures, built to move.

When standing still, their natural coloring tends to call one's attention to difference. Indeed, in this state of being they are the very model of disambiguation. However, when they are running, their stripes appear to merge. So, too, is it when we are in motion. That is when our disparate parts unite and engage each other with a commonality of purpose. What appears to be separate then becomes reconciled, changing perception in its wake. Stasis has one look, motion another. They are complimentary yet never mutually exclusive ~ one always blending into the other. Motion treats individual elements in such a way so that they function as a whole.

Our personalities are just like the zebra's stripes. They, too, call attention to difference. However, their role is to camouflage as well as reflect the uniqueness of each soul.

'Twas in *Hamlet* where Shakespeare said it best: **what a piece of work is man! How noble in reason! How infinite in faculties! In form and moving, how express and admirable! In action, how like an angel! In apprehension, how like a god!** It's a most apt observation, don't you think?

The zebra reminds us that we need to apply the principles of integration to all aspects of our lives. In order to do so, however, we must work both from within and without.

The primary task in each incarnation is to integrate the personality with the soul. On the personality side of the equation, there are usually karmic devices, dangling participles that must be confronted and effectively dealt with in order for us to feel more complete. If we can but accomplish this within our allotted time, then we shall have indeed been quite productive.

Unfortunately, the variances of personality can usually only be noticed during our all-too-rare moments of reflection. It's primarily when we pause that we can see our individual parts more clearly. If we're too busy, life becomes a blur. To live life only in the fast lane misses the mark. It's equally important for us to experience both stillness and movement, to be able to feel them deep down inside. Integration can only occur when we do.

The tuxedo, perceived by many as a symbol of wealth, is not quite as black and white as one might assume. It, too, speaks of integration. You may recall that in some of my films I was required to wear just such a garment. Each time I moved or danced across the screen, especially in tails, my characters became all the more whole and, right before your eyes!

I leave you with this thought. In the doing all gets done. And, as we do, we all become At-One.

AFTERWORD

It's been a lovely ride.
Again, my sincerest thanks to everyone who made it possible.

Now, if I may, allow me to quote
A lyric that Irving Berlin once wrote
A wise man was he
Mr. Berlin, indeed, knew how to 'be'
So now it is fitting, yes, quite apropos
To end this book by saying 'let's go on with the show.'

R. Valentino Guglielmi

CODA

The Life and Times of Rudolph Valentino
1895 – 1926

When people saw Rudolph Valentino speak in silent films, what they heard in their minds was the language of love. That is why, even to this day, the mere mention of his name still evokes the image of a great lover.

Valentino lived a short but fabled life, dying unexpectedly at the age of 31. Nevertheless, he had many accomplishments, only some of which I shall attempt to detail here.

First and foremost, he was a talented actor. To understand why you need only to watch him in one of his most famous roles, as Julio in *The Four Horsemen of the Apocalypse,* where he soared, captivating critics and the general public alike with his performance.

June Mathis, the screenwriter who adapted this film from the novel of the same name, was the person most responsible for his success at Metro Pictures, the forerunner of MGM. After having seen Valentino do a terrific job with a small part in *Eyes of Youth,* she lobbied to get him the lead in *The Four Horsemen.*

This film, one of the greatest of the silent era and the first ever to earn more than a million dollars, is perhaps best remembered for the tango scene where Valentino uses the structure of the dance not only to establish his character, but also to exude his own brand of sensuality. It was quite a feat, akin to Elvis Presley's first appearance on television. That he had prior experience as a dancer, of course, was very helpful. But the role also required him to turn himself inside out emotionally, something he was able to do quite well.

Following the release of *The Four Horsemen of the Apocalypse,* Valentino began his trajectory as a star. After making several other films at Metro, he signed with Paramount, the studio that provided him with two of his biggest hits, *The Sheik* and *Blood and Sand.*

The latter, according to critics, was perhaps his best film, again showcasing his ability to convey an incredible range of emotion.

Other major Valentino films were *Son of the Sheik, The Eagle, Cobra, Monsieur Beaucaire* and *Beyond the Rocks* with Gloria Swanson. So-called lesser ones are also of interest, for example, *Camille, The Married Virgin, The Conquering Power, Moran of the Lady Letty* and *The Young Rajah.* All of these movies survive and are available today in either DVD or VHS format.

What made Valentino one of the most remarkable film stars of all time?

- He had the right combination of looks and talent, also perfect timing and grace.
- As an icon of love, he became a lightning rod for public opinion.
- He fully inhabited his screen characters, living intensely whoever he portrayed.
- He was able to speak volumes within the framework of silence.
- He stood out in every scene he was in without even trying.
- His appeal was universal. He was, therefore, in some sense an 'everyman.'

Valentino was also known for his soulful gaze ~ **il suo sguardo.** When his eyes peered out from the screen, people felt compelled to take note. Why? Because apart from anything else he was attempting to convey, they were always filled with love. Again, that is what moviegoers were really reacting to as they watched his films.

Valentino's skills as an actor, I believe, can be traced back to Castellaneta, the little town in southern Italy where he was born. Upon visiting, I found the people there to be cordial, generous of spirit and **molto simpatico.** Simply put, I felt very welcomed. I was also able to get a sense of how that environment might have affected Valentino in his formative years. The old town center, built high on a hill in the middle of a plain, provides its residents with a spectacular view of the surrounding area. As a result, the second floor windows of the apartment he lived in as a child would have enabled him to see for miles.

I contend that from an early age Valentino liked to keep his eyes on the horizon. In fact, he always tried to keep the bigger picture in mind. Even in death this is so, his crypt immediately adjacent to a beautiful stained glass window depicting mountains, trees, water, and the beginning of a stairway to the clouds.

Any viewing of a Valentino film reveals the luminosity he infused into all his roles. What was his gift? He sparked our imaginations, encouraging us to believe in our own magic. Such was the strength of his powerful yet unassuming charisma.

For female fans, Valentino was the 'IT' man well before that term was first used as a code word for sex. As such, he was alternately praised and reviled, just as someone with an erotically charged image might have expected to be. Some claimed he was a heart-throb, others that he was nothing more than a gigolo. In either case, however, it was the consensus that his often hypnotic effect on women was that of an **homme fatal.**

Rudolph Valentino broke through the existing stereotypes of American masculinity by re-defining how a man could choose to look and act in relation to the world around him.

Whether or not Valentino truly was the perfect paramour was never really documented. However, allusions were certainly made to that effect, both during his life-time and after. The important point to make here is that Valentino was able to personify love and sex to a greater degree than just about any other public figure before him. In so doing, he provided fresh perspectives on both, at a time when they were not always being openly discussed. Why was he so successful in these endeavors? Again, because moviegoers saw him as infinitely relatable, someone capable of baring his soul to millions of people.

Among other things, Valentino reminded the Roaring Twenties generation:

1. That love and sex always have primal components as well as spiritual, emotional and esoteric ones.
2. That we may live love as something that's beyond the skin,

transcending time.

3. That feeling comfortable with one's own sexuality is a must.

4. That love is what both fills and fulfills us.

None of these ideas are new. However, it fell to Valentino to shine a spotlight on them, something it seems that he was destined to do.

The following quote is taken from an article Rudy wrote for *Photoplay Magazine* in 1923. In it he examines his own phenomenon. Note that he speaks of himself in the third person. **You tell me that I bring romance into your lives. You say that I offer you color, beauty and dreams. I feel as though I am simply a medium through which these things are being given to you. The Rudolph Valentino you have manifested on the screen is quite different from the Rudolph Valentino who really is. The public personality of the Valentino you know must dedicate himself to the creative work that you expect. He must show you the beauty and joy of love and the radiance of life. He must try to live out dreams that you may not have been able to work out for yourself. His life is such that he can no longer belong completely to himself.**

Valentino's sudden death in August of 1926 came as a result of complications from an operation to repair a ruptured stomach ulcer. Within hours of the news, there was a huge outpouring of grief. Indeed, thousands of fans converged on Campbell's Funeral Home in Manhattan, queuing up to pay their respects. After funeral services there and in Beverly Hills, his body was laid to rest in a setting that could not be more fitting, *Hollywood Forever* cemetery on Santa Monica Blvd. in Los Angeles, home to many a former star. In fact, Paramount Pictures is just a stone's throw away, literally right next door.

Post-death, perhaps Valentino's most well-remembered role was that of a sheik in two different but plot-related films, *The Sheik*, 1921, Paramount, and *Son of the Sheik*, 1926, United Artists, his final picture. In addition to having been given a certain priority by their respective studios, these two films owe much of their success to the fact that he was so at home in the role. Indeed, the desert was in his blood ~ and it showed!

Valentino's personal magnetism created a polymorphous image upon which audiences projected their own romantic and erotic desires. He was the canvas. They were artists. Together, they conspired to conceive one of the greatest lovers the world has ever known.

EPITAPH

And this thou perceivest, to make thy love more strong, to love that well that thou must leave ere long. One of Shakespeare's best pieces of advice and how Rudolph Valentino chose to live his life.

REFLECTIONS

Through film did not Valentino send a message to all mankind
That love, indeed, is the energy that doth bind?
Yes, he did ~ in what we know of as the here and now
Hmm, what a simple idea that is, wow!
Just think of it, harness the power of a loving kiss
And this world might no longer be quite so amiss.

So much more than 'just an actor' was Rodolfo V
For now it's Guglielmi that you get to see

Love he sends to one and all
Read this book, have a ball
Life requires alert and focused consciousness, that's all.

RVG

Photo courtesy of the Academy of Motion Picture Arts & Sciences.

PARTIAL BIBLIOGRAPHY

Dark Lover by Emily Leider, 2003 ~ the most complete biography to date.

Valentino Forever by Tracy Terhune, 2004 ~ A history of the Valentino Memorial Services.

The Valentino Mystique by Allan Ellenberger, 2005 ~ Valentino post-funeral events and analysis.

Valentino, The Unforgotten by Roger Peterson, 1937 ~ edited and republished in 2007 by Tracy Terhune. Eye witness accounts of those who visited Valentino's final resting place.

Intorno a Rodolfo Valentino ~ Materiali Italiani ~ edited by Silvio Alovisio and Giulia Carluccio, 2009 ~ an anthology of Italian language articles written about Valentino during his lifetime and after.

Rudolph Valentino: The Silent Idol; His Life in Photographs by Donna Hill, 2010 ~ a pictorial history of Valentino's life, it contains more than 400 photos, many of which have not been seen in over 80 years.

Day Dreams by Rudolph Valentino, 1923 ~ republished in 2010. A collection of metaphysically-oriented poems, sourced from "the other side" via automatic writing.

How You Can Keep Fit by Rudolph Valentino, 1923 ~ exercise booklet posted on the internet at <u>www.sandowplus.co.uk/Macfadden/Valentino/valentino-intro.htm</u>.

OTHER BOOKS BY WAYNE HATFORD

Letters from Janice; Correspondence with the Astral Plane, Uni-Sun, 1987. Also a channeled book. A dear friend recounting her experiences with the transition called death.

VALENTINO-RELATED BOOKS IN PROGRESS

Jeanine Villalobos, Rudolph Valentino's great-grandniece, is putting the final touches on what promises to be perhaps the most definitive book on his life thus far, sourced from family documents and correspondence in Valentino's own hand.

Affairs Valentino by Evelyn Zumaya ~ awaiting publication. The memoirs of George Ullman, Valentino's business manager and personal friend. Information on this book and its contents can be found at www.affairsvalentino.com

INTERNET RESOURCES

www.rudolph-valentino.com ~ Filmography, photos, podcasts. A wealth of information on Rudolph Valentino as well as a virtual tour of Falcon Lair, his former home. Maintained by Donna Hill, author of *Rudolph Valentino: The Silent Idol.*

www.edoardoballerini.com ~ Actor, writer, director. He wrote, directed and starred in the short film, *Goodnight Valentino,* to great acclaim. He has also written a script for a full-length feature film based on Valentino's relationship with his second wife, Natacha Rambova. Please go to the website for information on Mr. Ballerini's current projects.

www.valentinoforever.com ~ This website is maintained by Tracy Terhune, author of *Valentino Forever.* Contains rare photos and information on the yearly Valentino Memorial Services in Los Angeles.

www.valentinospeaks.com ~ Quotes. Media. Contact. Link to *Voce Valentino* Blog ~ Updates and Author's musings plus outtakes and sidebars sourced from the essence of Rudolph Valentino. Maintained by Wayne Hatford, author of *Valentino Speaks.*

There are also two on-line Valentino discussion groups. Both can be accessed at www.yahoo.com/groups

MUSEUM

Museo Valentino in Castellaneta, Italy ~ dedicated to the memory of Rudolph Valentino.

MEMORIAL SERVICE

Annual Memorial Service for Rudolph Valentino at *Hollywood Forever* Cemetery on Santa Monica Blvd. in Los Angeles every August 23rd at 12:10 PM. Open to the Public. The year 2011 marks the 84th anniversary of this service.

About the Author

Wayne Hatford is a teacher, writer, editor and author dedicated to bridging the gap between the physical and non-physical worlds. Born in the Midwest, he has lived on both coasts of the US while also traveling extensively, spending significant amounts of time in Chile, France, Spain and Italy. It is Italy, however, the birthplace of Rudolph Valentino, where he feels a special rapport and, in scholarly pursuits, has visited multiple sites associated with the "Great Lover."

Wayne speaks French, Spanish, Italian and English, the languages in which Valentino himself was conversant. As a result, he was able to provide Valentino with the perfect palette, allowing him to share his thoughts with the same texture and vibrancy he employed during his last incarnation.

A life-long student of metaphysics and transformation whose previous book, *Letters from Janice: Correspondence with the Astral Plane* is available via several major online book sellers and valentinospeaks.com, Wayne Hatford now resides in Palm Springs, California where he and the essence of Rudolph Valentino are currently collaborating on another writing project.

Photo by K. Stenlund.

22388877R00199

Made in the USA
Lexington, KY
25 April 2013